Future of Business and Finance

The Future of Business and Finance book series features professional works aimed at defining, analyzing, and charting the future trends in these fields. The focus is mainly on strategic directions, technological advances, challenges and solutions which may affect the way we do business tomorrow, including the future of sustainability and governance practices. Mainly written by practitioners, consultants and academic thinkers, the books are intended to spark and inform further discussions and developments.

Öncü Hazır • Maria Elena Bruni
Editors

Tomorrow's Data Empowered Project Management

Agile Decision Making, Sustainability and AI

Springer

Editors
Öncü Hazır
Rennes School of Business
Rennes, France

Maria Elena Bruni
University of Calabria
Rende, Italy

ISSN 2662-2467 ISSN 2662-2475 (electronic)
Future of Business and Finance
ISBN 978-3-031-84019-7 ISBN 978-3-031-84017-3 (eBook)
https://doi.org/10.1007/978-3-031-84017-3

This Springer imprint is published by the registered company Springer Nature Switzerland AG
The registered company address is: Gewerbestrasse 11, 6330 Cham, Switzerland

Foreword

In a professional context, a *project* can be defined as a collaborative enterprise that develops over a period of time and is intended to achieve a particular goal. A project is structured in small and manageable tasks that are interrelated. The tasks share common resources, including a limited budget. The need to complete a task before the execution of some others can start constraining the scheduling of the tasks. Several individuals and companies may be involved in the execution of the tasks. *Project management* is the application of processes, technologies, methods, and skills to efficiently and effectively complete a project, that is, to achieve the goal of the project within the predefined requirements that include respecting constraints on the duration of the project and the availability of resources. The interrelations between the tasks, the fact that usually various teams of people are involved, and the uncertainty that makes the duration of a task difficult to predict make project management a challenging activity.

While project management is an area studied by numerous researchers and practitioners, it remains worth investigating further especially because of the changes in the professional environments and organizations and of the development of new technologies.

This book aims at providing a broad overview of up-to-date topics in the area of project management. The title of the book communicates the vision of the editors and provides a clear message about why project management will be different in the future. *Agile decision making* refers to the fact that information and communication technologies have created the conditions for agile decision making. Frequent reassessment of decisions is replacing stable decisions; frequent redesign is replacing high-level static design. In 1987, the United Nations Brundtland Commission defined *sustainability* as "meeting the needs of the present without compromising the ability of future generations to meet their own needs." A society cannot be sustainable without the active commitment of companies. This is the reason why companies are more and more requested by society and by institutions to be sustainable, in the different dimensions of sustainability: environmental, economic, and social. The third expression in evidence in the title is *artificial intelligence (AI)*. In fact, while the creation of the expression dates back to the eighties of the past century, only recently AI methods started having a big impact on all the professional, industrial, and institutional sectors, due to some recent innovations, in particular machine learning methods and the field of AI known as generative AI. Project management will need to be more agile, to contribute to the sustainability goals of the company, and to benefit from the availability of AI tools that just started to be deployed.

From the scientific point of view, project management is an area that involves several different competences and disciplines, from operations research to computer science, from management to organization science, from human resources to financial management. This book aims at covering a broad variety of contributions and offers an overview of the topics that will impact project management in the future. The interdisciplinary character of the book makes it of particular value.

The book is intended to be of interest to academicians and to practitioners, in particular to project professionals. It will provide knowledge on the state-of-the-art research in the various and diverse aspects of project management and stimulate reflections. It will be an important reference for researchers to be aware of the frontier of research in the field and for practitioners to be prepared to tackle future challenges.

Università degli Studi di Brescia
Brescia, Italy

M. Grazia Speranza

Preface

Project management (PM) has been an essential area that deals with various decision-making problems. It offers opportunities to conduct academic studies, formulate new models to solve business problems, and develop software and decision support systems (DSS). It has been attracting the attention of academicians and professionals involved in project teams who studied different disciplines. This book aims to discuss contemporary industry problems and trends and related promising research areas, shedding light on the future of project management. It includes chapters that focus on new technology applications and organizational trends. The chapters are grouped into new technologies and recent developments in organizing projects.

The chapters address a diverse audience of undergraduate and graduate students and practitioners seeking to develop their project management knowledge. An important characteristic is to gather the managers and academics who conduct theoretical studies in this field to discuss the future of project management.

The discussion topics include how data analytics and artificial intelligence developments might shape project life cycle management and how the fourth/fifth Industrial Revolution and the new technologies will transform project management practices. The importance of sustainability in project management practices is elaborated on. Recent developments in the organization of projects, such as adopting agile techniques, establishing project management offices, and open innovation and collaborative projects, are discussed.

Rapid artificial intelligence and data analytics developments in recent years have created significant opportunities and risks for project managers and have already started changing business practices. At the same time, these practices' ethical and sustainability dimensions have been crucial. This textbook is intended to discuss theoretical and practical aspects of project management for graduate students and practitioners seeking to foster their knowledge of project management.

The chapter "The Use of Blockchain and Smart Contracts in Project Management: A Review and an Outlook" presents the principles of blockchain systems and argues how they can impact project life cycle management. Smart contracts and their use in project management are discussed in detail.

The chapter "Big Data for Project Management" addresses project management in the era of big data and discusses how developments in data analytics might support managers in achieving project management.

The chapter "The Use of Artificial Intelligence in Supply Chain Project Management: Insights from German Organizations" presents the results of the interviews conducted with managers with experience in supply chain and project management areas. The interview questions address artificial intelligence's current and future use in their profession.

The chapter "Transforming Startups with Generative Artificial Intelligence" focuses on startup companies and their projects. It details how startups can benefit from generative artificial intelligence to optimize and automate their processes and formulate and develop new processes, products, and business models.

The chapter "Planning and Controlling Startup Projects Applying Critical Chain Project Management" addresses startup projects and examines the usefulness of a planning and monitoring methodology, Critical Chain Project Management (CCPM), to manage the projects.

The chapter "Generative AI Supporting Project Management: Vertical Integration Using OPENAI MYGPT" discusses how generative artificial intelligence can support project managers. It includes a demonstration of creating an AI Chatbot use case for generating deliverables such as Project Charters, Work Breakdown Structures, and Schedule.

The chapter "Stakeholder Engagement and the Mindset Open to Innovate in the Digital Era" discusses the role and importance of stakeholder management and engagement in a complex innovation ecosystem from multiple theoretical and practical perspectives. The contribution theorizes on the connections between stakeholder engagement and project managers, offers novel concepts to broaden the discussion, and raises some critical questions.

The chapter "Digital Technologies and Sustainability in Project Management: Current Trends and Future Perspectives" presents the results of the literature review of digital technologies to enhance sustainability in project outcomes. It elaborates on the future of sustainability in project management.

The chapter "Exploring the Agile Project Management in the Software as a Service Sector" emphasizes the use of agile management techniques and investigates the projects in software as service sector (SaaS).

The chapter "Harmony of Discord: The Paradoxes of Artificial Intelligence and Innovative Teams" investigates the paradoxes within innovative project teams and emphasizes the interplay between technology and practice and the tensions in AI implementations.

The chapter "Biases in Modern Project Management: Opportunities Connected to Artificial Intelligence" explores cognitive biases inherent to project managers that affect decision-making and management, often in subtle and unconscious ways. Through a detailed analysis, the chapter examines how these biases can manifest, influencing decisions and management.

As editors, we would like to thank the authors for their contribution and to Springer for their support.

We are also deeply grateful to Maria Grazia Speranza for writing the foreword for this book. Her words bring unique perspectives and provide insightful reflections on the vision of this book. We are honored to have received her support in bringing our vision of tomorrow's project management.

Rennes, France Öncü Hazır
Rende, Italy Maria Elena Bruni

Contents

Part I New Technologies That Transform Project Management Practices

The Use of Blockchain and Smart Contracts in Project Management: A Review and an Outlook 3
Öncü Hazir, Ilter Önder, and Tolga Inan

Big Data for Project Management 31
Tuba Bakici and Öncü Hazir

The Use of Artificial Intelligence in Supply Chain Project Management: Insights from German Organizations 43
Dirk H. Hartel and Öncü Hazır

Transforming Startups with Generative Artificial Intelligence 57
Emine Gokce Phillips

Planning and Controlling Startup Projects Applying Critical Chain Project Management 81
Denis Solan

Generative AI Supporting Project Management: A Vertical Integration Using OpenAI MyGPT 101
Alberto Michele Felicetti, Daniele Rao, and Salvatore Ammirato

Part II Recent Developments and Challenges in the Organization of Projects

Stakeholder Engagement and the Mindset Open to Innovate in the Digital Era 123
Elisabetta Bracci and Maria Elena Bruni

Digital Technologies and Sustainability in Project Management: Current Trends and Future Perspectives 147
Leila Moslemi Naeni and Roksana Jahan Tumpa

Exploring the Agile Project Management in the Software as a Service Sector 169
Lauriane Saint-Denis

Harmony of Discord: The Paradoxes of Artificial Intelligence and Innovative Teams 181
Seyda Zeki Deligonul

Biases in Modern Project Management. Opportunities Connected to Artificial Intelligence (AI) 199
Roberto Linzalone, Antonio Bassi, Alberto Michele Felicetti, and Salvatore Ammirato

About the Editors and Contributors

About the Editors

Öncü Hazır is a professor at Rennes School of Business in France. He received his BS in Industrial Engineering and MBA from the Middle East Technical University, Ankara, Turkey. He completed his Ph.D. at the Department of Business Administration at Bilkent University in 2008. His dissertation was on project scheduling. He worked as a post-doctorate researcher in Laboratoire d'Informatique de Paris 6 and Ecole Nationale Supérieure des Mines de Saint-Etienne and as an associate professor at TED University. His research interests mainly cover project scheduling and control, earned value management, production planning, and operations management. He participated in various research projects and gave seminars and lectures. He published several articles in operations research and management journals. He co-authored the textbook, *An Introduction to Project Modeling and Planning*, published by Springer.

Maria Elena Bruni is Professor of Operations Research at the University of Calabria and a collaborating member of the CIRRELT, Montreal. She received a Ph.D. in Operations Research at the University of Calabria and an M.S. in Public Economy from the University of Sapienza (Rome). Her research activity focuses on designing solution methods for combinatorial problems under uncertainty and risk, with applications mainly in scheduling, routing, and healthcare. She is author of more than 90 papers accepted in refereed international journals and author of three Springer book chapters. She received the best paper prize of the *IMA Journal of Management Mathematics* in 2016 and best poster awards for the ICORES conferences in 2018, 2019, and 2022. She is an associate editor of international journals, a workshop organizer, and a member of program and scientific committees for several international conferences.

Contributors

Salvatore Ammirato Department of Mechanical, Energy and Management Engineering, University of Calabria, Rende, Italy

Tuba Bakici EDHEC Business School, Roubaix, France

Antonio Bassi Department of Innovative Technologies, Scuola Universitaria Professionale della Svizzera Italiana, Polo universitario Lugano, Lugano, Switzerland

Elisabetta Bracci Cluster Manager, Clust-ER Innovate of Emilia-Romagna Region, Bologna, Italy

Maria Elena Bruni University of Calabria, Rende, Italy

Seyda Zeki Deligonul St. John Fisher University, Rochester, USA

Alberto Michele Felicetti Department of Mechanical, Energy and Management Engineering, University of Calabria, Rende, Italy

Dirk H. Hartel Baden-Wuerttemberg Cooperative State University, Stuttgart, Germany

Öncü Hazır Rennes School of Business, Rennes, France

Tolga Inan Artificial Intelligence Engineering Department, TOBB ETÜ, Ankara, Turkey

Roberto Linzalone Department of Mechanical, Energy and Management Engineering, University of Calabria, Rende, Italy

Leila Moslemi Naeni University of Technology Sydney, Sydney, NSW, Australia

Ilter Onder InfoSec Team, GRC Group, Klarna Bank AB, Stockholm, Sweden

Emine Gokce Phillips Crypto Index Series Limited, London, UK

Daniele Rao Department of Mechanical, Energy and Management Engineering, University of Calabria, Rende, Italy

Lauriane Saint-Denis Barcelona, Spain

Denis Solan Technion – Israel Institute of Technology, Haifa, Israel

Roksana Jahan Tumpa Central Queensland University, Sydney, NSW, Australia

List of Abbreviations

AI	Artificial Intelligence
AIGC	Artificial Intelligence Generated Content
API	Application Programming Interface
AR	Augmented Reality
APM	Association for Project Management
BIM	Building Information Modeling
B2B	Business-to-Business
CAC	Customer Acquisition Costs
CLV	Customer Lifetime Value
CPM	Critical Path Method
CCPM	Critical Chain Project Management
CRM	Customer Relation Management
CTR	Click-Through Rates
DL	Deep Learning
DLT	Distributed Ledger Technology
DSS	Decision Support System
EI	Emotional Intelligence
EVM	Earned Value Management
FL	Fuzzy Logic
GenAI	Generative Artificial Intelligence
GPT	Generative Pre-trained Transformer
HCD	Human-Centered Design
HR	Human Resources
IoT	Internet of Things
IP	Intellectual Property
IQ	Intelligence Quotient
KPI	Key Performance Indicator
LLM	Large Language Model
ML	Machine Learning
MVP	Minimum Viable Product
NN	Neural Networks
NLP	Natural Language Processing
OEM	Original Equipment Manufacturer

PERT	Program Evaluation and Review Technique
PM	Project Management
PMBOK	Project Management Body of Knowledge
PMI	Project Management Institute
PMO	Project Management Office
PKI	Public Key Infrastructure
RFID	Radio Frequency Identification
SaaS	Software as a Service
SC	Supply Chain
SCM	Supply Chain Management
SCPM	Supply Chain Project Management
SDG	Sustainable Development Goal
SLR	Systematic Literature Review
SPM	Sustainable Project Management
TOC	Theory of Constraints
VUCA	Volatile, Uncertain, Complex, Ambiguity
WBS	Work Breakdown Structure

Part I

New Technologies That Transform Project Management Practices

The Use of Blockchain and Smart Contracts in Project Management: A Review and an Outlook

Öncü Hazir, Ilter Önder, and Tolga Inan

Abstract

In this chapter, we study the state-of-the-art developments in the use of Blockchain in project management. We establish a link between the design principles of Blockchain systems and project management practice. We investigate the benefits of using Blockchain systems in project life cycle management and list the advantages of implementation in agile project management. The findings of the literature review and the discussions presented in this paper can support researchers identify the research gaps in the adoption and implementation of Blockchain systems to enhance project management decision-making.

1 Introduction

New digital technologies have rapidly changed the business practices in manufacturing and service systems in the digital era. They have been transforming the work processes in manufacturing and service systems through big data analytics and artificial intelligence. Organizations can now access, store, and analyze massive amounts of data and design and implement smart, connected information systems.

Ö. Hazir
Rennes School of Business, Rennes, France
e-mail: oncu.hazir@rennes-sb.com

I. Önder (✉)
InfoSec Team, GRC Group, Klarna Bank AB, Stockholm, Sweden
e-mail: ilter.aptula@klarna.com

T. Inan
Artificial Intelligence Engineering Department, TOBB ETÜ, Ankara, Turkey
e-mail: tinan@etu.edu.tr

Ö. Hazır, M. E. Bruni (eds.), *Tomorrow's Data Empowered Project Management*, Future of Business and Finance, https://doi.org/10.1007/978-3-031-84017-3_1

Accessibility to high quantity and variety of data allows managers to improve their decisions using data analytics and decision support tools. Simultaneously, new information-sharing technologies and interconnected devices enable them to monitor and control geographically distributed projects.

While digital transformation brings many new opportunities to organizations in managing projects and portfolios (Pajares et al., 2017; Simion et al., 2018), at the same time, unknown risks such as cyber-attacks and vulnerability of data appear (Tupa et al., 2017). The security of sharing and processing these documents has become an organizational concern as more digital documents are produced. In this regard, Blockchain systems provide opportunities to enhance information management in organizations by improving the efficiency and traceability of transactions and providing secure data-sharing systems (Bodkhe et al., 2020). Blockchain-enabled smart contracts support decentralized managerial decision-making by enhancing trust and improving efficiency by eliminating unnecessary intermediaries and processes (Wang et al., 2019). According to Ferguson (2018), the development of Blockchain technologies can lead to a paradigm shift in business making, and organizations will need to change how they manage their operations and reconsider their missions and business models.

Considering this potential paradigm shift, we study how Blockchain technologies can be employed in projects to support managers in adopting new digital systems and decision-making approaches. We scrutinize the use of Blockchain and smart contracts in project management and present a comprehensive literature review. To present the Blockchain applications in the existing literature, we examine the project management studies from two different perspectives: knowledge areas and the project lifecycle phases. We demonstrate that Blockchain adds value from whatever perspective we examine the project management practices. The contribution of this study can be summarized as follows:

- We point out the correspondence of the design principles of Blockchain in managing projects and review the literature based on this correspondence.
- We investigate the use of Blockchain within the project life cycle framework.
- We list the benefits of using project management within each knowledge area of project management.
- We examine the use of Blockchain both in traditional planned-based and agile project management approaches.
- Focusing on the project life cycle analysis and knowledge areas, we present a comprehensive literature review highlighting the research gaps and potential directions.

Figure 1 shows the contribution of this review study.

Before discussing the potential benefits of using Blockchain in projects, we will define the essential concepts of Blockchain that we will refer to in our discussions.

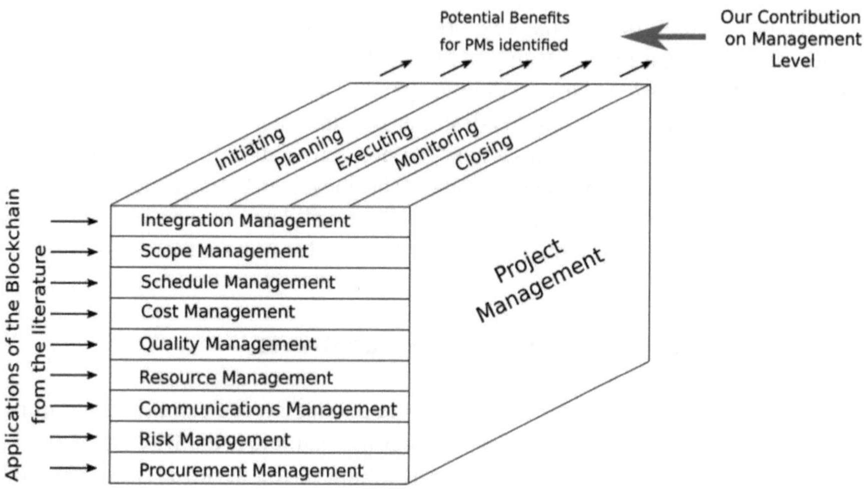

Fig. 1 The mapping of Blockchain use and potential contributions to project management

1.1 The Meaning of Blockchain

Cryptography professionals have studied Blockchain to avoid altering timestamps since the '80s. However, Nakamoto (2008) came up with a practical and innovative idea of using a decentralized approach to manage transactions, which led to the development and broader use of Blockchain systems. The main idea is to organize data in blocks and link them in a chain connected by immutable mathematical means. Each block contains a cryptographical digest of the previous block, called the hash, designed to give completely different values with proven mathematical entropy, even for a single bit change.

Nakamoto (2008) proposed using chained blocks as a part of a transaction scheme called BitCoin, the first cryptographic currency. This public Blockchain system is based on an open network where all the network nodes copy all the blocks and verify the chain's integrity so that a complete, consistent, correct, safe software system, which is free of errors and corruption, is maintained (Drescher, 2017). The hashes that connect the blocks eliminate the double-spending problem. A reward system is designed to ensure that the nodes actively participate in the record-keeping of the transactions. The distributed storage and verification of the Blockchain is also called Distributed Ledger Technology (DLT).

Even though the DLT terminology is used interchangeably with Blockchain, the implementation does not necessarily depend on the ledger distribution among various nodes. Single-node systems can be created in multiple software implementations, like core banking (Insights, 2021), log management, and government records. Blockchain ensures that the events are linked in different blocks signed with a timestamp, ensuring that nobody can alter the records backward. The node administrator cannot change the past, as the hashes will not hold in the later blocks. This property is the main advantage of single-node Blockchain implementations.

Nakamoto (2008) defines the network as a collection of nodes that record and broadcast all the transactions, trying to find the best proof of work and checking all previous transactions to ensure no double-spending is registered. Nodes also check proof of work broadcast by other nodes to ensure the integrity of the whole chain. The owning entities sign all transactions, so non-repudiation is integrated into the blocks by design. This network system allows businesses to manage their operations in a decentralized manner where transactions are validated based on a consensus mechanism. The basic concepts are defined in Table 1.

1.2 Blockchain Systems and Smart Contracts

The public Blockchain systems are open to the public; anyone can contribute if the network rules are followed. The most well-known example is the BitCoin network. The private Blockchains differ as the participation in the network is limited, and only authorized nodes can receive transaction broadcast information and become part of the network. The limitation can be enforced by a single entity or based on predefined criteria distributed to all nodes. The network can decide if a candidate node is accepted in the network. Consortium Blockchain expands the idea of private Blockchain from a single authoritative entity in private Blockchain to a consortium of entities, like companies in the same industry that need a platform to share information. These systems help the network participants to access up-to-date data and enhance the transparency of the network. We refer to the comprehensive review of Bouraga (2021) for the details of the blockchain consensus protocols.

Traditionally, written and signed documents and contracts have correspondence in the digital world. Contracts correspond to the agreements made with two or more parties' voluntary participation and have possible legal obligations. They ensure that promises between individuals/parties are kept. They can incentivize the parties to maximize the performance of the work that they deliver. Moreover, they can also include solutions for the cases if a party fails to fulfil its responsibility. At this point, smart contracts, which refer to the programs or protocols that execute automatically when specific criteria are met, have been used in many industries.

Table 1 Definition of the basic concepts

Concept	Definition
Node	Entities, part of the Blockchain network, can read and contribute to the info shared.
Transaction	All data shared in the Blockchain network that goes in the block related to the progress and management of the project.
Private Blockchain	Blockchain network where only authorized entities can join.
Consortium Blockchain	Private Blockchain is where the authorization decision is shared between several entities interested in collaboration.
Public Blockchain	The Blockchain that anyone can contribute and become a node if they follow the technical specifications.

Szabo (1997) defined Smart contracts in 1997, long before Nakamoto (2008) invented BitCoin, and Szabo's (1997) concepts have been put into practice within the Blockchain framework. The programs or protocols produced using a Turing-complete language on a distributed network have emerged as Smart contracts. Turing complete languages can simulate a universal Turing machine, an abstract and generalized representation of a programmable computation machine with infinite memory. In this way, a Smart contract infrastructure powered by a Turing complete language enables a wide range of computation and applications. The Blockchain network provides an infrastructure suitable for implementing Smart contracts.

A Smart contract defined in clear and transparent terms can be a viable and reliable solution for all parties as it automatically triggers an action when legal, economic, financial, industry-specific, or contract criteria are met. An application programming interface (API) call or similar action corresponding to a milestone event can trigger implementation. These Blockchain-enabled applications allow companies to improve the efficiency of the management control systems, eliminating unnecessary processes and intermediaries and improving the system transparency and security (Wang et al., 2019).

1.3 Use of Blockchain for Project Management

In the project management framework, the private and consortium Blockchain networks could be preferred to public options, as the data shared would be confidential in many cases. Most organizations give authority and responsibility to project managers to achieve the project goals. Project managers can decide whom to admit to the private Blockchain network as part of their monitoring and control responsibilities. Moreover, in private Blockchains, a token (bitcoin) is in each block, as the participants already have an interest in receiving broadcast information on the project or publishing transactions in the network for their business. Since mining new coins will not be required, the computing power requirements can be reduced as mining is a resource-intensive task.

If Blockchain is used to track a project managed by a central authority, an authoritative source exists to approve the transactions. However, if the authority is distributed among different parties, one does not have authoritarian power over the other in consensus-based decision-making (Matosyan, 2019). Smart contracts offer various benefits to enhance decentralized decision-making in projects, as contracting is a crucial aspect of project management. We refer to Ulusoy and Hazır (2021) for the basics and types of project contracts and Kerkhove and Vanhoucke (2016, 2020) for a literature review on the design and implications of the contracts.

We have introduced Blockchain systems and Smart contracts and given some preliminary insights into the transformation of business practices in the digital age. Despite the various potential benefits, the use of Blockchain and smart contracts in project management practices has been limited. Literature is scarce in this regard. Only recently, some researchers have started to study the use of blockchain systems in project management. We must thoroughly understand the adoption and implementation of blockchain systems for project management and their potential impacts on managerial practices and project outcomes. In this regard, we review the few academic studies published on this topic and discuss the potential application areas and managerial implications. We provide insights by answering the following questions:

- What is the current state of Blockchain and Smart contracts in the project management literature?
- How can we link the design principles of Blockchain systems with project management practices?
- How can Blockchain systems contribute to project life cycle management?
- Which knowledge or decision-making areas/problems of project management can benefit most from the developments in Blockchain systems?
- How can Blockchain systems contribute to agile project management?
- How can Blockchain technologies shape the future of project management practices?

The discussions that address these questions help researchers to identify the research gaps in digital transformation and project management. The results guide managers using Blockchain systems to enhance their project management practices.

In the sequel, we first discuss the state-of-the-art developments and summarize the existing studies in the literature. In Sect. 3, we introduce the essential characteristics of the Blockchain systems and discuss their adoption and implementation to support management. Section 4 scrutinizes the potential of using Blockchain systems in project life cycle management, conclusions, and promising research directions.

2 State of the Art

We systematically reviewed the project management literature and conducted an in-depth content analysis of the existing studies. For this purpose, we conducted a structured keyword search in Scopus and Scholar Google. We searched for the combinations of terms in the article title, abstract, and keywords. The specific combination of terms we used is: "project management" and ("Blockchain" or "Smart contract"). The Scopus search returned an initial result of only 17 journal articles and conference papers. A few articles have also been added to the list through Scholar Google search. After reading their abstracts and introductions, some have been classified as out of scope. Our final list includes 27 papers to be considered for the content analysis. We need more than this limited number of papers to prevent us from performing a reliable statistical analysis. Instead, we will classify these papers by presenting their main characteristics in the sequel. Another limitation is the information content of the publications. The existing literature is mainly composed of short conference papers or reports. Journal articles and detailed reports or theses are very few as this is a recent topic on which researchers have started to work only lately. We will summarize the findings of a few studies, which mainly address their use in the construction industry.

Kim et al. (2020) performed a comprehensive analysis of the use of Blockchain in the construction industry. According to them, the construction industry has embraced the great potential to implement Blockchain technologies due to the vast number of transactions involved across many parties, such as contractors and subcontractors. However, survey results show that the application of Blockchain technologies has been limited in this industry. Among the possible application areas mentioned in the survey by Kim et al. (2020), Smart contracts have been found to offer the most potential, which could be expected due to the importance of contract management in this industry.

Even though the implementation of Blockchain systems in the construction sector is in its early development stages (Penzes, 2018), the construction industry can benefit considerably. These technologies can improve resource management and cost efficiency, decrease project duration, and decrease payment disputes (Li et al., 2019). These benefits would be fostered by the wide adoption of Building Information Modeling (BIM) technologies as more digital documents are produced and shared (Hargaden et al., 2019; Turk & Klinc, 2017). The systematic literature analysis of Kiu et al. (2020) also shows BIM as a significant potential area, along with contract and supply chain management (SCM).

In projects, communication and negotiation between the different actors—the client, the contractor, and subcontractors—, and monitoring and controlling the financial transactions among these actors have always been challenging. In this regard, contract preparation and management are crucial in projects as the contracts constitute legally binding documents that specify the work content of the project, a baseline time plan, the cost of the project to the client, and a payment schedule. Other items are stated to establish a cooperative business environment and prevent disagreements and disputes. Considering these vital functions, managers must prepare effective contracts and securely manage their execution. Contract design has been essential in project management research (Kerkhove & Vanhoucke, 2016, 2020). According to Hall (2016), it offers several research opportunities, such as investigating different cooperation models and project contracting schemes.

Blockchain technologies provide various opportunities for organizations to support contract management. During the project execution, they can aid project managers in verifying and validating the required transactions. This way, they can monitor the work in progress, resource availability, and cost figures more effectively. Also, these systems can enhance the transparency of the payment systems and allow project partners to share their payment records securely. Elghaish et al. (2020) address the need for more trust due to payment delays in construction projects and propose using a Blockchain-based automated financial system. The Blockchain technology and the collaboration platform, accessible only to project partners, enable the automatic execution of financial transactions. As project partners can check their own and other partners' cost records, they will trust the outputs of the Smart contract.

According to Wang et al. (2017), Smart contracts can minimize cash flow problems due to late payments in projects. Payment delays have been commonly encountered in projects in all industries, and there is a rich literature on project planning with known and uncertain cash flows (Hazır & Ulusoy, 2020; Leyman & Vanhoucke, 2016; Vanhoucke et al., 2001, 2003). Blockchain technology offers a significant improvement opportunity in controlling payments as funds transfers can be automated by Smart contracts or instantaneous cryptocurrency transfers can be used as payment options to replace traditional funds transfers. Payments to contractors, subcontractors, and suppliers could be automatically made as milestone activities are terminated and validated according to the contract requirements. Lenarduzzi et al. (2018) also highlight the use of smart contracts to make project payments automatically. They propose using smart contracts in the acceptance criteria phase of agile projects and implementing blockchain-based automated testing and payment systems.

Smart contracts could be the most promising implementation area of Blockchain systems in project management. Despite the increasing number of applications, especially in some sectors such as finance and energy, there are still many challenges to overcome (S. Wang et al., 2019). In this regard, Zou et al. (2019) note that standards, regulations, and best practices are lacking. Several difficulties might be faced during implementation, especially in modifying, debugging, and verifying the code.

Besides fostering the reliability of financial operations, Blockchain technologies have supported the projects logistics operations. Based on the findings and discussions of the comprehensive supply chain management (SCM) review articles, such as Dutta et al. (2020), we observe that the literature and implementation of Blockchain in the logistics sector are more abundant compared to many other sectors. Combining the current SCM practices and sectoral requirements, the work of Kifokeris and Koch (2019) focuses on using Blockchain in construction logistics and presents a literature review.

Along with the improvement possibilities in contract and SCM practices of the sector, Wang et al. (2017) list the potentials in resource management, specifically in equipment leasing, and give an example of Blockchain-enabled crane leasing. Time and cost-efficiency of the equipment leasing could be enhanced and trust-building between the parties could be facilitated. Das et al. (2020) note the need for more trust among the participants of the construction projects and propose securing the interim payments, which are subject to unfair practices in many construction projects using Blockchain-based systems.

3 A Detailed Analysis of the Use of Blockchain in Project Management

First, we will link the design principles of Blockchain systems with project management practices. Then, we will study the use of Blockchain in project life cycle management, which is essential in traditional project management practices, and in agile management, which has become increasingly adopted.

3.1 Design Principles of Blockchain and Their Correspondence in Managing Projects

Blockchain benefits have been classified into different categories by different researchers. Perera et al. (2020) propose 12 categories: Decentralization, anonymity, security, immutability, auditability, veracity, transparency, disintermediation, trust, Turing-complete, performance, and scalability. Koo et al. (2019) propose five categories: Decentralization, transparency, traceability, immutability, and collaboration. These categorizations are based on technical aspects. As business-oriented classification might be more valuable for project managers, we refer to the practical implications of Tapscott and Tapscott (2016). They conceptualize Blockchain principles in seven categories:

- Networked integrity
- Security
- Rights preserved
- Inclusion
- Distributed power
- Value as incentive
- Privacy

In the sequel, we will explain the meaning of all these principles within the project management framework. In our discussions, the Blockchain network will represent the network created by project stakeholders to use all principles of Blockchain systems in managing projects. Nodes will represent the project stakeholders that authorize and make transactions in the Blockchain network (Fig. 2).

Networked integrity refers to the principle that no external authoritative entity is required to verify the data integrity in the Blockchain network. Up to now, business transactions have been mainly processed through intermediaries. However, due to this principle, Blockchain systems can be used as a trusted medium to process transactions among project parties without intermediaries. Once a transaction is processed and the block is closed, the hashing mechanism and the chaining of the block ensure that the transaction will not be altered. For project work shared between different entities/contractors or done at various geographical locations (often observed in project portfolio management), network integrity will undoubtedly establish a project system where project deliveries and payments are made on time.

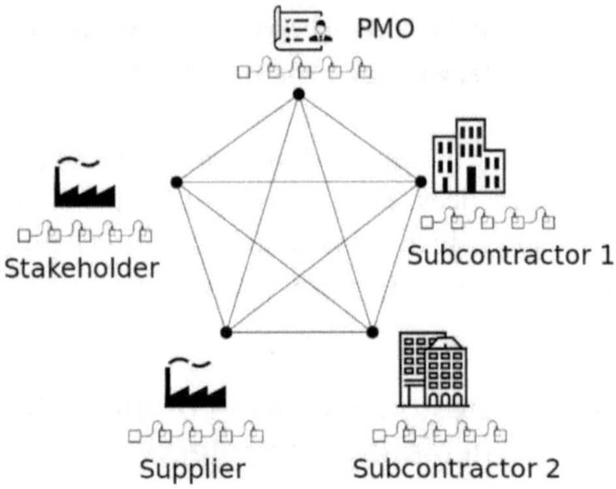

Fig. 2 The structure and interconnection of the Blockchain network

Networked integrity becomes crucial when the contractors work in different geographical locations, and there needs to be a clear legal framework to ensure the integrity of the data and documents. Blockchain technology ensures data integrity in the network using mathematics in a verifiable way without being dependent on external regulations. Based on the interview results, Matosyan (2019) underlines that eliminating intermediaries is a significant advantage of Blockchain systems. The interviewed project managers, even the most reserved ones in using these systems in project management, recognize this advantage.

Security principle in this context defines non-repudiation and authenticity of the information in the Blockchain records. Authenticity is guaranteed by having a copy of the whole chain information on all nodes connected to the chain; thus, all participants have a copy of the chain. On the other hand, non-repudiation is achieved by using Public Key Infrastructure (PKI). Since PKI is the primary identification method, cryptographic methods protect the falsification of information and the authenticity of information shared on the chain.

Many weapon development projects undertaken in the defence industry must be managed confidentially. For these secret projects, deciding when the details and intermediate outputs will be revealed is critical. The project managers try to protect confidentiality on the one hand and finish the project at the planned time on the other. Hall (2016) notes that a secret project has a value that depends on the actions of the competitors. The competitors are generally reluctant to share information but might want to show that they have achieved some milestones. Securing the confidentiality of essential project information is a critical role of managers in secret projects. Data vulnerability requires project organizations to securely store personal information and trade secrets. Achieving security through legacy systems can require extensive investments, while security is integral to Blockchain technology.

Rights preserved principle ensures that ownership and transactions on the chain are transparent and enforceable. Many of the projects need the work of several subcontractors, and their tasks could be time or resource-dependent on each other. Blockchain mechanism is beneficial since it allows all parties to see each other's transactions. As the required information of these tasks will be shared across all nodes in the network, each node can check if their counterparty created a transaction for starting a package of work or if an entry of a predecessor task completion has been posted on the network. Nodes in the network can use the information available and enforce it to the other stakeholders and project participants to preserve their rights. The rights preserved principle also supports project managers in communication management, as all network members get instantly notified of the progress instead of waiting for a notification.

Inclusion is the principle of Blockchain being open to all parties wanting to join the network. Private Blockchain would be the de facto implementation in project management, limiting the inclusion of stakeholders and resources identified by the project manager. When new resources and stakeholders are included in the project, they can become nodes in the network and start processing transactions. The advantage of Blockchain in this situation is that all nodes have access to the information. They become part of the Blockchain network, allowing them to check and verify other stakeholders' deliverables.

The Distributed power principle stresses the advantage of not having a central authority that oversees the transactions, and all peers in the network have control over the network as long as the previously defined criteria are met. In many projects, the project manager is the central authority to ensure the project is tracked and followed up correctly. Distributed power principles can create huge benefits in automating the tracking of project progress calculations based on Earned Value Management (EVM). We refer to the book of Vanhoucke (2009) for the principles of EVM methodology. In addition to traditional planning and control-based project management, the distributed power principle is used in distributed agile software management projects like open-source software development collaboration.

Value as an incentive is a principle specific to coin mining, an integral part of cryptocurrencies that motivates the storage of Blockchain data and participation in the network. Although in project management, all stakeholders will have their motivation to be part of the network, and this principle seems less relevant in project management, public Blockchain implementation of Smart contracts is based on cryptocurrencies. The industry 4.0 incentive and project management moving more to incorporate Smart contracts in projects would increase the impact of this principle in real-life applications.

The Privacy principle has been defined as one of the basic building blocks of BitCoin by Nakamoto (2008). Any participant can create a PKI key pair and issue transactions without needing the key pair to be linked to a real-life person or entity in the BitCoin design. This principle has valuable implementation benefits for "secret projects," slightly deviating from the initial notion. For secret project implementations, the privacy principle can be used to make sure that subcontractors and contributors remain anonymous to each other and do not have a direct interaction. The medium of interaction is the Blockchain network itself, where necessary information is made available to all contributors, and the project manager has complete visibility while keeping the actual identities of real-life entities limited to himself/herself.

We categorized the reviewed articles in Table 2 and examined their coverage of the abovementioned principles. Table 2, A (Acknowledged), shows that the study

Table 2 Implementations and possible benefits of the Blockchain principles

Study	Network integrity	Security	Rights preserved	Inclusion	Distributed power	Value as incentive	Privacy
Abodei et al.(2019)	A	A	A	A	A		
Ahmed et al. (2020)			A	A	A		
Choi (2020)		I				I	
Das et al. (2020)	A	A	A	A	A	A	A
Dutta et al. (2020)	A	A	A	A	A	A	
Elghaish et al. (2020)	I		I	I		A	
Hargaden et al. (2019)	A	A	A	A	A		A
Hewavitharana et al. (2019)	A	A	A	A	A		
Kifokeris and Koch (2019)	A			A	A		A
Kim et al. (2020)	A	A	A	A	A		A
Kiu et al. (2020)	A	A	A	A			A
Koo et al. (2019)	A	A	A	A	A		
Layaq et al. (2019)	A	A	A		A		A
Lee and Yoon (2019)	A		A				A
Li et al. (2019)	A	A	A	A	A	A	A
Liu et al. (2020)	A	A	A	A	A	A	A
Luo et al. (2019)	A	A	A	A	A		
Matosyan, Y. (2019)	A	A	A	A	A	A	A
Perera et al. (2020)	A	A	A	A	A	A	A
Tijan et al. (2019)	A	A	A		A	A	
Turk and Klinc (2017)		A	A	A			A
Wang et al. (2017)	A			A	A		
Wang et al. (2019)	A	A	A		A		

authors have acknowledged the principle as a benefit of the Blockchain. In contrast, I (Implemented) represents the original contribution of the study that the authors presented for the corresponding principle. It can be seen in Table 2 that even though most of the studies in the literature state possible benefits of Blockchains in project management, only some mention real-life implementation of the principle identified. Moreover, the business value added by each implementation needs to be explained in detail. The studies are more focused on the specific technology required for implementation and discuss the consequences of using this technology.

On average, around 80% of the authors identified Network integrity, Security, Rights preserved, Inclusion, and Distributed power as possible contributions of Blockchain technologies to project management; however, this value decreases to 30% for Value as an incentive and 50% for Privacy. We also observed that although most articles mention the benefits of Smart Contracts and Industry 4.0, less than 5% of these studies contain a novel approach to implementation ideas or represent an application of the acknowledged benefits.

In the following section, we demonstrate the potential benefits of Blockchain for each step of the project life cycle.

3.2 Project Life Cycle Management and Blockchain

Projects have life cycles. We perform a detailed analysis of the use of Blockchain throughout the life cycle. From the project initiation to its termination, it is possible to identify the phases: the conceptual design, definition, planning, monitoring, controlling, and termination (Ulusoy & Hazır, 2021). Different managerial approaches could be adopted at each phase, and different methods could be implemented. Blockchain systems could be used for different purposes at these stages, depending on the decision-support requirements of the managers. We will scrutinize each phase separately and discuss how Blockchain systems can support managerial practices in these phases. None of the existing studies investigate the use of Blockchain within the project life cycle framework. Our analysis considers the five-project life cycle stages and provides practical examples for each stage.

3.2.1 Initiating

Project charters are the primary documents used to establish the general framework for project implementation (Haugan et al., 2001). Even though their contents and format can differ depending on the project characteristics, the organizational requirements, and the business environment, they reflect the consensus between the undertaking organization and the stakeholders. Hence, they provide project managers a robust framework for their relations with these entities throughout the project lifecycle. Blockchain technologies could be used in the preparation of these documents.

The project charter can be the first transaction of the first block of the Blockchain, where all stakeholders can check and verify approved project requirements, constraints, and assumptions. In projects where Blockchain is used as the trusted network, the rules for creating and distributing transactions within the network are included in the project charter. When Smart contracts are used, the public/private Blockchain used to track the project progress employing EVM shall be defined in the project charter. In pure Blockchain implementation, the genesis node (first node) shall include a hash of the project charter and define the rules for containing new nodes in the chain. Block definitions can be customized based on project management requirements in private Blockchain implementations. The project charter can list identifiers for different types of inputs to the block. For example, risk registry files are to be identified with "R" before the hash, deliverables identified with "D," and new stakeholders with "S."

In traditional project management, stakeholder management comprises risks. Especially in big projects, there is a risk of not involving some of the important stakeholders or the emergence of new stakeholders. Blockchain can include stakeholders at any time they are required as resource(s)/providers with the benefit of the inclusion principle defined above.

3.2.2 Planning

Once the project objectives and scope are specified and the charter is signed, the project team and manager prepare time, resources, cost, and risk plans. Even though these plans might have to be revised several times during the project execution, they constitute the critical elements of the scope, change management, resource, and risk management.

The documentation regarding these managerial functions could be done through Blockchain systems. In this way, a historical record of all the decisions made will be kept, and the details of the revisions can be easily traced and shared with the stakeholders or third parties. Record-keeping is vital in projects where falsifying records or creating back-dated system entries cannot be allowed or tolerated. An excellent example of these projects would be the pharmaceutical industry vaccine or drug development projects. The COVID-19 pandemic showed that vaccine development involves enormous projects that span more than one geographical location and require verifiable and trustworthy information for assessment. Blockchain-based solutions for planning and executing these projects ensure that old records cannot be falsified and the data integrity since the planning stage can be proven (Networked integrity principle).

Another example is defence projects, which are always carried out with high confidentiality. The planning phase should be carried out in secrecy in defence projects, including critical processes such as bringing together the project team, preparing the procurement list, determining work packages, calendar, budget planning, and risk planning. Many defence projects are carried out with the contribution of many participants from different locations, which makes ensuring confidentiality at the Initiating and Planning stages even more challenging. Using Blockchain and distributed ledger will make it easier for all project participants to access project documentation securely and avoid manual documentation prone to error. Smart contracts will enhance process automation and reliability in the Initiating and Planning stages.

3.2.3 Executing

Once baseline plans are prepared and the criteria for performance assessment are set, the execution of the project begins. Even though the plans might have been crafted meticulously, unexpected events that jeopardize achieving the goals are often encountered. Unfortunately, many projects fail due to various uncertain events. Tracking the decisions taken is crucial for accountability and learning from the errors. Blockchain systems can track the risk events, budget execution, and change requests and revisions during the execution. Referring to the Blockchain transactions will provide a transparent view of the whole project to all stakeholders and enhance the accountability of the successes and failures.

Blockchain networks can be used to disseminate information on the execution of activities while avoiding administrative delays. With Smart contracts, payment orders can be executed immediately following the execution of the tasks, thereby increasing trust between parties and client satisfaction.

If the project is not transparent to all stakeholders, zero-knowledge proof (ZKP) methods can be used to track progress without revealing the actual information. This is a mathematical proof method to ensure that both parties have the same information without disclosing this information. Practical applications can be observed in software development for secret projects. Morais et al. (2019) presented some application examples. Moreover, in projects where the project manager prefers that subcontractors are not aware of each other or have limited visibility on the whole project, ZKP can support the Privacy principle of the Blockchain implementation.

3.2.4 Monitoring and Controlling

During project execution, deviations from the plans are expected rather than exceptions, and managers need to do corrective actions to minimize the deviations from the project goals. In this regard, monitoring and controlling activities of the managers play critical roles in ensuring successful project completion. Project managers can benefit greatly from establishing a structured monitoring and control system (Hazır, 2015). Blockchain can be used as a trusted medium to monitor progress. The transactions of the activity executions and budget use in the Blockchain ledger can simultaneously be used to track project progress and identify possible bottlenecks. As deviations are detected, corrective actions can be implemented, and the plans can be updated relatively quickly. Outputs of standard project management tools like Microsoft Project can be published as transactions, allowing all stakeholders to have a verified project progress report. They will not need to verify the contents with the project manager. Instead of sending emails to verify that an activity or a module is complete, a transaction in the last block can be used.

In secret projects, it is necessary to establish reliable and secure communication with material suppliers. The presence of material suppliers in the Blockchain infrastructure will make the supply chain safer and faster. With the support of smart contracts (Ahmad et al., 2021), secret projects such as defence projects, monitoring, and controlling can be performed without experiencing authentication and validation problems.

3.2.5 Closing

At the end of the life cycle, the project terminates as the deliverables are transferred to the customer. The project performance is assessed, final reports and documents are prepared, and the team is dissolved. Organizations would continue to undertake other projects. In this regard, every project provides valuable information to organizations. Documenting the lessons learned to have a sustainable organization with continuous learning is essential.

Blockchain can also be used in the closing stage. Since activity finish times and deliverables/milestones can be tracked through the transaction records, the task would be to collect the documents through the transactions. Similarly, feedback on the end product can be collected and recorded by ensuring that the feedback is also part of the chain as an indicator of the quality of the end product. Participants can use the Blockchain to give and collect feedback on their performance and communicate the lessons learned with their counterparties. Most importantly, for the project closing, there should be a final/terminal transaction of the chain, where all nodes in the chain agree that the project is closed.

We summarize the importance of Blockchain principles at different project life cycle stages in Table 3. The importance is reflected at three levels: low, medium, and high, using three example project types: single organization, distributed development, and secret projects. A distributed development project requires the contribution of many organizations, which can be located in various geographical locations, to develop products or services. As we already discussed, information security is critical in secret projects.

The low-level importance refers to limited or no significant improvement introduced by Blockchain. Medium-level importance has been assigned if the usage of Blockchain introduces some improvements when used as an alternative to standard centralized project management practices. A high level is set when using Blockchain, simplifying the paperwork and eliminating unnecessary checks and controls. We use the open-ended interviews conducted by Renwich and Tierney (2020) to decide on the rankings. Their study identified the following constructs: transparency, control, dynamic status updates, incentives, and trust.

Table 3 shows that network integrity and inclusion are the essential enablers for distributed and secret projects. The benefits of using Blockchain to manage a single organization project could be low. This factor slows down the adoption of Blockchain for project management by companies. Since most companies prefer to test the Blockchain internally before implementing it with stakeholders/subcontractors, the impact is only visible with a distributed or secret project. This prevents companies from investing in this new and emerging technology.

We discussed the potential benefits of using Blockchain within the project lifecycle phases. In the following section, we investigate the use of Blockchain, considering the knowledge areas.

3.3 Blockchain and Project Management Knowledge Areas

In this section, we analyze project management from the perspectives of the knowledge areas defined by PMI. Project management covers the following knowledge areas (PMI, 2017).

- Integration Management
- Scope Management
- Schedule Management
- Cost Management
- Quality Management.
- Resource Management
- Communications Management
- Risk Management
- Procurement Management

Although PMI (2017) considers **stakeholder management** to be a dedicated knowledge area, we will include it in the **communications management** area for simplicity. We also refer the readers to PMBOK-Guide, PMI 2017 for the definitions and scope of these areas. All these knowledge areas can benefit from Blockchain technology (Matosyan, 2019). We conducted a literature review, briefly discussed the selected studies based on their contribution to these areas, and summarized the findings in Table 4.

In Table 4, we matched the articles with the project management knowledge areas. If the article has identified a practical application, this is considered as an Acknowledgement (A) of the applicability of Blockchain to that knowledge area. Improvements (I) notation is used for cases where it is mentioned that Blockchain will bring significant improvements without specific case studies. Table 4 is more scarce compared to Table 2. It can be explained by the fact that studies usually concentrate on specific areas and the industry dependence on the problems mainly addressed focuses on the construction industry.

Kiu et al. (2020) examine the use of Blockchain in procurement, communications, and cost management. Elghaish et al. (2020) address cost management by presenting a payment platform for construction projects. In their construction logistics review, Koo et al. (2019) discuss using Blockchain in schedule, resource, and quality management. They perform scope management in pharmaceutical construction projects by using Blockchain.

Dutta et al. (2020) discuss the potential benefits of Blockchain in resource and procurement management for various industries, including manufacturing, healthcare, and software development. Layaq et al. (2019) present Blockchain as a potential solution for managing supply chain risks. Liu et al. (2020) developed a multicriteria decision-making procedure for supplier selection and discussed the benefits of blockchain tracing anti-counterfeiting platforms in procurement management.

Table 3 Life cycle stages and Blockchain principles concerning three project types

	Project type	Network integrity	Security	Rights preserved	Inclusion	Distributed power	Value as insscentive	Privacy
Initiating	Single organisation	Med.	Low	Low	Med.	Low	Low	Low
	Distributed	High	Med.	High	High	Med.	High	Low
	Secret	High	High	High	High	Med.	Low	High
Planning	Single organisation	High	Low	Low	Low	Low	Low	Low
	Distributed	High	Low	Low	Low	Med.	High	Med.
	Secret	High	Med.	Med.	Med.	Med.	Low	High
Executing	Single organisation	Low	Med.	Med.	Low	Low	Low	Low
	Distributed	Med.	Med.	High	High	Med.	High	Med.
	Secret	Med.	High	High	High	High	Low	High
Monitoring and controlling	Single organisation	Med.	Low	Low	Med.	Low	Low	Low
	Distributed	High	Low	Med.	High	Med.	High	Med.
	Secret	High	Med.	Med.	High	High	Low	High
Closing	Single organisation	Med.	Low	Low	Med.	Low	Low	Low
	Distributed	High	Med.	High	High	Low	Med.	Low
	Secret	High	High	High	High	Low	Low	High

Kim et al. (2020) conducted surveys in the construction sector to identify the potential impact of blockchain on each project management activity. The construction sector has been experimenting with Blockchain in project management. The sectors specific requirements can explain this early adoption of the technology. As it is a highly regulated industry, construction projects require different layers of blueprint drawings and various calculations to be made in the correct order to get regulators' approval. Since the drawings are already done using CAD, there is a strict predecessor-successor dependency. Blockchain is a good solution as it can be integrated into CAD software, supporting distributed processes, and consequently, dependencies can be tracked.

The construction industry is also highly dependent on subcontractors to prepare the necessary documentation, the tracking of which can be supported by Blockchain (Kifokeris & Koch, 2019). Another factor affecting the adoption of Blockchain in the construction industry is that managing the supply chain is critical for success. Today materials used for construction are acquired by various suppliers operating in different countries. Smart contracts offer opportunities to make procurement more efficient and reliable. As a result, the industry has become familiar with Blockchain technology. Companies like IBM and Samsung have developed supply chain management tools using Blockchain. Despite the increasing investments of many companies in digital transformation, Kim et al. (2020) note that the literature on the use of Blockchain technologies in the construction industry still needs to be expanded compared to finance and logistics industries.

Traditional project management emphasizes managing the project cycle while focusing on time and cost targets. We have discussed using Blockchain, considering the phases of the project life cycle. Agile project management has been replacing the plan-focused life cycle-based approaches in several industries, such as software development. Traditional pre-planning, monitoring, and control-based management approaches might need to be revised due to frequent scope changes in these industries. Next, we will investigate the use of Blockchain in agile project systems.

3.4 Use of Blockchain in Agile and Hybrid Project Management

Agile project management is based on delivering project outcomes through iterative development and delivery cycles. The main advantage of adopting an iterative approach is the inherent flexibility to adapt to changes. For this reason, organizations in industries that are subject to frequent changes and high uncertainty, such as the software industry, have largely adopted agile management methods (Weflen et al., 2022). However, the risk of failure is considerably high in many agile projects. Sahota (2012) notes that the failure rate of agile transformation projects goes up to 86%. Since resources will remain scarce, several critical elements of traditional approaches, such as structural planning, optimization of the resources, monitoring, and control of performance, and adopting systematic approaches to problem solving, could also be beneficial in these projects. In this regard, hybrid

Table 4 Implementations and possible applications of Blockchain in the knowledge areas

Study	Integration	Scope	Schedule	Cost	Quality	Resource	Communications	Risk	Procurement
Abodei et al. (2019)				I	A	I			I
Choi (2020)				I		A			
Das et al. (2020)	A	A		I		I	A		
Dutta et al. (2020)	A	A	A	A		A	A		A
Elghaish et al. (2020)	I			I		I	I		I
Hargaden et al. (2019)				A	A	A	A		A
Hewavitharana et al. (2019)	A			A	A	A	A		A
Kifokeris and Koch (2019)	A	A				I	I		A
Kim et al. (2020)	A	A	A	A	A	A	A	A	A
Kiu et al. (2020)	I			I		I	I		I
Koo et al. (2019)			A			I	A		
Layaq et al. (2019)				I	A		I	I	I
Lee and Yoon (2019)			A			A	A		
Li et al. (2019)				A		A	A		A
Liu et al. (2020)	A	A				A			A
Luo et al. (2019)	I			I		I	I		I
Matosyan (2019)	A	A	A	A	A	A	A	A	A
Perera et al. (2020)						A	A		A
Tijan et al. (2019)				A		A	A		A
Turk and Klinc (2017)							A		A
Wang et al. (2017)				A		A	A		
Wang et al. (2019)	I		A	I			I		I

approaches have been adopted to adjust the control requirements, especially for the budget and the flexibility of continuous development. One possibility could be opting for the plan-driven or the agile, depending on the project phase. Agile techniques could also be used until the requirements are known. Afterward, more detailed plans could be prepared, and traditional approaches could be used (Larson & Gray, 2021).

We have identified a close similarity between the principles of Blockchain technology and the Agile Manifesto (Beck et al., 2001). Agile methodology is built on providing value to the customer, reducing work that does not add business value, and acting fast based on customer requirements. Similarly, Blockchain provides a flattened view where customers, developers, and management can be part of a single network, increasing the impact on the customer. Like extensive documentation, work that does not add business value can be avoided by using Blockchain. When the definition of done criteria is met, and the customer accepts this, the project can move to the next phase. Blockchain also enables acting fast, and the best example is Smart Contracts, which will be discussed in the next section.

When we look at the individual principles of the Agile manifesto, we can see these similarities for each principle (see Fig. 3). The inclusion principle supports better project management using Blockchain compared to traditional methods. Since customers can be directly part of the Blockchain network, customer collaboration envisioned by the Agile Manifesto can be realized. Customers can contact all the teams involved directly and monitor the progress. The network identity principle defined above assures the customer about the progress. The rights preserved principle of Blockchain facilitates responding to changes in the Agile Manifesto. Blockchain can be used to ensure that the software developed is not modified afterward in line with the security principle. The idea of working software instead of comprehensive documentation can be checked and verified by the stakeholders using the verifiability of the Blockchain and the software provided by the developer using conventional means. Individuals and interactions stressed by the Agile Manifesto are one of the building blocks of Blockchain as a distributed network instead of a single standardized authoritative source.

Practically Sprints or Kanban boards used by agile teams can be integrated into Blockchain mechanisms. We see an opportunity to improve secret and distributed projects for remote project managers to verify that work packages are handled as planned and that necessary resources are allocated correctly to the tasks in consideration. Participants of a distributed project, where the internal works of other participants are secret to their counterparties, track the progress of the agile sprint on a high level and plan their actions based on the information available in the network.

Significant improvements to documentation and the ability to audit against requirements for highly regulated industries in software development can be achieved by using Blockchain. The finance and banking industries are practical examples where changes introduced to the code base must be verified through an approval process after the development. Tests need to be documented, and audit records of these actions must be stored for a specific time for auditing purposes. Nearly all the highly regulated industries CI/CD pipeline steps need to keep audit records about the changes. These records can be integrated into the project Blockchain. The project managers will also use these records maintained for auditing purposes to track the project progress. The immutability property of these records will be utilized for auditing purposes. At the same time, distributed information storage will make it easier to track development progress for teams distributed in separate geographical locations.

As indicated before, one of the main advantages of Blockchain is providing immutable records. Blockchain systems are highly suitable for keeping records, such as information that needs to be unchangeable. Blockchain offers several opportunities to enhance the security of projects. In agile project management, where the requirements evolve, having broad documentation and a full sign-off on all requirements at the beginning of the project is only sometimes possible. The Blockchain provides immutable documentation where changes, approvals, and progress can be tracked without unnecessary paperwork. The collection of user requirements, the collaboration between teams, and project progress can be simplified using Blockchain integrated into the agile development framework. The maximum benefit of the Blockchain in agile is possibly achieved on secret projects with distributed teams. Classical requirements management based on paperwork can be replaced by sharing the documents online and using the Blockchain network to prove the document authenticity within minutes to replace creating and sharing authorized copies.

To sum up, Blockchain in agile development will bring significant benefits to agile project management. However, this requires a defined framework and much more development effort than the Blockchain for traditional project management. Since agile methodology emphasizes product delivery, the documentation requirements could be less. Traditional approaches create much documentation. Such records serve as practical artifacts for communication. Agile methodologies encourage lean thinking and reducing overhead, particularly documentation. The knowledge in agile development is usually tacit and needs to be communicated through documents written by the development team members (Nerur et al., 2005). However, the end product acceptance criteria must be added to the Blockchain network. To implement agile project management using Blockchain, the product acceptance

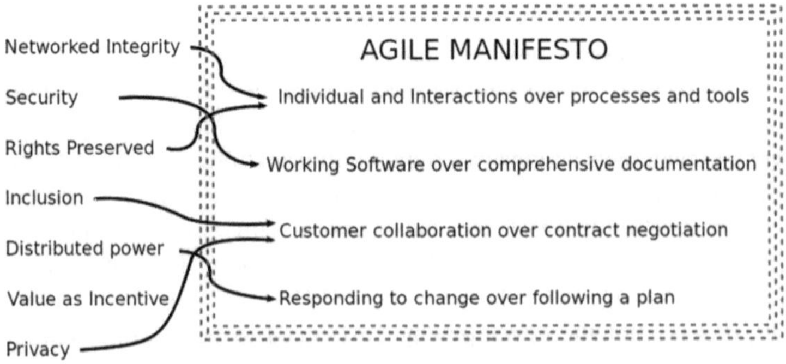

Fig. 3 Blockchain design principles and their linked agile manifesto statements

criteria need to be defined in agile terms, and a method of propagation of the statement of done needs to be developed. The transformation to agile in traditional project management can be achieved easily, as the documentation is already created, it can be used in transactions envisioned as part of the Blockchain. Next, we focus on one of the most promising applications of Blockchain in project management: Smart contracts.

3.5 Smart Contracts and Project Management

Smart contracts allow a specific step of a distributed program to be executed on the network when certain conditions are met. When the execution of the step is completed, the Blockchain is updated. Within the Blockchain structure, the completed transaction is no longer adjustable and can only be monitored by the authorized parties. These characteristics of Smart contracts offer several opportunities that can considerably change business management processes. Smart contracts can be used at each project life cycle stage. A multilateral consensus can be achieved quickly in the initiation and planning stages. Many processes of the execution, monitoring, and controlling activities can be carried out automatically, with the secure participation of the parties.

Using Smart contracts effectively will also be beneficial in dealing with project complexity. Vidal and Marle (2008) note that "project complexity is the property of a project which makes it difficult to understand, foresee and keep under control its overall behaviour, even when given almost complete information about the project system." There are transparent cause-and-effect relationships for projects with simple complexity (Snowden & Boone, 2007). The stakeholders share a common understanding. Therefore, simple projects can be fully automated by Smart contracts.

On the other hand, projects with complicated complexity have known unknowns. There need to be identified cause-and-effect relationships. Monitoring the project status and keeping the project progress under control will be more accessible by using Smart contracts. The processes will become more transparent and rapidly traceable. Changes in customer requirements and expectations are common in complex projects. Re-planning might require the consent of the parties. In cases where re-planning is required, Smart contracts allow a new consensus to be achieved transparently and quickly.

4 Conclusions and Future Research Directions

We conducted a literature review of the use of Blockchain in management. We discovered that most studies investigating Blockchain use in project management address the construction industry. However, when appropriately implemented, Blockchain is a suitable tool for project management with massive potential in various industries. Our literature review shows a need for studies that will address the practice in various other industries.

We pointed out a wide range of application areas throughout the text by referring to the Blockchain design principles. For example, the benefits of using Blockchain in defence projects were listed. We also discussed how Blockchain can improve project life cycle management and contribute to project management knowledge areas. We noted that agile practices are aligned with the design principles of Blockchain and underlined the substantial benefits of agile project management.

Despite the increasing popularity of blockchain technologies and the recognition of their high improvement potential, most organizations still need to adopt or consider adopting these technologies to enhance their project management practices. We also note that Smart contracts are in their infancy phase in project management. However, they will have a general industry acceptance with the popularization of the Internet of Things (IoT), as IoT devices can easily be used to create and maintain Smart contracts. In the construction industry, BIM systems have been increasingly adopted to support knowledge management (Wang & Meng, 2019). In this industry, we expect a wider use of Blockchain-based software and integration with BIM.

We highlighted several research gaps in this review. The findings can serve as a basis for future research on Blockchain adoption and implementation in project management. In this regard, the factors affecting the adoption and implementation of Blockchain technologies and the sectoral differences in adoption and implementation in project management could be investigated.

References

Abodei, E., Norta, A., Azogu, I., Udokwu, C., & Draheim, D. (2019). Blockchain technology for enabling transparent and traceable government collaboration in public project processes of developing economies. *Conference on E-Business, e-Services and e-Society*, 464–475.

Ahmad, R. W., Hasan, H., Yaqoob, I., Salah, K., Jayaraman, R., & Omar, M. (2021). Blockchain for aerospace and defense: Opportunities and open research challenges. *Computers & Industrial Engineering, 151*, 106982.

Ahmed, M., Ullah, A. S. B., & Pathan, A.-S. K. (2020). *Security analytics for the internet of everything*. CRC Press.

Beck, K., Beedle, M., Van Bennekum, A., Cockburn, A., Cunningham, W., Fowler, M., Grenning, J., Highsmith, J., Hunt, A., Jeffries, R., et al. (2001). Manifesto for agile software development.

Bodkhe, U., Tanwar, S., Parekh, K., Khanpara, P., Tyagi, S., Kumar, N., & Alazab, M. (2020). Blockchain for industry 4.0: A comprehensive review. *IEEE Access, 8*, 79764–79800.

Bouraga, S. (2021). A taxonomy of blockchain consensus protocols: A survey and classification framework. *Expert Systems with Applications, 168*, 114384.

Choi, T. M. (2020). Financing product development projects in the blockchain era: Initial coin offerings versus traditional bank loans. *IEEE Transactions on Engineering Management*.

Das, M., Luo, H., & Cheng, J. C. (2020). Securing interim payments in construction projects through a blockchain-based framework. *Automation in Construction, 118*, 103284.

Drescher, D. (2017). *Blockchain basics: A non-technical introduction in 25 steps*. Apress.

Dutta, P., Choi, T.-M., Somani, S., & Butala, R. (2020). Blockchain technology in supply chain operations: Applications, challenges and research opportunities. *Transportation Research Part E: Logistics and Transportation Review, 142*, 102067.

Elghaish, F., Abrishami, S., & Hosseini, M. R. (2020). Integrated project delivery with Blockchain: An automated financial system. *Automation in Construction, 114*, 103182.

Ferguson, M. (2018). Preparing for a blockchain future. *MIT Sloan Management Review, 60*(1), 1–4.

Hall, N. G. (2016). Research and teaching opportunities in project management. In *Optimization challenges in complex, networked and risky systems* (pp. 329–388). INFORMS.

Hargaden, V., Papakostas, N., Newell, A., Khavia, A., & Scanlon, A. (2019). The role of blockchain technologies in construction engineering project management. In *2019 IEEE International Conference on Engineering, Technology and Innovation (ICE/ITMC)* (pp. 1–6).

Haugan, G. T., et al. (2001). *Project planning and scheduling*. Berrett-Koehler Publishers.

Hazır, Ö. (2015). A review of analytical models, approaches and decision support tools in project monitoring and control. *International Journal of Project Management, 33*(4), 808–815.

Hazır, Ö., & Ulusoy, G. (2020). A classification and review of approaches and methods for modeling uncertainty in projects. *International Journal of Production Economics, 223*, 107522.

Hewavitharana, T., Nanayakkara, S., & Perera, S. (2019). Blockchain as a project management platform. 137–146. https://doi.org/10.6084/m9.figshare.10326821.v1

Insights, I. F. (2021). *Truly digital core banking: You are more ready than you think*. https://doi.org/IDC. Doc #AP15021X.

Kerkhove, L.-P., & Vanhoucke, M. (2016). Incentive contract design for projects: The owner's perspective. *Omega, 62*, 93–114.

Kerkhove, L.-P., & Vanhoucke, M. (2020). Multi-mode schedule optimisation for incentivised projects. *Computers & Industrial Engineering, 142*, 106321.

Kifokeris, D., & Koch, C. (2019, July 10). *Blockchain in construction logistics: State-of-art, constructability, and the advent of a new digital business model in Sweden*. Proceedings of the 2019 European Conference on Computing in Construction.

Kim, K., Lee, G., & Kim, S. (2020). A study on the application of blockchain technology in the construction industry. *KSCE Journal of Civil Engineering, 24*(9), 2561–2571.

Kiu, M., Chia, F., & Wong, P. (2020). Exploring the potentials of blockchain application in construction industry: A systematic review. *International Journal of Construction Management*, 1–10.

Koo, D. D., Kang, K., Lee, J. J., & Hu, Q. (2019). Enhancing comprehensive quality assurance of construction projects toward smart city sustainability using blockchain technology.

Larson, E., & Gray, C. (2021). *Project management: The managerial process 8e*. McGraw Hill.

Layaq, M. W., Goudz, A., Noche, B., & Atif, M. (2019). Blockchain technology as a risk mitigation tool in supply chain. *International Journal of Transportation Science and Technology, 5*(3), 50–59.

Lee, E., & Yoon, Y. I. (2019). Project management model based on consistency strategy for blockchain platform. In *2019 IEEE 17th International Conference on Software Engineering Research, Management and Applications (SERA)* (pp. 38–44).

Lenarduzzi, V., Lunesu, M. I., Marchesi, M., & Tonelli, R. (2018). Blockchain applications for agile methodologies. In *Proceedings of the 19th International Conference on Agile Software Development: Companion* (pp. 1–3).

Leyman, P., & Vanhoucke, M. (2016). Payment models and net present value optimization for resource-constrained project scheduling. *Computers & Industrial Engineering, 91*, 139–153.

Li, J., Greenwood, D., & Kassem, M. (2019). Blockchain in the built environment and construction industry: A systematic review, conceptual models and practical use cases. *Automation in Construction, 102*, 288–307.

Liu, A., Liu, T., Mou, J., & Wang, R. (2020). A supplier evaluation model based on customer demand in Blockchain tracing anti-counterfeiting platform project management. *Journal of Management Science and Engineering, 5*(3), 172–194.

Luo, H., Das, M., Wang, J., & Cheng, J. C. (2019). Construction payment automation through smart contract-based blockchain framework. *ISARC. Proceedings of the International Symposium on Automation and Robotics in Construction, 36*, 1254–1260.

Matosyan, Y. (2019). *Potential of using the Blockchain technology for project management* [Master's Thesis]. Vysoká škola ekonomická v Praze.

Morais, E., Koens, T., Van Wijk, C., & Koren, A. (2019). A survey on zero knowledge range proofs and applications. *SN Applied Sciences, 1*(8), 1–17.
Nakamoto, S. (2008). Bitcoin: A peer-to-peer electronic cash system. *Decentralized Business Review, 21260.*
Nerur, S., Mahapatra, R., & Mangalaraj, G. (2005). Challenges of migrating to agile methodologies. *Communications of the ACM, 48*(5), 72–78.
Pajares, J., Poza, D., Villafañez, F., & López-Paredes, A. (2017). Project management methodologies in the fourth technological revolution. In *Advances in management engineering* (pp. 121–144). Springer.
Penzes, B. (2018). *Blockchain technology in the construction industry*. Accessed August 1, 2022, from https://www.ice.org.uk/ICEDevelopmentWebPortal/media/Documents/News/Blog/Blockchain-technology-in-Construction-2018-12-17.pdf
Perera, S., Nanayakkara, S., Rodrigo, M., Senaratne, S., & Weinand, R. (2020). Blockchain technology: Is it hype or real in the construction industry? *Journal of Industrial Information Integration, 17*, 100125.
PMI, P. (2017). *Project management body of knowledge (PMBOK® guide)*. Project Management Institute.
Renwick, R., & Tierney, B. (2020). Are Blockchain-based systems the future of project management? A preliminary exploration. *The Journal of the British Blockchain Association, 12586.*
Sahota, M. (2012). An agile adoption and transformation survival guide.. Lulu.com.
Simion, C.-P., Popa, S.-C., & Albu, C. (2018). Project management 4.0–project management in the digital era. In *12th International Management Conference: Management Perspectives in the Digital Era* (pp. 93–100). Editura ASE.
Snowden, D. J., & Boone, M. E. (2007). A leader's framework for decision making. *Harvard Business Review, 85*(11), 68.
Szabo, N. (1997). Formalizing and securing relationships on public networks.. First Monday.
Tapscott, D., & Tapscott, A. (2016). *Blockchain revolution: How the technology behind bitcoin is changing money, business, and the world.* Penguin.
Tijan, E., Aksentijević, S., Ivanić, K., & Jardas, M. (2019). Blockchain technology implementation in logistics. *Sustainability, 11*(4), 1185.
Tupa, J., Simota, J., & Steiner, F. (2017). Aspects of risk management implementation for Industry 4.0. *Procedia Manufacturing, 11*, 1223–1230.
Turk, Ž., & Klinc, R. (2017). Potentials of blockchain technology for construction management. *Procedia Engineering, 196*, 638–645.
Ulusoy, G., & Hazır, Ö. (2021). Introduction to project modeling and planning. In *An introduction to project modeling and planning* (pp. 1–21). Springer.
Vanhoucke, M. (2009). *Measuring time: Improving project performance using earned value management* (Vol. 136). Springer Science & Business Media.
Vanhoucke, M., Demeulemeester, E., & Herroelen, W. (2001). On maximizing the net present value of a project under renewable resource constraints. *Management Science, 47*(8), 1113–1121.
Vanhoucke, M., Demeulemeester, E., & Herroelen, W. (2003). Progress payments in project scheduling problems. *European Journal of Operational Research, 148*(3), 604–620.
Vidal, L.-A., & Marle, F. (2008). *Understanding project complexity: Implications on project management.* Kybernetes.
Wang, H., & Meng, X. (2019). Transformation from IT-based knowledge management into BIM-supported knowledge management: A literature review. *Expert Systems with Applications, 121*, 170–187.
Wang, S., Ouyang, L., Yuan, Y., Ni, X., Han, X., & Wang, F.-Y. (2019). Blockchain-enabled smart contracts: Architecture, applications, and future trends. *IEEE Transactions on Systems, Man, and Cybernetics: Systems, 49*(11), 2266–2277.
Wang, J., Wu, P., Wang, X., & Shou, W. (2017). The outlook of blockchain technology for construction engineering management. *Frontiers of Engineering Management*, 67–75.

Weflen, E., MacKenzie, C. A., & Rivero, I. V. (2022). An influence diagram approach to automating lead time estimation in Agile Kanban project management. *Expert Systems with Applications, 187*, 115866.

Zou, W., Lo, D., Kochhar, P. S., Le, X.-B. D., Xia, X., Feng, Y., Chen, Z., & Xu, B. (2019). Smart contract development: Challenges and opportunities. *IEEE Transactions on Software Engineering, 47*(10), 2084–2106.

Big Data for Project Management

Tuba Bakici and Öncü Hazir

Abstract

In this chapter, we discuss the use of big data analytics to enhance project management. We present a literature review, summarize the current practices and point out the potential application areas. The use of big data analytics has recently attracted the attention of researchers and practitioners, but we still lack knowledge on the implementation of big data tools in projects.

1 Understanding Big Data

In the digital landscape, "big data" emerges like an untamed frontier for many organizations. It represents a world of large and intricate data sets that traditional methods and processing tools struggle to manage them. Beyond neatly categorized and filed structured data such as transactions, there is a rich potential in unstructured and semi-structured data. This includes social media posts, tweets, geolocation data, emails, calls, surveys, biometrics, and sensor readings, which remain largely unexplored (Chen et al., 2012; Negash, 2004).

The proliferation of the Internet of Things (IoT), Radio-frequency identification (RFID), smart devices, open data, cloud computing, web, and social media has ignited this explosion of data—growing in volume (amount of data), variety (type of data), and velocity (the speed at which data is generated). With advancements in

T. Bakici (✉)
EDHEC Business School, Roubaix, France
e-mail: tuba.bakici@edhec.edu

Ö. Hazir
Rennes School of Business, Rennes, France
e-mail: oncu.hazir@rennes-sb.com

Ö. Hazır, M. E. Bruni (eds.), *Tomorrow's Data Empowered Project Management*, Future of Business and Finance, https://doi.org/10.1007/978-3-031-84017-3_2

modern data storage and processing, companies can now unlock valuable insights from this diverse information, leading to better business decisions, enhanced productivity, process automation, innovation of new business models, products, and services, as well as improved transparency and operational efficiency (Akter et al., 2016; Manyika et al., 2011; Shim et al., 2015). Olsson and Bull-Berg (2015) further highlight several key developments that have driven the adoption of big data analytics in organizations:

- The availability of vast amounts of data, including internet data and information from sensors and tracking technologies such as IoT, GPS and telematics systems.
- The rise of targeted advertising, particularly on digital platforms, exposes consumers to more personalized content.
- Growing demand for making data accessible and transparent, leading initiatives like open data.
- The availability of affordable storage and analytical capabilities.
- The development of IT platforms that contextualize data, such as digital maps for geolocation data and Building Information Models (BIM) for construction and infrastructure projects.

However, big data is just a lot of data, and we cannot gain value until it has been processed. Specialized techniques are required to handle big data collected from various sources and business functions. These include data mining, machine learning, neural networks, social network analysis, signal processing, pattern recognition, optimization methods, and visualization (Chen & Zhang, 2014). Additionally, these techniques necessitate specific applications such as distributed file systems (e.g., Hadoop MapReduce framework), NoSQL databases, massively parallel processing (MPP) systems, cloud computing platforms, in-memory database processing, and various data mining tools (Furht & Villanustre, 2016). By processing this extensive data, two additional characteristics of big data can be assessed, namely its veracity (data's integrity) and value (contribution) (Górecki, 2018).

Gandomi and Haider (2015) explained several commonly used big data analytical techniques for structured and unstructured data:

- Text analytics, called text mining, involves extracting information from textual data such as "social network feeds, emails, blogs, online forums, survey responses, corporate documents, news, and call center logs, using statistical analysis, computational linguistics, and machine learning".
- Audio and video analytics are applied to analyze and extract information from unstructured audio data such as spoken audio and video streams.
- Social media analytics involves "analyzing user-generated content (e.g., sentiments, images, videos, bookmarks) and the relationships between network entities (e.g., people, organizations, products) from social media channels". This includes content-based analytics, which examines data posted by users, and structure-based analytics, which analyzes the relationships within the network.

- Predictive analytics uses various techniques to predict future outcomes based on historical and current data. These techniques fall into two main groups: those identifying historical patterns (e.g., moving averages) and those capturing interdependencies between outcome variable(s) and explanatory variables (e.g., linear regression). They can also be categorized by methodology: regression techniques (e.g., multinomial logit models) and machine learning techniques (e.g., neural networks). Additionally, they are classified by the type of outcome type: continuous (e.g., linear regression for predicting sale prices) or discrete (e.g., Random Forests for classifying credit status).

Keeping this description in mind, let's try to find answers to the following questions:

- How does big data contribute to more informed, agile, real-time decision-making?
- In what ways do big data analytics impact and enhance project management processes?
- How might big data revolutionize project management practices and influence the future trajectory of organizations?

2 Current State of Big Data in Project Management

While applications of big data and big data analytics in several areas, such as operations management, healthcare, and marketing, have increased rapidly (Choi et al., 2018; Erevelles et al., 2016; Luo et al., 2016), the actual use of big data analytics in project management remains very limited (Bakici et al., 2021). Many organizations need more resources, capability, maturity, and managerial support to use big data tools in their projects, or they are at the early stage of the adoption process (Bakici et al., 2021).

This can be partially attributed to the unique nature of projects despite many of the activities and processes being repetitive or well-known. Unlike ongoing operations, projects are instead temporary endeavors with distinct timelines. Projects can involve different teams, stakeholders, and resources in a dynamic environment, which introduces variability and complexity not typically in routine operations. This nature of projects makes applying standard big data analytics techniques directly challenging. Nonetheless, since many projects share common activities and resources, organizations can significantly benefit from incorporating big data and big data analytics into their project management practices. Let's see how next.

3 The Role of Big Data in Project Management

In the realm of project management, big data emerges as a powerful ally, providing deeper insights and more accurate predictions as project management becomes more inherently related to the use of data. By analyzing vast amounts of data from various sources, project managers can uncover patterns, anticipate potential risks, ensure timely project completion, increase productivity, and make more informed decisions (Mohammad et al., 2020; Ibrahim et al., 2017). Among these various benefits, the foremost advantage of big data tools would be in project decision-making (Hazır, 2015). Especially, each project management process, namely planning, execution, monitoring, and closing, requires continuous decision-making. Hence, success of project management is inherently tied to tools such as big data analytics for decision-making support (Raymond & Bergeron, 2008; Wamba et al., 2015).

But how exactly does big data support decision-making? Decision-making, the process of selecting the right choice among alternatives, is crucial for business success and often depends on the data availability and processing capabilities (Desgourdes & Ram, 2024). Big data enables access to vast, complex data and advanced processing capabilities that support decision-making beyond human cognitive limits (Janssen et al., 2017; Sammut & Sartawi, 2012). For instance, tools like data visualization enhance project managers' cognition by leveraging perception (Nguyen et al., 2017). They provide clear graphical representations, including tables and maps, to summarize complex large datasets, facilitating sense-making and analysis for informed decision-making (Burnay et al., 2019).

The unique nature of data and the capacity to collect and analyze it, such as incorporating previously inaccessible unstructured data, also provide better insights that would lead to better decisions (Bhimani, 2015). These datasets encompass structured, semi-structured, and unstructured data, offering a holistic view of various factors influencing business outcomes. By analyzing these extensive datasets, organizations can uncover hidden patterns, trends, and correlations previously undetectable. This depth of insight supports analytics, enabling businesses to anticipate future trends and behaviors. Consequently, decision-makers such as project managers can develop strategies based on data-driven evidence, reducing uncertainty and enhancing the precision of their decisions. Thus, the vast and complex datasets provide comprehensive insights that enable more informed decisions. In this regard, companies must collect data at every stage of the project life cycle. Currently, a big challenge is the availability and authenticity of data. Lack of reliable data can limit us to benefit enough from the rapid development of data analytics and AI tools (Acemoglu, 2024).

Working with real-life project data is also crucial for researchers. Until now, researchers primarily generated data sets artificially to test their algorithms. However, as big data analytics have developed rapidly, it has become imperative to use real-life project databases and make the tests using empirical data (Batselier & Vanhoucke, 2015; Ulusoy & Hazir, 2021).

Another essential aspect of decision-making is its effectiveness, which can be measured by accuracy and speed (Shamim et al., 2020). Prior studies have shown that big data and big data analytics significantly enhance decision-making quality (e.g., Awan et al., 2021). However, this process can be further improved by ensuring data quality and reliable sources, thereby reducing inaccuracies and biases and ultimately improving decision-making quality through big data (Janssen et al., 2017; Desgourdes & Ram, 2024). Big data allows for a detailed analysis of transactions, customer interactions, and market trends, revealing patterns and correlations that might otherwise remain obscured.

Furthermore, integrating advanced analytical techniques like machine learning, artificial intelligence, and data sources such as the IoT enables real-time data collection and analysis. This capability ensures project managers access the most current and relevant information, facilitating timely and accurate decisions (Jeble et al., 2017). The continuous influx of data also allows decision-making processes to be more agile, continuously improving as new data is collected and analyzed. Ultimately, leveraging big data and its analytics enables project managers to be more agile and reactive, making more informed, real-time decisions.

Now, let us see how big data can be applied to support decision-making in the project lifecycle.

4 Application Areas of Big Data in Project Management

4.1 Project Risk Management

Big data analytics significantly enhance project risk management by identifying relevant risks and predicting their probabilities and impacts more accurately. Especially during the initiation phase, big data analytics can help identify potential risks early on. For instance, Owolabi et al. (2018) demonstrated that predictive data analytics techniques, such as machine learning and regression, can predict construction project completion times. Among these techniques, random forest was identified as the most effective. However, many industries still do not fully utilize these opportunities. For example, a survey by Górecki (2018) found that Polish construction professionals show very little interest in implementing big data analytics.

During the project planning, the risks associated with each project can be thoroughly examined using descriptive and predictive data analytics models (Owolabi et al., 2018). Predictive analysis and risk modeling can also anticipate potential quality issues and plan for contingencies proactively. Big data analytics also revolutionized risk assessment methodologies, offering novel approaches in logistics, construction, finance, economics, and industrial systems (Choi & Lambert, 2017; Owolabi et al., 2018). By analyzing current and anticipated risks, project managers can enhance the likelihood of achieving project targets for each project (Pondel & Pondel, 2015).

Big data analytics can also play a crucial role in reducing financial risks. Accurate cost predictions are vital in tender pricing for infrastructure projects like highway and railway constructions, which require significant investments. Inaccurate predictions can result in too low or too high bids, jeopardizing project budgets and financial viability. Big data analytics can aid managers in conducting more effective pre-contract analyses and feasibility studies, thereby reducing financial risks associated with inaccurate bidding.

Similarly, the risks associated with each project can be thoroughly examined using descriptive and predictive data analytics models (Spalek, 2018). By analyzing current and anticipated risks, project managers can enhance the likelihood of achieving project targets (Pondel & Pondel, 2015). This transformative approach turns uncertainty into opportunity and empowers decision-makers to take decisive actions based on data insights. In the project selection process, identifying and assessing risks, probabilities, and potential impacts on project success is paramount. By leveraging data analytics models, managers can increase the likelihood of achieving project objectives, optimizing project outcomes and minimizing risks (Spalek, 2018; Pondel & Pondel, 2015).

During execution, risk management remains critical. In software development, for example, risk analysis within the agile management framework—emphasizing continuous design and development—can be enhanced by data analytics. Batarseh and Gonzalez (2018) explored how data analytics can predict failures during the software development lifecycle, helping to manage risks more effectively. Rekha and Parvathi (2015) underscored the ubiquitous nature of risks across all phases of software projects. They emphasized the potential of big data analytics in identifying these risk factors and analyzing their impact and likelihood throughout the project lifecycle. Overall, integrating big data offers organizations a powerful tool for maintaining and improving project quality and identifying and mitigating risks.

4.2 Resource Planning and Allocation

Big data analytics can support efficient resource planning and allocation. By harnessing the vast volumes of data generated throughout the project lifecycle—such as historical project data and external market information—project managers can leverage advanced analytics to optimize planning processes. This approach enhances the accuracy of project planning. By leveraging predictive models, project managers can generate more accurate forecasts of project durations and milestones and better anticipate potential roadblocks, and this enables better planning and resource allocation. This leads to optimized time schedules and enhances overall project efficiency and performance (Whyte et al., 2016; LaValle et al., 2010).

Additionally, by incorporating big data analytics, project managers can effectively address potential schedule risks, uncertainties, resource constraints, and capacity limitations when formulating plans. This proactive approach enables project managers to implement contingency plans and mitigate potential disruptions. It facilitates the creation of robust plans and schedules, empowering project managers to adopt proactive strategies to reduce risks before they escalate, enhancing project outcomes and minimizing disruptions (Bakici et al., 2021).

Big data-driven optimization and analytics also streamline resource allocation, network optimization, and operational cost minimization (Han et al., 2017; Zheng et al., 2016). Organizations can leverage advanced analytics to make data-driven decisions that maximize resource utilization, minimize waste, and enhance productivity. Regarding human resources, N'Cho (2017) studied the aerospace industry's recruitment processes and advocated for using data analytics to analyze candidate information, thereby forming better project teams. In the UK construction industry,

Kusimo et al. (2019) further identified major problems in resource management resulting from poor data management. They suggested that an effective resource database that gathers information from all an organization's projects could help eliminate these issues.

Additionally, big data enables organizations to incorporate real-time data streams, including weather forecasts, traffic information, market demand, and supplier and material availability, into their resource allocation decisions from sources such as the IoT, RFID, geolocation services, and other advanced systems. This ensures that their plans are dynamically adjusted to reflect changing conditions. Overall, integrating big data analytics into resource planning and allocation processes offers significant benefits such as optimized resource usage and agile planning, ultimately driving greater value from their resources.

4.3 Project Evaluation and Performance

Big data brings clarity to the increasing number and complexity of projects. For instance, it helps organizations choose between several project ideas and select the right portfolio of projects by examining relevant data through data analytics. Moreover, big data analytics enables organizations to conduct predictive analysis and scenario modeling, allowing them to anticipate potential issues and plan for contingencies before they arise. It will enable us to weigh possible project alternatives and prioritizing the most promising ones while considering various resource constraints (Singh, 2015).

Big data analytics also facilitates project performance evaluation and enhances monitoring and control. Olsson and Bull-Berg (2015) focused on building and transportation infrastructure projects, highlighting how new data categories, such as internet traffic and movement-related data, can be utilized. Vanhoucke et al. (2016) emphasized the importance of periodically assessing time and cost performance during the project lifecycle. They argued that big data analytics enables project managers to measure progress better and predict future outcomes, allowing for data-intensive innovations in scheduling, risk analysis, and control.

Vanhoucke (2015) directed attention to the role of big data in monitoring and controlling projects, advocating for applying big data statistical analysis to enhance project control. Similarly, Colin and Vanhoucke (2014) adopted a statistical approach to monitor project progress, employing simulations based on control charts to identify deviations in project performance promptly. Alleman and Coonce (2014) introduced an innovative method for analyzing trends and predicting project time and cost performance, utilizing the autoregressive-integrated moving average algorithm. This approach uncovered underlying trends that traditional earned value management calculations could not detect, enhancing the ability to track performance effectively and make informed decisions to maintain project success. These instances collectively illustrate how big data facilitates the expansion of project control to tackle complex project management challenges.

In project management, real-time project performance tracking to monitor Key performance indicators (KPIs), market trends, and resource usage through big data analytics offers organizations complete visibility and control over their projects. Big data analytics enable organizations to track project performance in real time by aggregating and analyzing data from various sources, including project management systems, time-tracking tools, and financial databases. This capability allows project managers to make swift adjustments, ensuring projects adhere to their timelines and budgets (Kitchin, 2014). These practices are vital for accurately evaluating project progress and performance. Leveraging big data for real-time monitoring allows project managers to promptly identify deviations from the planned schedule or budget, empowering them to make agile adjustments to maintain project alignment. This proactive approach significantly enhances the likelihood of projects staying within budget constraints and achieving successful completion.

Narbaev et al. (2024) presented a reliable forecasting machine learning algorithm for project costs. Using this algorithm, managers can assess their performance during execution and estimate the project cost if they continue with similar performance. They can decide on the corrective actions by comparing the forecasts with the targets. While big data offers valuable insights for evaluating project success, Ekambaram et al. (2018) emphasized the importance of considering the costs associated with utilizing big data and comparing them with more conventional methods.

4.4 Expanding Big Data Applications in Project Management

Big data analytics can be expanded to support various decision-making areas in project management, including project selection and portfolio management, pre-project analysis and bidding, forecasting and performance assessment, resource analysis and planning, and project quality planning and analysis. The predictive and prescriptive algorithms used in supply chain management to match companies' demand and supply can also be used in project procurement.

Furthermore, the future role of big data in project management may shift towards more real-time, adaptive project management methodologies. With the proliferation of the IoT and sensor technologies and edge computing, organizations will have access to vast streams of real-time project data, allowing for continuous monitoring, analysis, and adjustment of project plans and workflows.

One area of development is the further integration of artificial intelligence (AI) and machine learning (ML) technologies for big data analytics, as presented by Shoushtari et al. (2024) and Uddin et al. (2024). As AI and ML algorithms mature, they are expected to play an increasingly central role in project management, offering organizations advanced capabilities for predictive analytics, risk forecasting, and decision support. By harnessing the predictive capabilities of AI and ML, organizations can analyze large volumes of project-related data, identify patterns, predict outcomes, and make decisions with unprecedented accuracy and efficiency.

Sheoraj and Sungkur (2022), for instance, developed an AI framework to meet the deadlines in software development projects. Such predictive analytics tools can identify the tasks that have not been performed appropriately or are at risk of late completion. Then, the team members performing these tasks could be guided or offered suggested training. Intelligent AI assistants and chatbots could tutor, communicate, and collect information.

Generative AI (GenAI), such as ChatGPT and Copilot, can also be integrated to further enhance project management by relying on deep learning models to generate content that mimics human writing, even when given complex and varied prompts (Lim et al., 2023). Training could be customized to meet personal needs; live feedback could be given to keep team members engaged in achieving project goals. GenAI can also support post-project analysis and be used to prepare reports quickly. Lessons learned can be documented easily if project data is provided. According to Sarafanov et al. (2023), AI can make assumptions even if the data is insufficient. In these cases, analysis based on these assumptions can be used in selecting and planning new projects. Additionally, GenAI can be used for project planning. Barcaui and Monat (2023) compared the performance of the AI and human generated project plans and found out that associating two approaches can be the best solution as each has unique pros and cons.

Eventually, big data is expected to play a central role in fostering a culture of data-driven decision-making and innovation within organizations. The role and training of project managers will increasingly require data literacy. Hence, organizations will invest in comprehensive training and development initiatives to equip their teams with the skills and knowledge necessary to leverage big data effectively.

In summary, the future role of big data in advancing project management practices holds immense promise and potential. By integrating with emerging technologies, embracing real-time methodologies, and fostering a culture of data-driven decision-making and innovation, organizations can leverage big data to navigate the complexities of modern projects with greater agility, resilience, and success.

5 Conclusions

These previous studies collectively emphasize the interconnectedness of big data and project management, highlighting the significant benefits project managers can derive from leveraging the knowledge embedded within big data. The wealth of data, drawn from countless sources and analyzed with advanced techniques, equips project managers to navigate complex projects with precision and agility. While summarizing the various application areas and outcomes, it becomes evident that despite its relatively limited implementation, big data holds substantial promise in supporting project managers and decision-makers throughout project management processes. However, it is noteworthy that the current applications are limited to specific industries, particularly construction. It will be an exciting research project to investigate the sectoral differences in adopting and implementing these big data analytics tools in project management.

Even though the number of research studies on the use of data analytics and AI is increasing, we still need more knowledge on the implementation of big data tools in managerial decision-making in projects and the results demonstrate their impact on project success.

References

Acemoglu, D. (2024, June 06). *Don't believe the AI hype, project syndicate*. project-syndicate.org

Akter, S., Wamba, S. F., Gunasekaran, A., Dubey, R., & Childe, S. J. (2016). How to improve firm performance using big data analytics capability and business strategy alignment? *International Journal of Production Economics, 182*, 113–131.

Alleman, G., & Coonce, T. (2014). Earned value management meets big data. In G. Alleman & T. Coonce (Eds.), *Presentation at the ICEAA Workshop, Denver Colorado* (pp. 1–11).

Awan, U., Shamim, S., Khan, Z., Zia, N. U., Shariq, S. M., & Khan, M. N. (2021). Big data analytics capability and decision-making: The role of data-driven insight on circular economy performance. *Technological Forecasting and Social Change, 168*, 120766.

Barcaui, A., & Monat, A. (2023). Who is better in project planning? Generative artificial intelligence or project managers? *Project Leadership and Society, 4*, 100101.

Bakici, T., Nemeh, A., & Hazır, Ö. (2021). Big data adoption in project management: insights from French organizations. *IEEE Transactions on Engineering Management, 70*(10), 3358–3372.

Batarseh, F. A., & Gonzalez, A. J. (2018). Predicting failures in agile software development through data analytics. *Software Quality Journal, 26*(1), 49–66.

Batselier, J., & Vanhoucke, M. (2015). Construction and evaluation framework for a real-life project database. *International Journal of Project Management, 33*(3), 697–710.

Bhimani, A. (2015). Exploring big data's strategic consequences. *Journal of Information Technology, 30*(1), 66–69.

Burnay, C., Dargam, F., & Zarate, P. (2019). Data visualization for decision-making: an important issue. *Operational Research, 19*, 853–855.

Chen, H., Chiang, R. H., & Storey, V. C. (2012). Business intelligence and analytics: From big data to big impact. *MIS Quarterly, 36*(4), 1165–1188.

Chen, C. P., & Zhang, C. Y. (2014). Data-intensive applications, challenges, techniques and technologies: A survey on Big Data. *Information Sciences, 275*, 314–347.

Choi, T. M., & Lambert, J. H. (2017). Advances in risk analysis with big data. *Risk Analysis, 37*(8), 1435–1442.

Choi, T. M., Wallace, S. W., & Wang, Y. (2018). Big data analytics in operations management. *Production and Operations Management, 27*(10), 1868–1883.

Colin, J., & Vanhoucke, M. (2014). Setting tolerance limits for statistical project control using earned value management. *Omega, 49*, 107–122.

Desgourdes, C., & Ram, J. (2024). The role of big data analytics for decision-making in projects: Uses and challenges. *Enterprise Information Systems, 23*(17), 2317153.

Ekambaram, A., Sørensen, Ø., Bull-Berg, H., & Olsson, N. O. E. (2018). The role of big data and knowledge management in improving projects and project-based organizations. *Procedia Computer Science, 138*, 851–858.

Erevelles, S., Fukawa, N., & Swayne, L. (2016). Big Data consumer analytics and the transformation of marketing. *Journal of Business Research, 69*(2), 897–904.

Furht, B., & Villanustre, F. (2016). *Big data technologies and applications*. Springer.

Gandomi, A., & Haider, M. (2015). Beyond the hype: Big data concepts, methods, and analytics. *International Journal of Information Management, 35*(2), 137–144.

Górecki, J. (2018). Big data as a project risk management tool. *Risk Management Treatise for Engineering Practitioners, 787*, 788.

Han, S., Chih-Lin, I., Li, G., Wang, S., & Sun, Q. (2017). Big data enabled mobile network design for 5G and beyond. *IEEE Communications Magazine, 55*(9), 150–157.

Hazır, Ö. (2015). A review of analytical models, approaches and decision support tools in project monitoring and control. *International Journal of Project Management, 33*(4), 808–815.

Ibrahim, K., Abanda, H., Vidalakis, C., & Wood, G. (2017, July). BIM big data system architecture for asset management: A conceptual framework. In *Proceedings of the joint conference on computing in construction (Jc3)* (pp. 289–296).

Janssen, M., Van Der Voort, H., & Wahyudi, A. (2017). Factors influencing big data decision-making quality. *Journal of Business Research, 70*, 338–345.

Jeble, S., Kumari, S., & Patil, Y. (2017). Role of big data in decision making. *Operations and Supply Chain Management: An International Journal, 11*(1), 36–44.

Kitchin, R. (2014). *The data revolution: Big data, open data, data infrastructures and their consequences*. SAGE Publications.

Kusimo, H., Oyedele, L., Akinade, O., Oyedele, A., Abioye, S., Agboola, A., & Mohammed-Yakub, N. (2019). Optimisation of resource management in construction projects: A big data approach. *World Journal of Science, Technology and Sustainable Development, 16*(2), 82–93.

LaValle, S., Lesser, E., Shockley, R., Hopkins, M. S., & Kruschwitz, N. (2010). Big data, analytics and the path from insights to value. *MIT Sloan Management Review*.

Lim, W. M., Gunasekara, A., Pallant, J. L., Pallant, J. I., & Pechenkina, E. (2023). Generative AI and the future of education: Ragnarök or reformation? A paradoxical perspective from management educators. *The International Journal of Management Education, 21*(2), 100790.

Luo, J., Wu, M., Gopukumar, D., & Zhao, Y. (2016). Big data application in biomedical research and health care: A literature review. *Biomedical Informatics Insights, 8*, BII-S31559.

Manyika, J., Chui, M., Brown, B., Bughin, J., Dobbs, R., Roxburgh, C., & Byers, A. H. (2011). *Big data: The next frontier for innovation, competition, and productivity*. McKinsey Global Institute.

Mohammad, B., Alzyadat, W., Al-Fayoumi, M., Hawi, R. E., & Alhroob, A. (2020, April). An approach to improve data quality from big data aspect by sensitive cost and time. In *2020 11th International Conference on Information and Communication Systems (ICICS)* (pp. 022–026). IEEE.

Narbaev, T., Hazir, Ö., Khamitova, B., & Talgat, S. (2024). A machine learning study to improve the reliability of project cost estimates. *International Journal of Production Research, 62*(12), 4372–4388.

N'Cho, J. (2017). Contribution of talent analytics in change management within project management organizations. The case of the French aerospace sector. *Procedia Computer Science, 121*, 625–629.

Nguyen, V. Q., Nguyen, G. T., Nguyen, S. N., Choi, J., & Kim, K. (2017). Big data analytics and visualization techniques: A case study from agriculture domain. In *KISM Fall Conference* (pp. 1–6).

Negash, S. (2004). Business intelligence. *Communications of the Association for Information Systems, 13*, 177–195.

Olsson, N. O., & Bull-Berg, H. (2015). Use of big data in project evaluations. *International Journal of Managing Projects in Business, 8*(3), 491–512.

Owolabi, H. A., Bilal, M., Oyedele, L. O., Alaka, H. A., Ajayi, S. O., & Akinade, O. O. (2018). Predicting completion risk in PPP projects using big data analytics. *IEEE Transactions on Engineering Management, 67*(2), 430–453.

Pondel, J., & Pondel, M. (2015). BI and Big Data solutions in project management. *Informatyka Ekonomiczna. Prace Naukowe Uniwersytetu Ekonomicznego we Wrocławiu, 4*(38), 95–109.

Raymond, L., & Bergeron, F. (2008). Project management information systems: An empirical study of their impact on project managers and project success. *International Journal of Project Management, 26*(2), 213–220.

Rekha, J. H., & Parvathi, R. (2015). Survey on software project risks and big data analytics. *Procedia Computer Science, 50*, 295–300.

Sarafanov, E., Valilai, O. F., & Wicaksono, H. (2023, September). Causal analysis of artificial intelligence adoption in project management. In *Intelligent Systems Conference* (pp. 245–264). Springer Nature Switzerland.

Sammut, G., & Sartawi, M. (2012). Perspective-taking and the attribution of ignorance. *Journal for the Theory of Social Behaviour, 42*(2), 181–200.

Shamim, S., Zeng, J., Khan, Z., & Zia, N. U. (2020). Big data analytics capability and decision-making performance in emerging market firms: The role of contractual and relational governance mechanisms. *Technological Forecasting and Social Change, 161*, 120315.

Sheoraj, Y., & Sungkur, R. K. (2022). Using AI to develop a framework to prevent employees from missing project deadlines in software projects-case study of a global human capital management (HCM) software company. *Advances in Engineering Software, 170*, 103143.

Shoushtari, F., Daghighi, A., & Ghafourian, E. (2024). Application of artificial intelligence in project management. *International Journal of Industrial Engineering and Operational Research, 6*(2), 49–63.

Singh, H. (2015). *Project management analytics: A data-driven approach to making rational and effective project decisions*. FT Press.

Shim, J. P., French, A. M., Guo, C., & Jablonski, J. (2015). Big data and analytics: Issues, solutions, and ROI. *Communications of the Association for Information Systems, 37*(1), 39.

Spalek, S. (2018). *Data analytics in project management*. CRC Press.

Uddin, S., Yan, S., & Lu, H. (2024). Machine learning and deep learning in project analytics: Methods, applications and research trends. *Production Planning & Control*, 1–20.

Ulusoy, G., & Hazır, Ö. (2021). Recent developments and some promising research areas. In *An introduction to project modeling and planning* (Springer Texts in Business and Economics). Springer.

Vanhoucke, M. (2015). On the use of schedule risk analysis for project management. *Journal of Modern Project Management, 2*(3), 108–117.

Vanhoucke, M., Coelho, J., & Batselier, J. (2016). An overview of project data for integrated project management and control. *The Journal of Modern Project Management, 3*(3), 158–158.

Wamba, S. F., Akter, S., Edwards, A., Chopin, G., & Gnanzou, D. (2015). How 'big data' can make big impact: Findings from a systematic review and a longitudinal case study. *International Journal of Production Economics, 165*, 234–246.

Whyte, J., Stasis, A., & Lindkvist, C. (2016). Managing change in the delivery of complex projects: Configuration management, asset information, and 'big data'. *International Journal of Project Management, 34*(2), 339–351.

Zheng, K., Yang, Z., Zhang, K., Chatzimisios, P., Yang, K., & Xiang, W. (2016). Big data-driven optimization for mobile networks toward 5G. *IEEE Network, 30*(1), 44–51.

The Use of Artificial Intelligence in Supply Chain Project Management: Insights from German Organizations

Dirk H. Hartel and Öncü Hazır

Abstract

In this chapter, we investigate the use of artificial intelligence (AI) to enhance the performance of supply chain projects. We conducted semi-structured interviews with German project managers with experience in supply chain management (SCM) and logistics. The results show that using AI in supply chain projects is very early, but the interviewees see a high potential for the future. The potential is discussed within a project life cycle framework.

1 Introduction

In today's highly competitive business environments, organizations have been transforming their manufacturing and service operations by using new digital technologies to improve business operations' effectiveness and efficiency. Artificial intelligence (AI) has played a critical role in this transformation by supporting managerial decision-making. Especially with big data analytics, several decision options generated by quantitative analysis tools can be presented to managers, and evidence-based, effective decisions can be taken. For instance, product availability could be increased, and transportation and inventory costs can be minimized by using supply chain analytics (Wang et al., 2016; Arunachalam et al., 2018).

D. H. Hartel (✉)
Baden-Wuerttemberg Cooperative State University, Stuttgart, Germany
e-mail: dirk.hartel@dhbw-stuttgart.de

Ö. Hazır
Rennes School of Business, Rennes, France

Ö. Hazır, M. E. Bruni (eds.), *Tomorrow's Data Empowered Project Management*, Future of Business and Finance, https://doi.org/10.1007/978-3-031-84017-3_3

In line with the rising importance of AI projects in practice, there is also a growing interest in research on AI in academia. The number of publications on AI studies in business management has rapidly grown. This research studies two essential business areas: project management (PM) and supply chain management (SCM). More specifically, we investigate the use of AI techniques in managing supply chain projects (supply chain project management, SCPM). There is no commonly used definition of SCPM; Meyer and Torres (2019) presented some of the definitions. Some authors prefer the "management of supply chain projects," and some use the term "supply chain management projects." We use SCPM to refer to developing and using project management techniques to enhance coordination within the supply chain and overall performance.

Companies undertake various projects within or across the supply chains, such as warehouse constructions, relocation of production or distribution facilities, changing the layout of the assembly lines or warehouses, automation of the procurement/production/distribution facilities, or ERP implementation projects. We refer to Hartel (2022) for classifying these projects and real-life case studies. The companies have invested in digital transformation projects to optimize their product procurement, production, inventory, and distribution management strategies. The success of these projects highly depends on the PM capabilities of the companies. Hallikas et al. (2021) investigated the opportunities and complexities of digitalization of supply chains. For them, information sharing and analytical capabilities are determinants in the performance of supply chains. Project management maturity plays a critical role in facilitating information sharing and developing a data-driven decision-making system.

The managers who will take the primary responsibilities in digitalization projects that will transform the supply chain should have experience in supply chain management and PM competencies. They need to bring change within the supply chain while ensuring the efficiency of the procurement, production, and distribution operations. In other words, they need to excel in SCPM. Two groups of studies are relevant for our research: AI applications in SCM and AI applications in PM. Although there are many published papers in these areas, the number of studies at the intersection of these sets is scarce. We address this intersection in this paper.

Pournader et al. (2021) review the AI applications in SCM. They study AI applications in three categories: sensing and interacting, learning, and decision-making. They note that SCM literature regarding AI applications in decision-making is quite rich. However, studies on learning, sensing, and interacting methods still need to be done. They also underline that the application areas of AI in SCM practice are vast. Rolf et al. (2022) reviewed the applications of reinforcement learning algorithms. They find out that the most common application area is inventory management. Information systems use, such as forecasting and risk management, is found to be the second most common area. Transportation, sourcing, and pricing areas follow these two major supply chain drivers. We focus on using AI techniques for learning and decision-making in this study. Learning from previous projects, examples, and experiences can enhance PM decision-making. For example, AI tools can identify and assess the list of risks of a project and estimate the chance of success of a project by learning from data on the projects undertaken.

AI also offers vast application areas in PM: AI is changing PM practices by improving PM productivity and the quality of work (PMI, AI @ Work report, 2019). AI can improve PM decision-making (IPMA report, 2020). Even though AI has vast application areas in business, its impacts have only recently been recognized (Steen et al., 2022).

Taboada et al. (2023) reviewed the studies that address the use of AI in PM. Based on their findings, the most common sectors are construction and IT. The papers mainly address project planning, measurement, and uncertainty. Machine learning (ML) is the most common technique. Forecasting is the most common AI function. Decision-making, optimization, automation, and estimation are other recurrent functions. Uddin et al. (2022) discussed how ML could be used in PM and presented a case study investigating the factors affecting cost overruns using Indian construction project data. Using ML, Narbaev et al. (2023) estimated the project cost, and Mariani et al. (2023) classified the project stakeholders. Ulusoy and Hazir (2021) and Bakici et al. (2021) listed many other application areas.

Wei et al. (2021) reviewed and analyzed the publications relevant to SCM and PM in PM journals. They noted that although both areas have typical research streams, only a few studies work on integrating SCM in PM. We can list some areas: risk management, planning and scheduling, monitoring and control, coordination and contracting, and procurement. Aloini et al. (2015) studied the antecedents of SCM introduction in projects and examined their relationships. The aim is to provide insights into the interdependencies so that managers can take practical actions to benefit from the SCM approach in projects. Naz et al. (2022) discussed AI's role in supply chain resiliency (SCR). They pointed out the lack of studies: "Future studies must integrate the role of project management in SCR post-pandemic because only a limited number of studies exists concerning project management and SCR" (Naz et al., 2022). Hamdani et al. (2022) addressed big data analytics in supply chain operations management and proposed an agile project management approach.

Thomé et al. (2016) underline the scarcity of research on resilience in both SCM and PM literature. Since 2016, many articles and books have been published on resilience in supply chains, but the coverage in PM literature is still lacking. The studies examining AI use in SCM stress the opportunities and gains of implementing AI techniques to manage various supply chain problems. However, they do not mention the use of AI in managing SC projects. They mainly focus on process. To the best of our knowledge, very few studies have addressed the use of AI in SC project management. We refer to Hartel & Hazir, 2022 for the results of a systematic literature review.

We aim to address this research gap by investigating the use of AI to enhance the management of supply chain projects. For this purpose, we analyze the current state of research and conduct semi-structured interviews with SCPM professionals. We addressed both traditional and agile project management approaches and investigated the potential use of AI techniques within the PM phases. Based on the findings, managerial implications and promising future research directions are presented.

2 Methodology

Exploratory nature (Schwandt, 1994) guided our study design. We conducted 14 semi-structured interviews with SCPM professionals. The interviewees are SCM professionals on different career levels: project managers, heads of supply chain management, team leaders, SCM interviewees, and program managers. Despite the different positions in their professional lives, they have the following common characteristics (see Appendix):

- Several years of professional experience in SCM (min. 4 years, max. 22 years)
- Several years of project experience, primarily as project manager or sub-project manager (min. 4 years, max. 13 years)
- Experience in international projects.
- Professional experience in Germany.

An overview of those participants and their roles is provided in Appendix. This sample allows for a broad view of the addressed topic, yet the commonalities allowed us to derive some focused statements. The interviews accompanying the constellations took between 34 and 57 min and were recorded. The professional levels of participants varied from minimum team lead level to General Management. Afterward, the interviews were fully transcribed. All interviews were held and transcribed in German and then translated into English. A native English speaker checked the translations and clarified open topics with the authors. The German researcher compared the relevant sections with the original interview texts as a final step of the transcriptions. This led us to minimize language-related errors. Then, the authors analyzed to determine the project management approach, the current and potential use of artificial intelligence in SCPM, and country and industry specifics in supply chain projects.

3 Results and Discussion

The interviewees are all professionals whose workplace is in Germany. Nevertheless, 12 of them stated that they also had international project experience and that comparing project management practices in Germany and other countries was possible. To make a comparison, we investigated the aspects of supply chain project management that the respondents consider "typically German." It was essential to ensure that this assessment was not understood as negative. The results can be summarized by considering the following aspects.

3.1 Organizational Aspects

The 14 interviewees identified country-specific organizational aspects regarding project management. These relate to clearly structured procedures and the existence of dedicated project planning. AI solutions can improve the quality of planning. Two interviewees also emphasize that efforts are made to involve all potential stakeholders, and that consensus-building is essential for their projects in Germany. The following quotes underline these points.

"very structured," "more in details," less "hands-on" (Interviewee 1)
"better planning of projects" (Interviewee 11)
"consequently following the adopted planning" (Interviewee 9)
"conflicts at the early stage of projects, but then very efficient; top-down communication; stakeholder management; case oriented; long approval paths; long decision paths" (Interviewee 4)
"huge documentation process, considering any stakeholder" (Interviewee 2)
"stringent working according to the plan: to integrate the team members; while in the US: let us make 60% and then we see" (Interviewee 8)
"definition of the standards" (Interviewee 7)
"lack of data scientists" (Interviewee 12)

Regarding managing the projects, three approaches could be followed: The traditional waterfall model follows a sequential approach from project initiation to completion. It requires a well-defined scope and a detailed plan at the beginning. On the other hand, the agile system is more dynamic, customer-focused, and iterative. It intends to accelerate project execution via sprints. The hybrid approach, which has become popular lately, combines the traditional and agile elements.

A clear preference emerged among the supply chain project managers surveyed in the interviews. Twelve of the 14 respondents stated that they follow a hybrid approach. The following statements support this preference:

"hybrid; the framework of the overall project is traditional, but subprojects are agile; because the scope was unclear" (Interviewee 14)
"Most of my projects are traditional, some are hybrid, but I do never agile" (Interviewee 9)

One group of interviewees pointed out that in the development of software modules, a pure agile approach is pursued while all other subprojects are handled traditionally. The following statements are interesting:

"traditional approach; only hybrid when the modules are relevant with agile" (Interviewee 3)
"hybrid means primarily traditional, but when it comes to IT, then agile" (Interviewee 5)

The other group emphasized the development over time in project management, i.e., first implementing projects traditionally and then incorporating agile aspects step by step:

"originally traditional, but more and more new methods, now hybrid" (Interviewee 1)
"started with traditional, now more and more agile, so definitively hybrid" (Interviewee 13)

Interestingly, two interviewees stated that they initially tried switching from traditional to Agile. After realizing that this complete change did not work, they opted for the "hybrid" compromise:

"They jumped quickly on Scrum in 2019, have converted many processes in the company, according to the agile principles but did not have success" (Interviewee 12)
"hybrid; first traditional, then all agile, now hybrid, for it is best" (Interviewee 7)

Only a few interviewees stated that they handle their projects agilely. However, only two interviewees mentioned the purely traditional approach as the usual approach to project management.

For the interviewees, AI experience relates to their day-to-day work. Regarding the use of AI in PM, they have a limited level of experience. Only three of the 14 interviewees have considerable experience using AI in SCPM. The following reasons are cited for the lack of experience:

- time pressure
- lack of knowledge
- project goals can be reached even without using AI
- unclear cost-benefit ratio

These obstacles can be matched with the lack of experience; time pressure is typical in project management. Despite the lack of experience and the cited reasons for not using AI in SCPM, the interviewees are optimistic about future AI solutions.

3.2 Data Protection and Psychological Concerns

Almost all respondents emphasized the importance of data protection. Particularly in AI-supported projects, data about individuals and their performance are critical. Nevertheless, the respondents, as well as their project team members, consider strong reservations or worries. The interviewees consider the strong position of the work councils as a characteristic both limiting and supportive. Although the involvement of the work councils leads to greater acceptance in the planning and implementation of the processes, it is also seen as a limitation due to general reservations on the part of employee representatives. The following quotes illustrate these points of view:

"respectful use of data as an advantage" (Interviewee 3)

"legal regulations to save employers and employees; also data security" (Interviewee 4)
"role of workers' council; while process mining information of errors per person absolutely taboo (not like in China)" (Interviewee 6)
"strong workers' council" (Interviewee 7)
"data security (in other countries like Americas and Asia: here are the data, make the best out of it) "(Interviewee 8)
"handling data with care and ethics due to German history; role of workers' council and participation of employees" (Interviewee 9)
"data security, strong role of workers' council" (Interviewee 10)
"power of workers' council; bureaucracy" (Interviewee 13)
"Occupational safety and health, data security" (Interviewee 14)

There is also a broad consensus regarding the fundamental attitude of project managers and team members toward new technologies, with some level of skeptical behavior. Most of the interviewees have some reservations about the technological changes in general and AI in particular, especially in comparison with project colleagues from China and the USA. This reluctance is related to monitoring the project team as well as a general lack of knowledge about the possibilities and limits of the tools:

"lack of awareness for AI" (Interviewee 7)
"lack of innovation, AI is still seen as a testing field" (Interviewee 5)
"Germans not as tech-savvy as the US" (Interviewee 9)
"reservations about AI" (Interviewee 11)
"critical view on AI, Apps and Tools" (Interviewee 14)

3.3 Project Life Cycle Management

3.3.1 Project Selection and Initiation

The interviewees consider that AI can be used to decide whether the project is needed. Instead of an unsystematic individual online search, an AI tool can search and systematically present the results. In the best case, this should answer the question of similar projects in SCM and check the Internet about trends, success factors, and best practices.

"Using big data analysis to get the information about project selection (instead of just Google research for 5 min to 1 hour)" (Interviewee 5)
"new project proposals by using AI data screening" (Interviewee 6)

In this context, one interviewee pointed out the opportunities and limits of obtaining relevant benchmark data without violating internal compliance rules.

"Learning from shared data, of course, sharable data, on a common platform" (Interviewee 8)

Chatbots were also cited within the knowledge management framework, for example, to discover if similar projects have been conducted at other locations or national companies. The supply chain managers of global corporations cited this purpose of use.

"chatbots to do a first research internally with similar projects: input factors, number of project members, complexity, number of sprints, use of Kanban boards, check-in/checkout-method to be used" (Interviewee 6)
"This is a major weakness in our company. The fact that we do not know which project team members are working on the same topic." (Interviewee 14)
"(permanent) screening of similar projects within the group" (Interviewee 3)

Finally, one interviewee mentioned the operational benefits of automating the project charter preparation or similar routine tasks.

"AI to deliver decision templates including statements regarding resources and consequences" (Interviewee 9)

Only one interviewee had no expectations of using AI during project initiation. The main concern is data availability.

"But I think that enough data is just available so that AI can support me" (Interviewee 11)

3.3.2 Project Planning

Twelve of the 14 interviewees cited some benefits of using AI methods during the planning phase of SCM projects. Almost all of them hope that AI can contribute to increasing planning quality. For them, more realistic (robust) plans could be prepared using data analysis.

"can be used to find the right PM approach (agile, hybrid, ...), to prepare project plans using the former projects, for capacity planning" (Interviewee 1)
"better resource planning, capacity planning, time scheduling" (Interviewee 2)
"better planning quality based on similar projects" (Interviewee 9)

By analyzing and evaluating similar projects, subjective planning decisions can be replaced with data-driven decisions. AI tools should rely not only on external data but also on internal data in order to increase the planning quality.

"for schedule generation, historical data can be consulted to such as to integrate how often an employee is absent…;" (Interviewee 14)
"realistic resource planning can be achieved" (Interviewee 8)

"objective planning instead of five planners who all develop different plans" (Interviewee 4)

3.3.3 Project Execution, Monitoring, and Control

The interviewees consider project implementation as the phase that can benefit from AI tools, i.e., the analysis of the project progress, update of the targets, and support for implementing the plans. This aligns with the Association for Project Management (APM) study (Dacre & Kockum, 2022). Only two interviewees were critical of using AI methods in project implementation. They consider that AI cannot replace humans in project implementation.

"no use for execution and we need staff, I would say in terms of mindset, I am sure that the implementation is something that the employees prefer to do themselves." (Interviewee 9)

In contrast, the 12 interviewees see a wide range of areas for the application. Data mining and machine learning are highlighted to analyze data more quickly. Data cleansing can be automated; for example, duplicates in large volumes of data can be eliminated, e.g., data collection of transport flows or purchase orders from previous years.

"to improve data quality to find data duplicates, like delivery addresses Mainstr. = Mainstreet; for today for each original equipment manufacturer (OEM) client we have the same delivery address for it is a multi-brand retailer" (Interviewee 10)

One interviewee mentioned that he imagines process mining for the process survey and analysis in project management.

"identification and analysis of processes by Process Mining" (Interviewee 13)

This interviewee considers process mining interesting because this AI method has already been used for process monitoring and cross-plant benchmarking. However, he also emphasizes the high cost of implementing it, which may not justify its use in SCM projects. Another interviewee also shares this doubt:

"no to Process Mining as part of analysis in projects because it could be too time-consuming" (Interviewee 14)

Finally, these two interviewees cited the considerable preparation effort and thought the method could not be used in daily work.

Twelve participants view AI methods as possible supporters of problem-solving. Like in the project planning phase, the principal added value is linked to the facilities that search engines and chatbots offer to generate and evaluate alternative problem-solving approaches.

"better prediction for the next 12, 18 or 24 months" (Interviewee 6)
"intelligent search systems to find out the projects inside and outside the company for best practices or lessons learned; to find out the legal regulations in other countries" (Interviewee 2)
"scenario analysis including alerts and messages that warn you probably will not reach the goals" (Interviewee 8)
"material flow planning, layout planning, definition of scenarios, simulations" (Interviewee 1)

Simulation approaches help develop and evaluate solutions, for example, in material flow planning and for the subsequent implementation of the preferred solution in the project. In this way, they could increasingly serve virtual mapping of future operational processes, for example, to train employees in implementing new picking processes. Here, several interviewees refer to the possible use of Artificial or Virtual Reality in projects using smart glasses to simulate the processes.

"use of augmented reality (AR) to project a 3D world" (Interviewee 4)
"training of staff regarding new processes, e.g. new BI system with Google Glasses instead of YouTube tutorials" (Interviewee 5)
"onboarding of new distribution processes with AR glasses" (Interviewee 12)
"AR before implementing the new material flow in a warehouse" (Interviewee 13)

Apart from one interviewee, all other respondents also see potential uses for AI methods in project monitoring and control. The answers given are categorized as follows:

- target/realization comparison
- detection of failure risks, proactive interventions, and necessary project adjustments
- chatbots to support communication within the project team
- continuous and standardized project documentation with the help of text mining

Project control focuses on the permanent target-performance assessment: comparing the project goals with the respective degree of goal achievement. The interviewees emphasize that it is not just a matter of obtaining a target/realization comparison "at the push of a button", but AI can actively point out the possible failure projects and make suggestions for improvement, e.g., based on the screening of similar projects. We cite two good examples of cases from software projects: one predicting failures in agile development and the other using AI to prevent employees from missing project deadlines (Batarseh & Gonzalez, 2018; Sheoraj & Sungkur, 2022).

"AI to find weakness signals, to show interdependencies "(Interviewee 2)
"useful to see too big deviations, e.g. in the use of AGV regarding takt times" (Interviewee 4)
"Early detection of time deviations "(Interviewee 5)

"data collection and actively giving recommendations what is good and what goes wrong" (Interviewee 7)

3.3.4 Project Termination and Closure

The interviewees assess the opportunities AI offers for the closure phase similarly to those in the monitoring phase. The main benefit cited is the reduced workload of project managers for routine activities and a well-founded analysis of the achievement of the project goals, including the derivation of recommendations for future projects. In the closure phase, final reports are created, which could be categorized concerning the stakeholder groups in terms of scope, preparation, and focus with the help of AI. Text mining tools could provide appropriate support in this regard:

"Types of reports for different stakeholder groups" (Interviewee 3)
"To develop nice presentations and reports for each stakeholder group" (Interviewee 7)
"Text mining to produce reports, for reports are time-consuming including a workflow for future projects" (Interviewee 9)

In addition to these standard tasks, the interviewees also expect AI tools to be able to perform an interpretation and analysis of the project results and to derive recommendations for action not only for the completed project but also for future projects:

"Review of planning; recommendations for future projects" (Interviewee 5)
"rechecking results by AI at the end of the project (like reverse engineering), automated and objective best practice" (Interviewee 8)
"comparison of the targets with the reached goals (Where is the gap? Lessons learned for the future)" (Interviewee 9)

In addition, one interviewee pointed out that the use of AI tools can continue in other projects or operations at the end of the project. For example, process mining in his project continued by transferring the tasks from the project owner (supply chain project manager) to the process owner (procurement manager), making it easier to justify the initial effort spent on process mining.

4 Conclusions

We derived some concrete findings from the semi-structured interviews. First, the interviews revealed that more than half of the respondents already have experience using AI methods in SCM. However, this experience is based on operations they manage as a part of their supply chain manager roles. Despite their many years of project experience, many have yet to use AI tools while managing supply chain projects. In other words, the comprehensive combination of AI methods and SCPM is still lacking in operational practice. This is in line with earlier research results.

The interviewees cite various reasons for the low level of adoption. The following arguments are mentioned: the need for more experience with these tools is mentioned often. In this context, the lack of competence in AI methods is underlined. Several interviewees also expressed that there is still no reliable cost/benefit analysis for using AI tools today and that the benefits still need to be clarified from their point of view. It has also been pointed out that the time pressure in SCM projects is very high, and the project goals cannot be achieved without AI. All these reasons show that SCM professionals still have numerous reservations about using AI in projects.

Despite the lack of experience and reservations about using AI methods in supply chain project management, the interviewees see a high potential in applying these methods across all life cycle phases. Potentials are seen primarily in relieving routine activities in project management; for example, AI tools support documentation and assessing the project results. Another potential is the increase in project quality, as AI could improve the process/project analysis and decision-making and actively make suggestions for improvement using the data of similar projects.

This study has some limitations. The interviewees work in Germany. There is a need for further research in this area, such as interviewing outside Germany and conducting a cross-country comparative study. In addition, there needed to be a focus on a specific AI tool (e.g., machine learning) and a specific project phase (e.g., project planning). This is where future research projects could start by investigating tools and focusing on a specific project phase instead of a more generalist approach. A specific industry could be focused on as well. Consequently, based on a phase-by-phase project management approach, we underline the need for future research on AI methods, opportunities, impacts, and implications within SC projects.

Appendix

Interviewee no.	Position	Industry sector	SCM business experience in years	PM business experience in years
1	Supply Chain Manager	Technical Solutions	22	>10
2	Digitization Specialist	Consultancy	4	4
3	Digitization Specialist	Logistics Service Provider	5	5
4	Digitization Specialist	Automotive	9	9
5	Project Manager	Retail	10	10
6	SCM Specialist	Power Tools	5	3
7	Project Manager	Consultancy	11	11
8	Project Manager	Automotive	5	5

Interviewee no.	Position	Industry sector	SCM business experience in years	PM business experience in years
9	Commodity Buyer	Technical Solutions	15	13
10	Chief Digital Officer	Logistics Service Provider	13	10
11	Strategic Buyer	Consumer Goods	6	6
12	Founder and Owner	Consultancy	12	12
13	SCM Specialist	Power Tools	4	6
14	Head of Fulfillment Center	E-Commerce	13	8

References

Aloini, D., Dulmin, R., Mininno, V., & Ponticelli, S. (2015). Key antecedents and practices for Supply Chain Management adoption in project contexts. *International Journal of Project Management, 33*(6), 1301–1316.

Arunachalam, D., Kumar, N., & Kawalek, J. P. (2018). Understanding big data analytics capabilities in supply chain management: Unravelling the issues, challenges and implications for practice. *Transportation Research Part E: Logistics and Transportation Review, 114*, 416–436.

Bakici, T., Nemeh, A., & Hazir, Ö. (2021). Big data adoption in project management: Insights from French organizations. *IEEE Transactions on Engineering Management, 70*(10), 3358–3372.

Batarseh, F. A., & Gonzalez, A. J. (2018). Predicting failures in agile software development through data analytics. *Software Quality Journal, 26*, 49–66.

Dacre, N., & Kockum, F. (2022). *Artificial Intelligence in Project Management*. Association for Project Management. https://doi.org/10.61175/DOGX9829.

Hallikas, J., Immonen, M., & Brax, S. (2021). Digitalizing procurement: The impact of data analytics on supply chain performance. *Supply Chain Management: An International Journal, 26*(5), 629–646.

Hamdani, F., Quintero, I., Enjolras, M., Camargo, D., & Lelong, C. (2022). Agile supply chain analytic approach: A case study combining agile and CRISP-DM in an end-to-end supply chain. *Supply Chain Forum: An International Journal.*

Hartel, D. (2022). *Project management in logistics and supply chain management* (Springer Series in Supply Chain Management) (Global ed.). Springer Gabler.

Hartel, D. H., & Hazir, Ö. (2022). The applications of artificial intelligence in supply chain project management: A survey.

IPMA. (2020). *Report on artificial intelligence impact on project management.* International Project Management Association.

Mariani, C., Navrotska, Y., & Mancini, M. (2023). Unsupervised machine learning for project stakeholder classification: Benefits and limitations. *Project Leadership and Society, 100093.*

Meyer, C. M., & Torres, E. L. G. (2019). Success factors for supply chain management projects: An empirical analysis. *IFAC-PapersOnLine, 52*(13), 153–158.

Narbaev, T., Hazir, Ö., Khamitova, B., & Talgat, S. (2023). A machine learning study to improve the reliability of project cost estimates. *International Journal of Production Research*, 1–17.

Naz, F., Kumar, A., Majumdar, A., & Agrawal, R. (2022). Is artificial intelligence an enabler of supply chain resiliency post-COVID-19? An exploratory state-of-the-art review for future research. *Operations Management Research, 15*(1–2), 378–398.

PMI. (2019). *AI @ work: New projects, new thinking*. Project Management Institute.

Pournader, M., Ghaderi, H., Hassanzadegan, A., & Fahimnia, B. (2021). Artificial intelligence applications in supply chain management. *International Journal of Production Economics, 241*, 108250.

Rolf, B., Jackson, I., Müller, M., Lang, S., Reggelin, T., & Ivanov, D. (2022). A review of reinforcement learning algorithms and applications in supply chain management. *International Journal of Production Research*, 1–29.

Schwandt, T. A. (1994). Constructivist, interpretivist approaches to human inquiry. In N. K. Denzin & Y. S. Lincoln (Eds.), *Handbook of qualitative research* (pp. 118–137). Sage Publications.

Sheoraj, Y., & Sungkur, R. K. (2022). Using AI to develop a framework to prevent employees from missing project deadlines in software projects-case study of a global human capital management (HCM) software company. *Advances in Engineering Software, 170*, 103143.

Steen, J., Klein, G., & Potts, J. (2022). 21st-century general-purpose technologies and the future of project management. c(5), 435–437.

Taboada, I., Daneshpajouh, A., Toledo, N., & de Vass, T. (2023). Artificial intelligence enabled project management: A systematic literature review. *Applied Sciences, 13*(8), 5014.

Thomé, A. M. T., Scavarda, L. F., Scavarda, A., & de Souza Thomé, F. E. S. (2016). Similarities and contrasts of complexity, uncertainty, risks, and resilience in supply chains and temporary multi-organization projects. *International Journal of Project Management, 34*(7), 1328–1346.

Uddin, S., Ong, S., & Lu, H. (2022). Machine learning in project analytics: A data-driven framework and case study. *Scientific Reports, 12*(1), 1–13. https://doi.org/10.1038/s41598-022-19728-x

Ulusoy, G., & Hazir, Ö. (2021). Recent developments and some promising research areas. In G. In Ulusoy & Ö. Hazır (Eds.), *An introduction to project modeling and planning* (Springer Texts in Business and Economics) (pp. 457–469). Springer.

Wang, G., Gunasekaran, A., Ngai, E. W. T., & Papadopoulos, T. (2016). Big data analytics in logistics and supply chain management: Certain investigations for research and applications. *International Journal of Production Economics, 176*, 98–110.

Wei, X., Prybutok, V., & Sauser, B. (2021). Review of supply chain management within project management. *Project Leadership and Society, 2*, 100013.

Transforming Startups with Generative Artificial Intelligence

Emine Gokce Phillips

Abstract

Startups operate in an environment where time, resources, and funds are extremely scarce, making it essential to maximise efficiency and productivity without necessarily expanding the size of their teams or allocating extensive resources and funds toward activities that can be streamlined. In this high-pressure setting, Generative Artificial Intelligence (Gen AI) offers a suite of tools and techniques designed to optimise operations, reduce costs, and accelerate project timelines. By embracing Generative AI, startups can automate routine tasks, digitise manual processes, retrieve actionable insights from data, and focus their limited human resources on strategic planning and innovation. This not only enhances their competitive edge but also ensures that they can do more with less, paving the way for sustainable growth and scalability.

In this chapter, we introduce a three-step AI integration framework detailing how a startup can adopt Gen AI with the aim of optimising and automating processes as well as building new processes, products and business models. We also discuss how Gen AI tools can be actively used in startups by showcasing the author's experience with various startups.

E. G. Phillips (✉)
Crypto Index Series Limited, London, UK

Ö. Hazır, M. E. Bruni (eds.), *Tomorrow's Data Empowered Project Management*, Future of Business and Finance, https://doi.org/10.1007/978-3-031-84017-3_4

1 Introduction

Artificial Intelligence (AI) is a "system capable of rationally solving complex problems or taking appropriate actions to achieve different goals in many real-world circumstances" (NSTC, 2016). Since November 2022, with the rise of Generative Artificial Intelligence (Gen AI) especially after the launch of Chat GPT (OpenAI, 2024), the everyday use of AI has increased significantly. Gen AI is a branch of AI that employs machine learning models to produce new and original content, such as images, text, or music, by analyzing and imitating patterns and structures found in existing data (Gozalo-Brizuela & Garrido-Merchán, 2023).

Generative AI can be utilised in areas including, but not limited to, content generation, data augmentation, personalisation, problem solving and predictive analysis, automation of routine tasks, automated design and prototyping, simulation and modeling, natural language understanding and translation, Speech Synthesis and Recognition, Anomaly Detection, Image and Video Generation, Behavioral Modeling, Complex Decision Making and so on (Bandi et al., 2023; Oxford Analytica, 2023).

The use cases where these capabilities can be utilised are vast for individuals and organisations, especially startups. A startup initiative is often seen as a highly risky endeavour because it involves creating a unique outcome, such as a new product, service, or business model, within a limited timeframe and with very limited resources, all while operating under conditions of extreme uncertainty (Ries, 2011). Utilising resources and funds effectively and making use of any potential automation opportunity is of utmost importance to startup founders in order to have a chance to succeed. In this regard, Gen AI brings significant opportunities to optimise and automate operations, simplify project management as well as support innovation efforts in a startup setting.

In this chapter, we discuss how Gen AI tools can be actively used in startup projects and gradually integrated into the everyday life of startups by showcasing the author's experience with various startups.

In Sect. 2, we introduce a three-step AI integration framework detailing how a startup can adopt Gen AI with the aim of optimising and automating processes as well as building new processes, products and business models. The process is delineated into three primary steps: Discovery and Familiarisation, Knowledge Sharing and Utilisation, and AI-Powered Innovation. Section 3 introduces a case study following this framework, providing real-world examples of how startups can effectively implement AI technologies to enhance their operations and products. Section 4 summarises the learnings, considerations for larger organisations and open areas for further exploration.

2 AI Integration Framework

Gen AI has become a pivotal technology for startups aiming to innovate and streamline their operations. The framework for AI integration in startups can be broadly categorised into three stages: Discovery and Familiarisation, Knowledge Sharing and Utilisation, and AI-powered Innovation. Each stage is critical in ensuring that AI tools are not only adopted but also effectively utilised to bring tangible benefits to the startup.

2.1 Phase One: Discovery and Familiarisation

The first step in integrating AI into a startup involves the discovery and familiarisation phase. The main objective of this phase is to get the team acquainted with AI tools and select specific use cases to test these tools. This foundational step sets the stage for deeper integration and ensures that the team is well-versed with the potential capabilities of AI technologies.

During this stage, startup founders can select a group of team members who would be actively involved in AI adoption activities. It is important to include executive members who would potentially be accountable for the projects as a whole as well as senior and junior members of the team to raise awareness and motivate the use of AI tools and solutions across different functions.

In order to set objectives for the exercise, the selected team first determines the pain and improvement areas that need to be addressed within the startup. Pain areas usually refer to the lack of an activity, a sub-optimum functioning of a process, insufficient work or a manual process. Some examples may include, but not limited to, late responses to customers, lack of video marketing, insufficient code-testing, lack of resources for content generation, manual tasks in lead generation and email broadcasting and so on.

These pain areas can be related to processes or projects within business units such as sales, marketing, customer Service, HR, and product development departments. At this point, the founders may choose to adopt AI only in one department as a pilot initiative or include team representatives from each department and motivate adoption across the board. This decision mainly depends on how big the startup is and how motivated the leaders are. Smaller startups are more agile and may even involve the full team.

It is important to note that at this phase, the AI initiatives based on the selected pain areas ideally should not involve fully blown projects to generate a new process or a product. Instead, they can be seen as Kaizen activities to improve existing processes.

The process for this stage then follows the steps outlined below:

- **Identify Needs**: The team identifies pain areas within the startup that require optimisation, additional resources, or supplementary work. At this stage, it is recommended to select simple processes & tasks that need attention rather than complex problems as the team's knowledge in utilising AI solutions is minimal.
- **Tool Exploration**: Team members conduct a broad search to list all relevant Gen AI tools that could address the identified needs.
- **Narrowing Down**: During one of the workshops, the team members refine the list of AI tools by considering the specific scope and requirements of the startup.
- **Prioritisation**: The pain areas are then prioritised based on their importance for the startup and the most relevant AI tools are selected for initial trials.

- **Team formation**: Team members are assigned to relevant use cases, deadlines and KPIs are set for each use case. This is where the team can start treating each selected AI initiative as a defined project and make use of project management tools.

These activities are best carried out in a couple of workshop sessions. The initial workshop may include brainstorming to identify needs, pains and improvement areas. The team can then work on their own to study relevant AI tools. In the second workshop, the tools studied by the team can be discussed, filtered and prioritised for trial.

It is important to point out that startup founders can employ multiple project management activities during this stage. This involves identifying pain points, setting preliminary goals and the scope, and establishing a framework for evaluating AI tools.

2.2 Phase Two: Knowledge Sharing and Utilisation

Once the initial AI tools have been identified and tested as part of the selected AI Initiatives in the Discovery and Familiarisation Phase, the next phase focuses on Knowledge Sharing and Utilisation.

The goal of this phase is to ensure that AI initiatives in different settings are monitored, measured against the expectations, and learnings are shared amongst the team members. By sharing experiences with tools and iterating on implementations, the startup can build a robust AI-driven culture which becomes an integral part of the startup's operations and common knowledge.

This step is crucial for building internal expertise, understanding the capabilities & limitations of Gen AI and ensuring that AI tools are effectively leveraged across the teams. The process in this phase would follow the steps below:

- **Implement AI Initiatives**: The team begins using AI tools for the selected pain areas in order to optimise or enhance processes that are traditionally performed manually or semi-automatically.
- **Knowledge Sharing**: During the workshops and meetings, team members share the insights and learnings from these implementations with the broader team.
- **Iterative Implementation**: The process is repeated for other selected optimisation or automation opportunities to continuously expand the AI capabilities within the startup.

The duration of this phase is dependent on the length of the AI initiatives selected and the learning process of the team. Regular meetings and brainstorming workshops are recommended to ensure the continuity of the process as well as the sharing of learnings.

During this phase, the team can also decide to start new AI initiatives that may be more complicated than the ones selected in the first phase. Whilst the initial AI initiatives may focus more on optimisation of existing tasks & processes, the AI initiatives in the Knowledge Sharing and Utilisation Phase may also involve the automation of activities or the generation of new processes.

2.3 Phase Three: AI-Powered Innovation

The final stage in the AI integration framework is AI-Powered Innovation. At this point, the startup leverages its growing expertise in AI to drive innovative solutions that add direct value to the business.

The primary aim of this phase is to use AI creatively to develop new products and processes and drive business growth. By focusing on AI-powered innovation, startups can differentiate themselves in the market and increase their competitive advantage.

The tasks at this phase can be defined as follows:

Brainstorming & Ideation During this step, the team conducts brainstorming and ideation sessions to identify areas where AI can add significant value. These areas can be related to

- product enhancements where certain features may be missing in the products due to a lack of resources or time
- completely new product ideas where the current expertise of the team together with the power of AI tools and solutions can shape disruptive products in a much shorter time.
- completely automated, innovative processes that support internal or external targets (customer satisfaction score, sales objectives, etc.)

Notably, Gen AI solutions such as Chat GPT (OpenAI, 2024), Gemini (Google Deepmind, 2024) can also be utilised during the Brainstorming and Ideation sessions to increase the number of ideas and to multiply creativity.

Governance AI governance is crucial for ensuring that AI systems are used ethically, responsibly, and effectively. In small startups with limited resources, funds, and time, AI governance can still be implemented in a small scale through focused, pragmatic activities. These activities can help manage risks, maintain compliance, and promote trust in AI systems. This would ensure that the ownership of the projects is well communicated within the company, the ground rules are set, and the restrictions are established by design rather than an afterthought.

One of the first activities at this stage may involve having an AI Champion in the team. This may be one of the co-founders or a senior member of the team. Other governance activities may include, but not limited to (Mendes et al., 2023; Zysman & Nitzberg, 2020):

- Establishing AI ethics guidelines to create a concise set of ethical principles that guide the development and deployment of AI. These principles should cover fairness, transparency, accountability, and privacy.
- Privacy measures to ensure compliance with data protection regulations such as GDPR or CCPA. Implement data anonymisation and encryption techniques to protect sensitive information.
- Bias and fairness audits to detect and mitigate biases in data and algorithms.

- Model transparency and explainability studies to define and communicate the limitations and potential risks of AI models to internal users and clients.
- Risk management activities to document the risks and develop mitigation strategies.
- Promoting regulatory awareness to stay informed about relevant AI regulations and standards.
- Engaging stakeholders to provide basic AI ethics and governance training for employees to raise awareness and promote responsible AI use.

By focusing on these pragmatic AI governance activities, small startups can effectively manage the ethical, legal, and operational challenges associated with AI deployment. These measures, while resource-conscious, can significantly contribute to building trustworthy and reliable AI systems that align with the startup's goals and values.

Selection Criteria This step is where the team determines their selection criteria as the amount of time and resources that need to be dedicated to these AI-powered innovation projects will be much more significant compared to the AI initiatives carried out during the initial two phases. It is important to note that there are several factors in defining selection criteria such as:

- Business objectives to ensure strategic alignment
- Team's expertise to ensure cultural alignment
- AI worthiness to ensure the pain or the need is significant enough to integrate AI solutions.

A sample AI Initiative Scorecard to allow project scoring is given in Table 1 for reference.

Each criterion on the table aims to check the worthiness of the AI initiative from a different perspective. For instance, if the pain for which the AI tool is proposed requires high workload, but it is not a frequent task, the initiative is questionable. If

Table 1 AI initiative sample scorecard

Criterion (Score 1–10, 1 lowest & 10 highest)	Weight	AI Initiative-1	AI Initiative-2	AI Initiative-3
Business Alignment				
Staff Expertise				
Expected Return on Investment (eROI)				
Workload				
Volume				
Recurring Task				
Required Task				
Manual Task				
Optimisation Level				
Automation Level				
Innovation Level				
Disruptive Product				

the pain area requires quite a large amount of manual work, however, if it is an optional work (not a required work), then again, the worthiness of the project is open to discussion.

The team can add/edit the criteria and the weights scorecard based on their priorities.

Selection and Project Planning At this stage, the team selects the most promising use cases based on the chosen scorecard. Once the AI-Powered Innovation Initiatives are defined, the startups' own project planning and management process can be applied.

Project Management Institute's (PMI) A Guide to The Project Management Body of Knowledge (PMBOK® Guide) defines Project Management as "the application of knowledge, skills, tools, and techniques to project activities to meet the project requirements" (Project Management Institute, 2021).

Given the high uncertainty faced by startups, they often cannot afford a flawless project or business plan at the outset. According to Ash Maurya in his book 'Running Lean,' successful startups focus on finding a workable plan before depleting their resources, rather than striving for perfection from the start (Maurya, 2012).

In the Project Management Practice Guide for Startups (Phillips et al., 2020), co-authored by the author of this book chapter, *Outspeed Startup Glasses* is developed as a startup project management lifecycle. In this model, the life of a startup initiative is divided into two main phases: the pre-commitment phase and the post-commitment phase where the former includes the activities that need to be accomplished prior to the commitment decision, i.e., before spending any significant time & money, and the latter is where funding is secured and all available resources are put into use to realise the initiative as a product/service as shown in Fig. 1.

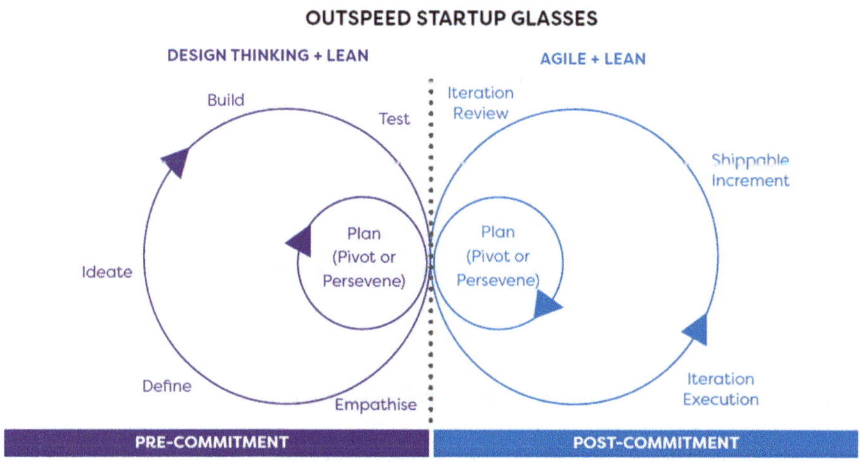

Fig. 1 Outspeed startup glasses—startup project management lifecycle (Phillips et al., 2020)

A similar approach can be followed in the planning and implementation of AI-powered innovation projects whereby after the selection of initiatives, the team can test the technical feasibility and the possibility of utilising AI tools & solutions first.

Once the results are satisfactory, the project can kick-off.

Implementation and Measurement During this step, the team can follow the project management techniques they have in place internally to implement the selected innovation projects. In the Project Management Practice Guide for Startups, the authors state the following guidelines for successful execution (Phillips et al., 2020):

- Continuously test and validate your hypotheses and assumptions.
- Engage with internal/external customers early to gather essential feedback.
- Review and, when feasible, validate work with real input.
- Maintain frequent communication with all relevant stakeholders.
- Regularly compare baseline plans with actual progress.
- Address changes and risks promptly.

For startups, it is crucial to have a quick feedback to decide whether to continue with the AI initiative or not, hence setting up a feedback loop, testing the results, and checking the KPIs at an early stage is of utmost importance to utilise startups' resources efficiently.

Maintenance Founders or the AI Champion in the team need to maintain the list of AI Initiatives running in the startup as well as the AI tools and models integrated as part of these initiatives. This is not only crucial to keep track of AI use in the company and to make the relevant changes when the tools/models change, but also for cross-departmental utilisation of these tools.

Startups also need to implement simple monitoring mechanisms to track the performance and impact of AI models based on performance data, user feedback, and changing business needs, and use these insights to make iterative improvements.

3 AI Integration Case Study

The practical implementation of the AI integration framework involves a series of steps tailored to the startup's unique needs and objectives. Below are detailed real-life examples for each phase from the author's own experience with various startups showcasing how startups can execute this process effectively.

3.1 Phase 1: Discovery and Familiarisation

Firstly, team members who will be actively involved in the exercise are selected and brought together in a workshop to identify the pain areas. One of the startups the author worked with has come up with the pain areas and pain descriptions shown in Table 2.

Table 2 Pain areas selected for the Discovery and Familiarisation Phase

Pain areas	Pain description
Content Generation/Blog writing	Content Generation is challenging due to the niche technical area that the startup operates. Developers have the knowledge of the potential topics for blogs, but they do not have the expertise or time to generate content, and the content generators do not know about the technical details of the products sufficiently to generate content.
Paraphrasing	The content writers are not English native speakers; hence paraphrasing is a challenge in content writing.
Video Marketing	There is no resource for video generation for marketing purposes in the startup.
Webinar Reels—Mini video clip creation	The startup organises webinars quarterly and would like to produce mini videos of these webinars, but is unable to do so due to lack of resources and talent in-house.
Wider Email Outreach	Lead Generation and sending mass emails are challenging.
Personalised Email Automation	There are several target audiences for different products and writing personalised emails for these different target audience groups is time-consuming and poses a challenge for the non-native Marketing staff.
Meeting Notes	At every business meeting, potential clients provide details about their business and needs. It is crucial to capture every detail during these meetings, however, this is a manual and error-prone task, and the person taking meeting minutes may miss important points.
Product Demo Videos	The technical nature of the products sometimes makes it difficult for institutional users to comprehend the product by reading the details on the website. Product demo videos would simplify the storytelling for these products, but there is a lack of resources to produce such videos.
Webinar	The webinars require too many manual tasks.
Presentation/ Document Generation	Sales and Marketing activities require the production of many documents and presentations such as Brochures, Product decks, Case Study documents, etc. All these take a considerable amount of time to prepare for Marketing staff.
Content Planning	To plan content weekly or monthly is a creative task that requires some knowledge of the products, priorities of the company, and scheduling of the sales activities. It is challenging to plan a variety of activities timely.
Search Engine Optimisation (SEO)	There is a lack of resources to monitor the SEO of the company website on a regular basis.
LinkedIn AI Posts/Insights	LinkedIn is one of the channels that is used heavily by this startup and creating consistent posts and visuals for LinkedIn daily requires a significant amount of work for Marketing staff.
Lead Generation	Although relevant potential customer names can be found in some channels and websites to target for sales activities, it is a challenge to find the correct e-mail addresses for these people.

More detailed pain descriptions have been noted down to record the existing situation as well as the ideal situation.

The startup then carried out wild research for Gen AI tools specifically in these areas. In this research, the information gathered included the tool name, website, features, relevant business function, specific area of expertise and pricing. This

Table 3 AI tool list sample

Tool name	Area	Department
Dorik (Dorik, 2024)	Website generator	Marketing
Krock.io (Krock, 2024)	Story Boards	Sales, Marketing
Octaparse (Octaparse, 2024)	Data Retrieval/Collection	Sales, Marketing
Perplexity (Perplexity, 2024)	Content Generator	Marketing
Descript (Descript, 2024)	Video Editing, Recording	Marketing
AssemblyAI (AssemblyAI, 2024)	Speech-to-text and sentiment analysis	Sales, Marketing, Data Analysis
Fireflies (Fireflies, 2024)	Speech-to-text, summarise, search	Sales, Marketing, Data Analysis
Krisp (Krisp, 2024)	Call Center AI Assistant	Customer Service

initial list included approximately 115 AI tools. Table 3 shows example rows out of this research except the website, features and pricing column to keep the table concise.

The team gathered in a workshop where the members who added the tool names in the AI Tool List discussed the tools briefly. Finally, the team selected several tools per pain area to be tested. The final list is shown in Table 4.

Each pain area listed above has been considered as an AI initiative and the team members were then assigned AI Initiatives based on their area of expertise and interests. The expectation here was for each project champion to figure out how the respective AI tools can address challenges faced in the pain area and whether or not utilising such an AI tool made sense in addressing the pain both technically and in a commercially viable manner.

3.2 Phase 2: Knowledge Sharing and Utilisation

The objective of this phase, as introduced in Sect. 2.2, is to ensure that AI initiatives in various settings are monitored and evaluated against expectations, with insights and learnings shared among team members. By exchanging experiences with tools amongst the team members and refining implementations, the startup can cultivate a robust AI-driven culture that becomes an integral part of its operations and collective knowledge.

This phase has started with a workshop where the following topics were discussed:

- experiences from AI initiatives selected during the initial phase
- the effectiveness of the tool(s) in addressing the initial pain with a review of respective KPIs
- the optimisation or the automation achieved
- cross-department use of the tools

Table 4 Pain area—AI tool matching list

No	Pain areas	Relevant AI tools
AI-01	Content Generation/Blog writing	Chat GPT (OpenAI, 2024), Gemini (Google Deepmind, 2024)
AI-02	Paraphrasing	Quillbot (Quillbot, 2024) Wordtune (Wordtune, 2024)
AI-03	Video Marketing	Runwayml (Runwayml, 2024), Synthesia (Synthesia, 2024)
AI-04	Webinar Reels—Mini video clips creation	Pictory.ai (Pictory, 2024), Vidyo.ai (Vidyo, 2024)
AI-05	Wider Email Outreach	Mailchimp (Mailchimp, 2024), Omnisend (Omnisend, 2024)
AI-06	Personalised Email Automation	Sendinblue (Sendinblue, 2024), Cargo (Cargo, 2024)
AI-07	Meeting Notes	Otter (Otter.ai, 2024)
AI-08	Product Demo Videos	Supademo (Supademo, 2024)
AI-09	Content Performance Insights	Semrush (Semrush, 2024), Buzzsome (Buzzsome, 2024)
AI-10	Webinar	Everwebinar (Everwebinar, 2024)
AI-11	Presentation/Document Generation	Prezi (Prezi, 2024), Lumen5 (Lumen5, 2024)
AI-12	Content Planning	Marketmuse (Marketmuse, 2024)
AI-13	SEO Optimiser	Writesonic (Writesonic, 2024)
AI-14	LinkedIn AI Posts/Insights	Taplio.com (Taplio, 2024)
AI-15	Lead Generation	Kleanleads (Kleanleads, 2024)

Based on the initial feedback, some initiatives were suspended due to the difficulty level of the tools or the lack of expertise in the area. Additionally, new initiatives kicked off as the experience with the tools grew and the process iterated.

Some of the AI initiatives covered during this phase are given below with information about the input (In), output (Out), AI tools utilised (AI), the human intervention (HI) still needed in the process as well as the Impact (I) of the change within the startup. The author selected the initiatives that utilised a variety of tools for different business units in the startup to give a better understanding of the wide area of use. Please note that AI initiatives 16–21 are later added at the workshops during this phase.

AI Initiative 01: Content Generation/Blog Writing

In: Provide prompts for content creation.

Out: Social media posts and technical blogs.

AI: Used ChatGPT (OpenAI, 2024), Bard (Google AI, 2024), or Quillbot (Quillbot, 2024) for generating text-based content, and Gencraft (Gencraft, 2024) or Canva (Canva, 2024) for creating images.
HI: Ensured relevance and value addition by checking the generated content for accuracy and alignment with the startup's goals.
I: Number of social media posts increased to 5 from 2. Blog writing was an irregular activity. The startup started publishing one blog article per week. The average time spent on content generation did not increase.

AI Initiative 03: Video Marketing
In: Series of prompts for video content.
Out: Product and company videos.
AI: Lumen5 (Lumen5, 2024) for slide generation, Gencraft (Gencraft, 2024), DALL-E (OpenAI, 2024), Canva (Canva, 2024) for images, and Capcut (Bytedance, 2024) for summarising prompts and voiceovers.
HI: Edited voiceovers and slides to ensure quality and relevance.
I: The startup generated five product videos and four company videos in 4 weeks without requiring additional resource or providing additional training to existing staff.

AI Initiative 11: Presentation/Document Generation
In: Use transcripts as inputs.
Out: Business and product presentations.
AI: Lumen5 (Lumen5, 2024) and Canva (Prezi, 2024) to generate slides.
HI: Edited and verified the slides to maintain correctness and coherence.
I: Modified product and company decks that were outdated within 3 days. New brochures have been created by using these new tools.

AI Initiative 16: Competitor Analysis
In: Provide prompts for competitor research.
Out: Information about competitors.
AI: Utilised ChatGPT (OpenAI, 2024) and Bard (Google AI, 2024) to compile a list of competitors.
HI: Analysed and refined the generated data to ensure comprehensive and actionable insights.
I: The time spent to analyse the activities of the competition in the market and to find new competitors has been cut down to one-fifth of the initial state. At a later project, the startup created a GPT for this specific purpose. More information about GPTs is given in Sect. 3.3.

AI Initiative 19: Code Writing Guidance
In: Provide coding prompts.
Out: Draft of a code for a specific function.
AI: ChatGPT (OpenAI, 2024), CodeConvert AI (CodeConvert, 2024) to generate code snippets.

HI: Validated the code for correctness and reliability.

I: Developers started actively using Chat GPT to create pieces of code (eg. functions) either to not start from scratch or to compare the code they have already written with the proposed piece of code. At a later stage, some of the Matlab code written by technical researchers has also been converted into C# by using CodeConvert (CodeConvert, 2024) to simplify the process for C# developers. The developers gave positive feedback about how AI simplified the coding, inspired them and provided alternative code snippets in certain scenarios. The efficiency gained here is yet to be measured.

AI Initiative 20: Technical Research

In: Detailed technical prompts.

Out: Literature review, summary of academic reports, insights.

AI: Chat GPT (OpenAI, 2024) and Scispace (Scispace, 2024) to summarise scientific content with support from CoPilot (Copilot, 2024) for further exploration.

HI: Provided in-depth prompts to ensure high-quality responses and checked the result to ensure correctness and relevance.

I: Finding relevant articles and retrieving insights from large reports have been simplified massively. In addition to contributing internal efforts in product development, this work later supported R&D grant applications which has generated additional funds for the startup.

Here are some of the observations and learnings shared at the final workshop of this phase:

- All these AI initiatives inspired the team to find new use cases where AI tools add value.
- Each new tool has had a different learning curve and both the managers and the team members were willing to dedicate this time to effectively utilise the AI tools.
- None of the Gen AI tools used in this case study required team members to have a technical background.
- The workshops facilitated the sharing of the experience and the learnings, especially between different functions such as Marketing, Product Development, Sales, HR, etc.
- Some activities such as Video Marketing had been an activity not performed in the startup due to lack of resources and expertise in the field, yet the AI tools simplified the process and made it possible.
- Human Intervention remained to ensure the quality and relevance of the outcome. This has also been important as a risk measure against hallucinations that AI tools may have. For instance, in Competitor Analysis, Chat GPT came up with fictional competitors and later admitted that.
- The tools increased the speed of the processes as well as the amount and quality of the outputs in all initiatives.
- Whilst the initial iterations of AI initiatives carried out can be seen as Kaizen activities focusing on optimisation of processes, the ones introduced during the latter iterations involved more complicated tasks.

Finally, this phase set the groundwork for AI-powered innovation as the team got familiar with the capabilities and limitations of the AI tools.

3.3 Phase 3: AI-Powered Innovation

At this phase, the startup utilised its expanding expertise in AI to develop innovative solutions that deliver direct business value. The main objective is to creatively apply AI to create new products and processes, thereby driving business growth.

To brainstorm ideas, the team got together in a workshop session.

At this stage, proposed AI initiatives, we call them AI-Powered Innovation Initiatives, require more time, resources and funds, hence it is important to have a good set of selection criteria to ensure strategic and cultural alignment as well as technical feasibility. A sample AI Initiative Scorecard based on author's experience with startups is given in Sect. 2.3.

Having gone through ideation, scoring, prioritisation stages, the team chose several projects to work on. Some example projects are provided in the rest of this section.

AI-Powered Innovation Project 1: Automated Social Media Posts based on a live product

In: The startup offers a News API (CIS News, 2024) that consolidates news articles from 40+ media outlets, tags and classifies the articles based on given classification, and finally assigns a sentiment score to each article. This is a product that the startup created by using AI in the past. This particular product was used as an input in this project.

Out: A structured social media post including a summary of the last 24 h, top five most positive and negative news of the day, highlights of the day

AI: Utilised Chat GPT (OpenAI, 2024) to summarise news content, highlight high-sentiment articles, and to create social media posts; ProposedMake.com (Make, 2024) or Zapier (Zapier, 2024) to provide automation in the process.

HI: Published the content on the website and social media channels, with plans for automation.

I: The impact of the project is detailed below.

This project initially envisioned complete automation with the process flow given in Fig. 2 where the startup's own News API (CIS News, 2024) would create a file with all the news of the day in .json format, send it to the Chat GPT 3.5 with the right prompts, and finally publish the post on LinkedIn via an AI tool aggregator.

At the time of the implementation of this project, Chat GPT's API version was only available for Chat GPT 3.5 which unfortunately did not accept files as input (although the Chat GPT 4 available to end users did). Hence this design, unfortunately did not work due to this limitation. Instead, the process flow had to be modified as shown in Fig. 3 to include human intervention.

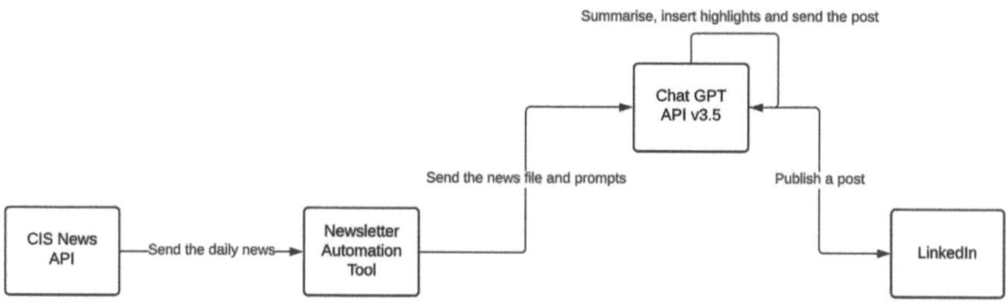

Fig. 2 Initial process flow designed for AI-Powered Innovation Project-1

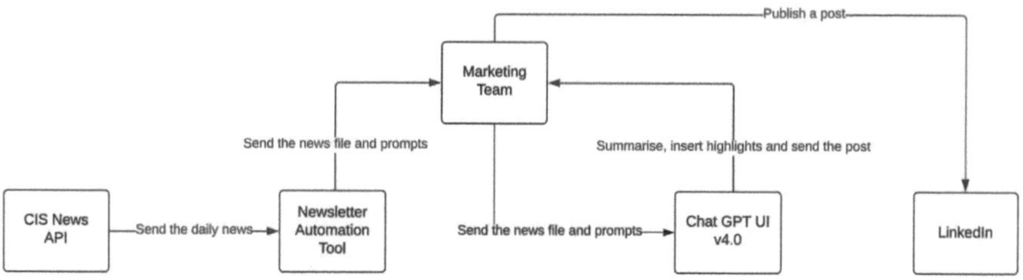

Fig. 3 Modified process flow designed for AI-Powered Innovation Project-1

In the new version of the process, the news automation tool developed by the in-house developers created the news file in .json format. This file has been given as an input to Chat GPT with a defined prompt to ensure a standardised output. This output has then been posted as a social media post daily.

This project is a good example showcasing the limitations of the AI tools that may not be visible during the project's design phase.

Despite the change in the process, the project created a new venue for Product-based Marketing for the News API product.

AI-Powered Innovation Project 2: Creating and Training GPTs to generate crypto asset reports

In: Series of prompts and files.
Out: Structured crypto asset reports in Word format.
AI: Create and train custom GPT (Generative Pre-trained Transformer) models within Chat GPT (OpenAI, 2024).
HI: Specify output formats and validate the content generated by the GPTs.
I: The impact of the project is summarised below.

This project aimed at combining the data from startup's products providing crypto asset data & analytics with other textual information about a crypto asset such as whitepaper, news, etc and generate a report focusing on one crypto asset at a time.

A GPT, or Generative Pre-trained Transformer, is an advanced neural network model for natural language processing. It employs the Transformer architecture,

Table 5 Structure of the crypto asset report and the sources

No	Report section	Source
0	Current State	Digital Asset Data API
1	Intro	Crypto Analysis Report GPT
2	Own Description	Digital Asset Data API
3	Executive Summary	Crypto Analysis Report GPT
4	Investment Thesis	Crypto Analysis Report GPT
5	Team & Governance	Crypto Analysis Report GPT
6	Market Analysis	Crypto Analysis Report GPT
7	Product Overview	Crypto Tech Report GPT
8	Technological Analysis	Crypto Tech Report GPT
9	Tokenomics	Tokenomics GPT
10	Technical Analysis	Digital Asset Data API + Chat GPT
11	News	News API + Chat GPT

characterised by self-attention mechanisms, to process and generate human-like text (Radford et al., 2018).

GPTs are initially trained on a wide-ranging corpus of text data to understand language patterns and contextual details and subsequently fine-tuned for particular tasks. Its capability to grasp long-range dependencies and the subtle context in the text makes it highly effective in various applications, such as text completion, summarisation, text analysis, and question answering.

During the design phase, the technical researcher in the team put together a list of different types of information about a crypto asset. This list included the sections shown in Table 5. The subsections are excluded in this book chapter for conciseness.

As shown in Table 5, the source for some of the information is startup's own products such as Digital Asset Data API and News API, and the sources for others are the given GPTs.

Initially, only one GPT was planned to be implemented to cover the sections that do not need analytical information from the startup's products, however, it has been observed that GPTs perform better if their purpose is more focused and defined, otherwise, they act lazy and provide shorter answers. Hence several GPTs have been created for this project. Additional documents about the crypto asset have been used in the instructions as base documents. The prompts within the GPTs followed the RICCE framework (Role, Instructions, Context, Constraints, Examples). The output from each GPT has been consolidated by a team member and checked by a Technical Researcher for correctness.

As future work for this project, the objective is to automate the consolidation process by calling these GPTs through an API and sending the final report for the quality check to the technical researcher directly.

The crypto asset reports generated in this project acted as a potential new product for the startup, hence proving the innovative potential of AI use in product development.

4 Learnings and Future Work

The journey of integrating Generative AI (Gen AI) into startup projects has provided several valuable learnings. These insights not only highlight the potential and benefits of Gen AI for startups but also shed light on the challenges and areas requiring further exploration not only for startups but also for larger organisations.

Section 4.1 summarises key learnings from the projects carried out. Section 4.2 highlights some of the considerations for larger organisations that have not been discussed in detail in this book chapter. Section 4.3 underlines the Project Management activities carried out in the AI Integration Framework and how these activities can also benefit from AI tools. Finally, Sect. 4.4 discusses the areas for potential future work.

4.1 Key Learnings

Gen AI tools significantly enhance operational efficiency and reduce operational costs by automating routine tasks and providing data-driven insights. Startups can thus focus their limited resources on strategic planning and innovation, fostering a more productive environment.

Successful AI integration requires a cultural shift within the organisation. This involves fostering a learning culture where team members are encouraged to experiment with AI tools, share knowledge, and continuously improve their skills. A series of workshops certainly supports the learning process and continuity of the AI integration process. In addition, encouraging the use of AI across different departments leads to more holistic improvements. For instance, integrating AI in marketing, sales, and customer service can create synergies that amplify the overall impact.

Despite the advanced capabilities of Gen AI, as shown in Sect. 3, human intervention remains essential to ensure the quality and relevance of AI-generated outputs. This collaboration is crucial to mitigate risks such as AI hallucinations and to maintain a high standard of work.

In addition to utilising Gen AI tools for optimisation and automation of processes, exploring their use in Innovation is also invaluable for startups. This involves using AI to create new products, services, and business models that can disrupt the market.

It is important to note that in the AI initiatives covered in this chapter, data privacy and IP protection were not a significant concern for the startups involved as the activities did not include sharing confidential, IP-related or customer-centered information with the public AI tools, however, for such initiatives, there should be measures in place, especially as part of the AI governance efforts.

Finally, in terms of achieving scalability and growth, the ability to automate repetitive tasks, innovate new products, and generate high-quality outputs at scale allows startups to grow sustainably without proportionally increasing their workforce.

4.2 Considerations for Larger Organisations

While startups can rapidly adopt and benefit from Gen AI, larger organisations must address additional considerations:

- Intellectual Property (IP) Concerns: Larger organisations have a bigger concern about protecting their proprietary information. Using off-the-shelf AI tools can expose them to IP risks. Therefore, developing in-house AI solutions or customising existing ones to ensure IP protection is crucial.
- Data Privacy and Cybersecurity: Handling vast amounts of sensitive data requires robust data privacy and cybersecurity measures. Organisations must comply with regulations like GDPR or CCPA and implement encryption and anonymisation techniques to safeguard data.
- Implementing Custom AI Models: Unlike startups, larger organisations often have the resources to develop their own Large Language Models (LLMs) tailored to their specific needs. This approach provides greater control over data usage and model performance.
- Complex Integration Processes: Integrating AI into existing systems in larger organisations can be complex due to legacy systems and multiple stakeholders. A phased approach with comprehensive change management strategies is essential for smooth integration.
- Project Management: For larger organisations integrating AI, it is crucial to apply robust project management methodologies. This necessity stems from the complexity and scale of AI projects requiring more scalable and more personalised solutions, which often involve multiple departments, substantial data sets, and significant investments. Effective project management ensures that AI initiatives are aligned with organisational goals, resources are efficiently allocated, and risks are managed proactively. It provides a structured approach to planning, executing, and monitoring AI projects, facilitating coordination among diverse teams and stakeholders.

These factors certainly do not form a comprehensive list, yet they present the need for a well-defined AI Strategy, a well-communicated AI Governance and Risk Management for larger organisations. The process laid out in this book chapter is specifically applied within startups in agile environments and can only be partly applied to larger organisations.

4.3 Project Management Activities in AI Integration Framework

Gen AI tools not only optimise workflows, automate processes and play a key role in innovation in startups but also has the potential to transform how new AI projects are managed, leading to increased efficiency and effectiveness.

Some of the areas showcasing how project management activities can benefit from Gen AI tools are provided below (Barcaui & Monat, 2023; Nieto-Rodriguez & Vargas, 2023).

- Planning and Scheduling: AI tools can automate and optimise planning and scheduling tasks, which are critical in project management.
- Resource Management: If data about resource use per project is available, then the project manager can also utilise AI in analysing historical project data and estimating current resource availability to allocate resources more efficiently for AI projects.
- Risk Management: Similar to resource management, provided that there is historical data, AI-driven predictive analytics tools can identify potential risks in a project by analysing historical data and current project variables. These tools can provide risk scores and suggest mitigation strategies to project managers.
- Communication and Collaboration: AI tools can enhance communication and collaboration by providing real-time language translation, summarising conversations, and automating meeting scheduling.
- Monitoring and Reporting: AI tools can be utilised to automate the generation of project reports, providing real-time insights into project progress, budget utilisation, and performance metrics.
- Decision-Making Support: Project managers can analyse vast amounts of project data as well as contraints by using AI tools to retrieve recommendations to support decision-making.
- Knowledge Management: AI tools can facilitate knowledge management by organising and retrieving project-related information efficiently. These tools are able to automatically tag and categorise documents, making it easier to find relevant information.

Integrating Gen AI tools gradually into project management activities offers numerous benefits, including increased efficiency, optimised resource utilisation, enhanced risk management, and improved decision-making. The areas discussed in this section are certainly not exhaustive yet provide examples illustrating the potential changes to project management tasks with the use of AI, showcasing the transformative impact of AI on project management in a startup setting.

As for the AI Integration Framework proposed in this book chapter, it is important to note that utilising AI for this purpose may be too early during the Discovery and Familiarisation Phase explained in Sect. 2.1. During this step, the team has very little knowledge of how AI tools can be integrated into their work routine. However, as soon as the team gets familiar with a wide spectrum of AI tools during the second and third phases, detailed in Sects. 2.2 and 2.3, the efforts to plan, schedule and implement AI initiatives can also heavily benefit from AI tools.

4.4 Future Work

The AI tools and solutions are constantly progressing in many ways. Some of the improvement areas for AI tools and solutions may include, but not limited to, the following areas (Zewe, 2023; Bandi et al., 2023):

i. **Multi-Modality**: Multi-modality refers to the capability of AI systems to process and generate data across multiple types of modalities, such as text, images, audio, and video. The latest version of Chat GPT (OpenAI, 2024) at the time of writing this book chapter, version Omni, offers multi-modality, yet many other tools lack this ability.

Multi-modality brings quick transformation of artifacts to one another. This means less work for startups in producing documents, videos, clips, visuals, graphics, etc. and as creating one supports the creation of the other by using AI, leading to less work specifically for Sales, Marketing, Customer Service and Technical Research departments. For example, a multi-modal AI could provide more comprehensive customer support by understanding and responding to queries that include both text and images.

ii. **Localisation**: Localisation involves adapting AI tools to cater to different languages, cultural contexts, and regional preferences. Startups specifically in the growth stage of startups will benefit immensely from simplified localisation through AI in expanding their reach into new markets, offering personalised and culturally relevant user experiences

iii. **Personalisation**: Personalisation in AI refers to the ability to tailor responses, recommendations, and interactions based on individual user preferences and behaviors. For startups, this means enhancing user experience by providing more relevant and customised content.

iv. **Explainability**: Explainability is about making AI systems more transparent and understandable to users. It involves developing methods and tools that can provide clear explanations for the decisions and outputs generated by AI models. For startups, this is crucial for building trust with users and stakeholders, particularly in industries where accountability and regulatory compliance are essential.

v. **Scalability**: Scalability refers to the ability of AI systems to efficiently handle increasing amounts of data and computational demands. Startups need scalable AI solutions to support their growth without compromising performance. Scalable AI enables startups to maintain high service quality as they expand their customer base and operations.

vi. **Real-Time Processing**: Real-time processing involves the capability of AI systems to analyse and generate data in real-time, providing immediate responses and actions. For startups, this means providing instant feedback and services to users, enhancing user engagement and satisfaction. Real-time AI is essential for applications such as live customer support, real-time analytics, and dynamic content personalisation.

vii. **Human-AI Collaboration**: Enhancing human-AI collaboration involves developing AI tools that can work seamlessly with human users, complementing their abilities and augmenting their productivity. For startups, fostering effective collaboration between AI and human teams can enhance productivity and innovation. AI tools can handle repetitive tasks, allowing employees to focus on more strategic and creative activities.

viii. **Integration with Existing Systems**: Improving the integration of AI tools with existing systems and workflows is crucial for facilitating their adoption. This involves developing APIs, plugins, and frameworks that allow AI solutions to be easily incorporated into current technologies and processes, enhancing their utility and efficiency. Startups can benefit from AI solutions that easily integrate with their CRM, ERP, and other essential business systems, leading to more cohesive and efficient operations.

The advancement of AI tools in these areas will certainly increase the level of adoption by startups and other larger organisations.

Additionally, the author also expects a shift in the understanding and utilisation of AI by knowledge workers. As the number of startups and other organisations expecting their staff to collaborate with AI increase, the qualifications in the recruitment process will modify to include experience with AI tools. This will certainly change the company culture over time.

As agile entities, startups may not spend too much time on AI governance initially, however, developing robust AI governance frameworks is essential to ensure ethical and responsible AI usage. This includes establishing clear guidelines on data privacy, bias mitigation, and transparency to build trust in AI systems. As technology evolves, the author also expects to see certain standards to be formed for governance.

Finally, the AI landscape is rapidly evolving, and organisations must continuously learn and adapt to new advancements. This requires ongoing training, knowledge sharing, and a willingness to experiment with emerging AI technologies.

5 Conclusions

The integration of Generative AI into startup operations presents a transformative opportunity to enhance efficiency, reduce costs, and drive innovation. Through a structured framework of discovery, knowledge sharing, and AI-powered innovation, startups can effectively harness the power of AI to achieve their strategic objectives.

The practical case studies highlighted in this chapter demonstrate the tangible benefits of AI adoption, from automating content generation to developing sophisticated data-driven products. These illustrations highlight how Gen AI has the power to transform startup operations and provide businesses with a competitive edge.

However, the journey is not without its challenges. Ethical considerations, the need for human oversight, and the continuous evolution of AI technologies require startups to adopt a proactive and adaptable approach. By fostering a culture of continuous learning and ethical AI implementation, startups can navigate these challenges and fully realise the potential of Gen AI.

In larger organisations, the integration of AI involves additional layers of complexity, such as managing IP concerns, ensuring data privacy, and developing custom AI solutions. These organisations must implement well-defined AI strategies through robust governance frameworks and cybersecurity measures to safeguard their operations and maintain compliance with regulatory standards.

In conclusion, the future of startup and enterprise success lies in the strategic integration of AI technologies. By leveraging Gen AI, organisations can unlock new possibilities, drive sustainable growth, and pave the way for a more innovative and efficient business landscape. As AI continues to evolve, those who embrace these technologies will be well-positioned to lead in an increasingly digital world.

References

AssemblyAI. (2024). *AssemblyAI* [Speech-to-text API]. https://www.assemblyai.com

Bandi, A., Adapa, P. V. S. R., Kumar, V. P., & Kuchi, Y. E. (2023). The power of generative AI: A review of requirements, models, input–output formats, evaluation metrics, and challenges. *Future Internet, 15*(8), 260. https://www.mdpi.com/1999-5903/15/8/260

Barcaui, A., & Monat, A. (2023). Who is better in project planning? Generative artificial intelligence or project managers? *Project Leadership and Society, 4*, 100101. ISSN 2666-7215. https://doi.org/10.1016/j.plas.2023.100101

Buzzsumo. (2024). *Buzzsumo* [Content research tool]. https://buzzsumo.com

Bytedance. (2024). *Capcut*. [Voice AI tool]. https://www.capcut.com

Canva. (2024). *Canva*. [AI presentation tool]. https://canva.com

Cargo. (2024). *Cargo* [Website builder]. https://cargo.site

CIS News. (2024). *Crypto Index Series*. [AI news sentiment tool]. https://cryptoindexseries.com/en/products-services/cis-news-sentiment-api/

CodeConvert. (2024). *CodeConvert.ai*. [AI Code generator / converter]. https://codeconvert.ai

Copilot. (2024). *Microsoft*. [AI search engine]. https://copilot.microsoft.com

Descript. (2024). *Descript* [Audio/video editing tool]. https://www.descript.com

Dorik. (2024). *Dorik* [Website building platform]. https://dorik.com

EverWebinar. (2024). *EverWebinar* [Webinar automation platform]. https://www.everwebinar.com

Fireflies.ai. (2024). *Fireflies* [Meeting transcription tool]. https://www.fireflies.ai

Gencraft. (2024). *Gencraft*. [Image generation tool]. https://www.gencraft.com

Google AI. (2024). *Bard*. [AI search engine]. https://bard.google.com

Google DeepMind. (2024). *Introducing Gemini: Our largest and most capable AI model*. https://ai.google/gemini-ecosystem

Gozalo-Brizuela, R., & Garrido-Merchán, E. C. (2023). *A survey of generative AI applications*. Accessed May, 2024, from https://doi.org/10.48550/arXiv.2306.02781

Kleanleads. (2024). *Kleanleads* [Lead generation tool]. https://kleanleads.com

Krisp. (2024). *Krisp* [Noise cancelling app]. https://www.krisp.ai

Krock.io. (2024). *Krock.io* [Project management tool]. https://krock.io

Lumen5. (2024). *Lumen5* [Video creation platform]. https://lumen5.com

Mailchimp. (2024). *Mailchimp* [Email marketing platform]. https://mailchimp.com

Make. (2024). *Make*. [AI aggregator]. https://make.com

MarketMuse. (2024). *MarketMuse* [Content optimisation tool]. https://www.marketmuse.com

Maurya, A. (2012). *Running lean: Iterate from plan A to a plan that works*. O'Reilly Media.

Mendes, L. S., Doneda, D., & Almeida, V. (2023). On the development of AI governance frameworks. *IEEE Internet Computing*. https://doi.org/10.1109/MIC.2022.3186030

National Science and Technology Council (NSTC) Committee on Technology. (2016). *Preparing for the future of artificial intelligence*. Executive Office of the President.

Nieto-Rodriguez, A., & Vargas, R. V. (2023). *How AI will transform project management*. Harvard Business Review.. https://hbr.org/2023/02/how-ai-will-transform-project-management

Octaparse. (2024). *Octaparse* [Web scraping tool]. https://www.octaparse.com

Omnisend. (2024). *Omnisend* [Email & SMS marketing]. https://www.omnisend.com

OpenAI. (2024). *ChatGPT (GPT-4)* [Large language model]. OpenAI. https://www.openai.com.

Otter.ai. (2024). *Otter* [AI transcription service]. https://otter.ai

Oxford Analytica. (2023). *GenAI will transform workplace tasks across industries.* Expert Briefings. https://doi.org/10.1108/OXAN-DB279960
Perplexity. (2024). *Perplexity* [AI search engine]. https://www.perplexity.ai
Phillips, E. G., Gümüş, B., Lenic, M., Gray, M., Mihailov, M., Erozan, A., & Mrzlikar, I. (2020). *Project management practice guide for startups.* https://www.projectmanagement.com/deliverables/807134/project-management-practice-guide-for-startups
Pictory.ai. (2024). *Pictory.ai* [AI video creation]. https://pictory.ai
Prezi. (2024). Prezi [AI presentation tool]. https://prezi.com
Project Management Institute (Ed.). (2021). *A guide to the project management body of knowledge (PMBOK® guide)* (7th ed.). Project Management Institute.
QuillBot. (2024). *QuillBot* [Paraphrasing tool]. https://quillbot.com
Radford, A., Narasimhan, K., Salimans, T., & Sutskever, I. (2018). *Improving language understanding by generative pre-training.* OpenAI. https://cdn.openai.com/research-covers/language-unsupervised/language_understanding_paper.pdf
Ries, E. (2011). *The lean startup: How today's entrepreneurs use continuous innovation to create radically successful businesses.* Crown Business.
RunwayML. (2024). *RunwayML* [Creative suite for AI]. https://runwayml.com
Scispace. (2024). *Scispace* [Academic research tool]. https://typeset.io
Semrush. (2024). *Semrush* [SEO & online visibility management]. https://www.semrush.com
Sendinblue. (2024). *Sendinblue* [Digital marketing platform]. https://www.sendinblue.com
Supademo. (2024). *Supademo* [Product demo creation]. https://supademo.com
Synthesia. (2024). *Synthesia* [AI video generation]. https://www.synthesia.io
Taplio. (2024). *Taplio* [LinkedIn growth tool]. https://taplio.com
Vidyo.ai. (2024). *Vidyo.ai* [AI video editing]. https://vidyo.ai
Wordtune. (2024). *Wordtune* [Writing assistant]. https://www.wordtune.com
Writesonic. (2024). *Writesonic* [AI writing assistant]. https://writesonic.com
Zapier. (2024). *Zapier* [AI aggregator]. https://zapier.com
Zewe, A. (2023, November 9). Explained: Generative AI. *MIT News.* https://news.mit.edu/2023/explained-generative-ai-1109
Zysman, J., & Nitzberg, M. (2020). Governing AI: Understanding the limits, possibility, and risks of ai in an era of intelligent tools and systems. *Social Science Research Network.* https://doi.org/10.2139/SSRN.3681088

Planning and Controlling Startup Projects Applying Critical Chain Project Management

Denis Solan

Abstract

A realistic evaluation of project progress relies on planning and controlling milestones. Startup companies face challenges in planning long-term and controlling short-term development. Previous studies have examined startup management practices, primarily focusing on business and financial planning, but rarely explored startup project management. This study investigates the contribution of the Critical Chain Project Management (CCPM) method for planning, monitoring, and controlling the entire startup project. Feedback from a startup company implementing the technique indicates that CCPM could benefit ventures in their early design and development phase.

1 Introduction

This chapter highlights the increasing contribution of startups to local and global economies (Global Startup Ecosystem Report, 2022). Startups often develop their ideas without comprehensively understanding who needs and will buy their products. Thus, unlike traditional project management that focuses on meeting the project requirements agreed upon with the customer (PMBOK Guide Seventh Edition, 2021), startups focus on reaching a minimum viable product (MVP) and getting feedback from potential customers to improve the value proposition (e.g., Reis, 2011; Sońta-Drączkowska & Mrożewski, 2019). During new product development, startups face intense competition in rapidly changing markets; therefore, entrepreneurs strive to maximize their product fit and minimize its time to market (Schilling & Hill, 1998).

D. Solan (✉)
Technion – Israel Institute of Technology, Haifa, Israel
e-mail: denis.solan@campus.technion.ac.il

Ö. Hazır, M. E. Bruni (eds.), *Tomorrow's Data Empowered Project Management*, Future of Business and Finance, https://doi.org/10.1007/978-3-031-84017-3_5

Entrepreneurship requires management skills (e.g., Reis, 2011). Previous studies have examined startup management practices, primarily focusing on business and financial planning (e.g., Davila et al., 2015; Mansoori & Lackéus, 2020; Shepherd & Gruber, 2021), but rarely explored startup project management. Project management methods include the Critical Path Method (CPM), Program Evaluation and Review Technique (PERT), Critical Chain Project Management (CCPM), and recently, agile project management. Agile project management is the most popular approach among entrepreneurs (e.g., Ghezzi & Cavallo, 2020) that involves short-term planning iterations (Azenha et al., 2021; Sońta-Drączkowska & Mrożewski, 2019).

As startups create new products or services in an uncertain environment, entrepreneurs encounter challenges in long-term planning. This research aims to address that gap by investigating the contribution of the Critical Chain Project Management (CCPM) approach to early-stage startups. The research results indicate that the CCPM could benefit startups in planning, monitoring, and controlling the entire project.

2 Literature Review

2.1 Project Management

Traditional project management focuses on meeting the planned scope, cost, and time (Gemino et al., 2021). The project progress review relies on planning and controlling activities and milestones. The duration of activities depends on subjective estimations associated with factors that might delay project completion (e.g., Blackstone Jr et al., 2009). For example, activities may take longer than expected, resources may become unavailable, and materials may arrive late (Herroelen & Leus, 2005). Therefore, predictions are highly uncertain, and buffering strategies are usually employed as protection mechanisms (e.g., Hazır & Ulusoy, 2020; Pellerin & Perrier, 2019). The scheduling of activities often occurs as the final step in the project planning process. The PMBOK Guide defines a project schedule as 'an output of a schedule model that presents linked activities with planned dates, durations, milestones, and resources' (PMBOK Guide Seventh Edition, 2021).

The resource-constrained project scheduling problem (RCPSP) has been studied extensively for several decades (Brucker et al., 1999) and is still the primary method for project planning (Pellerin & Perrier, 2019). The purpose is to schedule a set of activities to minimize project completion time within constraints of both activities' precedence relations and limited resource availabilities. Various exact and heuristic algorithms are available for generating a baseline schedule (also called a predictive schedule) under the assumption of a deterministic environment and complete information (Van de Vonder et al., 2008). In the case of stochastic activity durations, inserting time buffers between activities might improve the stability of the baseline schedule (Van de Vonder et al., 2008). The RCPSP complexity requires heuristic procedures to generate a baseline schedule in real-world projects (Herroelen et al.,

2002). Some industries drive variants and extensions of the RCPSP (e.g., Hartmann & Briskorn, 2010; Ikeziri et al., 2019).

The project management methods include the Critical Path Method (CPM), Program Evaluation and Review Technique (PERT), and Critical Chain Project Management (CCPM). The CCPM method is the Theory of Constraints (TOC) solution for planning, scheduling, and controlling projects. Project completion time is constrained by the critical chain representing the longest sequence of dependent events through a network of activities and resources (The TOCICO Dictionary Second Edition, 2012). The CCPM was introduced by Goldratt in his book *Critical Chain* in 1997 to minimize the inefficiencies identified in traditional project management methods such as the CPM and the PERT, developed in the 1950s. The CPM and PERT methods are often used for time management, but projects rarely meet their deadlines (Ordoñez et al., 2019; Pellerin & Perrier, 2019). Poor performance is related to the inherent uncertainty of projects (Van de Vonder et al., 2008). Furthermore, Leach (2014) argued that one of the biggest problems in project execution occurs when organizations allow or encourage multitasking, i.e., switching from one incomplete task to another. Multitasking increases the amount of time to accomplish all tasks, produces waste, and leads to mistakes (Leach, 2014).

The CCPM method provides a rigorous plan and simplifies project control (Steyn, 2000) by removing multitasking and safety in activities' time estimates and utilizing buffer management that reduces uncertainty and identifies any schedule disruption during project execution. Compared to CPM and PERT, the CCPM method offers better monitoring and control of project status. The CCPM method could benefit a company that strives to meet deadlines but lacks effective project management processes (Raz et al., 2003). Further, Van de Vonder et al. (2006) argued that the critical chain can provide good project duration protection in case of uncertainty. Hence, the CCPM method is popular among project management practitioners despite its oversimplification (Herroelen & Leus, 2005), especially for single projects (Herroelen & Leus, 2004). Yet, Herroelen and Leus (2001) reviewed the strengths and weaknesses of the critical chain scheduling approach. According to the authors, it is a simple tool for setting realistic due dates and monitoring projects. At the same time, their criticisms are based on theory and simulations and not on case studies of actual projects (Ricketts, 2008). Research is ongoing to improve the CCPM method (Ghaffari & Emsley, 2015), such as buffer sizing (e.g., She et al., 2021; Zarghami et al., 2020). Nevertheless, Pinto (1999) argued that project managers should understand the critical chain's pros and cons to apply the method where it is appropriate.

The recent agile project management approach contrasts with the traditional, front-end planning process through multiple iterations and incremental improvements via the development cycle (Serrador & Pinto, 2015). This approach is especially prevalent in software development and information technology projects (Gemino et al., 2021; Serrador & Pinto, 2015), where scope and requirements change rapidly during the project life cycle (Azenha et al., 2021). Hence, agile software development principles include satisfying the customer with early and continuous software delivery and welcoming changing requirements (https://

agilemanifesto.org/principles.html). Combined traditional and agile approaches are becoming popular in project management (Gemino et al., 2021).

2.2 Startup Project Management

Startup companies evolve around the founder's belief in solving a certain problem by developing a single product or service. Startups usually have a small team trying to implement the entrepreneur's idea. Startups operate in an uncertain environment and often lack the expected value to potential customers, resulting in high risks such as product development and market penetration. Thus, startups have a high failure rate.

During new product development, startups face intense competition in rapidly changing markets; therefore, entrepreneurs attempt to maximize their product fit and minimize the time to market (Schilling & Hill, 1998). In contrast to traditional project management, ventures make decisions without considering customers' requirements and involvement. Thus, a popular approach involves developing a minimum viable product (MVP) and obtaining feedback from early adopters to improve the value proposition (e.g., Reis, 2011; Sońta-Drączkowska & Mrożewski, 2019) or pivot to a different direction.

Ventures often encounter challenges such as a lack of financial resources and necessary commercial and managerial competencies (e.g., Noelia & Rosalia, 2020). Entrepreneurs seeking funding from investors or acceptance by entrepreneurial development programs are required to present a business plan. The business plan usually includes a Gantt chart with project activities and milestones, which relies on traditional project management principles. However, most traditional project management practices are not applied due to their complexity and a lack of entrepreneurs' management knowledge. Therefore, ventures use simple management methods and tools to plan project milestones.

Previous studies have examined startup management practices. Nevertheless, these studies primarily focus on business and financial planning (e.g., Davila et al., 2015; Honig & Samuelsson, 2021) but rarely examine startup project management. During project execution, startup initiatives may cause schedule disruptions, such as optimistic goal setting, activity duration changes, and resource shortages. Thus, the popular agile approach relies on iterations of short-term planning and constant replanning of work (Sońta-Drączkowska & Mrożewski, 2019).

3 Research Methodology

The author conducted a preliminary study in the U.S. and Israel between May 2019 and August 2020 to collect data on the management practices of early-stage startups. The main insight from the investigation was the necessity of providing training and project management tools to startup companies. As a result of the findings, the author investigated the relevance and application of the CCPM method for early-stage startup project planning, monitoring, and control. In the next stage, the author introduced the technique and guided a Food Tech startup company in planning and monitoring its project between June 2023 and December 2023.

3.1 Data Collection

For data collection purposes, we established a collaboration with several international incubators and accelerators for early-stage startups. The author collected the data through an online questionnaire and interviews with startup founders. The purpose of the questionnaire was to collect data about startup characteristics (e.g., founders' experience, number of employees, and product development stage). Additionally, the author conducted a 30-min interview to collect data on founders' management practices.

3.2 Research Sample

The author contacted 130 early-stage startups. Eighty-three startups from the U.S. and Israel responded to the questionnaire (63.8%). Of those, 73 were interviewed, resulting in a sample size of 73 startups (56.1%). About 65% of the startups were from the United States. Information technology and healthcare sectors accounted for about 60% of the startups. Over 72% of the sample are software startups. The typical founder was male (88.6%), 43 years old, with a Master's degree, founded a company, and had 10 years of experience. About 60% of the startups had a product. The typical startup age was 6.5 years, with 17 employees (a median size of 7).

4 Research Results

The research findings indicate that startup founders use management tools based on their experience, the number of employees, and the stage of product development. The most common tools are Excel, Asana (https://asana.com), Trello (https://trello.com), and Slack (https://slack.com). Entrepreneurs use these tools to plan and control activities in the short term. Several entrepreneurs noted the challenge of long-term planning and control of product development in the short term due to high uncertainty and subjective estimates. Interviewees mentioned the following concerns:

> "New product uncertainty makes it difficult to plan a long-term Gantt."
> "Estimation and measurement of weekly progress are hard because it relies on feelings."

In some cases, entrepreneurs noted a lack of integration between their master plan and agile sprints, resulting in wasted resources and inefficiencies. Interviewees asserted the following:

> "The agile incremental development is disconnected from the master plan."
> "Daily or weekly reflection of development progress and quarterly review of the master plan."
> "Integration of the master plan and agile sprints could improve the management processes."

According to the research findings, there is a need for a simple yet effective startup project management tool. Thus, this study analyzes the applicability of the Critical Chain Project Management (CCPM) method for early-stage startup project planning, monitoring, and control. Table 1 summarizes the relevance of the CCPM method for early-stage startups. Additionally, this study provides evidence of the contribution of the CCPM technique. A startup founder who employed the CCPM for half a year noted:

> "While the method has helped keep track of our tasks and manage their execution, it can be challenging to follow the plan."

The founder mentioned the main reasons, which include unexpected events that require preparation and attendance, repetitive tasks, and small tasks that need attention and prevent entire focus on a single task. Thus, the entrepreneur proposed:

> "Consider repetitive actions when planning and differentiate tasks into big and small stones."

The following section discusses how early-stage startups can implement the CCPM method.

4.1 Analysis of the CCPM Method for Early-Stage Startups

The theory of constraints states that managers should develop a good enough plan and buffer it to minimize the risk of the project enduring longer than expected. The CCPM method includes the following steps:

1. Removal of multitasking (switching from one incomplete task to another), student syndrome (delaying work until the last moment before the deadline), and Parkinson's Law (work expands to fill the available time for completion).
2. Development of a project network that includes activity and resource dependencies (without safety buffers in activities' time estimates).
3. Development of a schedule displaying the critical chain and the buffers.
4. A focused effort to complete an activity and hand it off immediately to a resource ready to take over, frequent report of work remaining.
5. Identification of schedule disruption based on buffer management.

Table 1 Summary of the relevance of the CCPM method for early-stage startups

#	Startup characteristics	Relevance of the CCPM method
1.	Startups develop new products under conditions of extreme uncertainty (Reis, 2011).	CCPM reduces uncertainty and indicates the project duration during the project's execution (Goldratt, 1997). Buffering strategies address the uncertainty (Pellerin & Perrier, 2019). CCPM can provide good project duration protection in the case of uncertainty (Van de Vonder et al., 2006).
2.	Startups need to minimize their product time to market (Schilling & Hill, 1998).	CCPM reduces a single project duration compared with the CPM (Ricketts, 2008; Steyn, 2000).
3.	Startups encounter a scarcity of financial resources (Noelia & Rosalia, 2020).	CCPM can be learned within a short period (Steyn, 2000). CCPM provides a rigorous plan and simplifies project control (Steyn, 2000). CCPM could benefit a company that lacks effective project management processes (Raz et al., 2003). CCPM reduces the duration of a single project (Ricketts, 2008; Steyn, 2000), thereby reducing its cost.
4.	Startups lack practices for entire project planning and control. The popular agile approach involves short-term planning and control (Sońta-Drączkowska & Mrożewski, 2019).	CCPM is a simple tool (Herroelen & Leus, 2001) for realistic due dates settings and project monitoring (Steyn, 2000). CCPM identifies schedule disruption and high-priority activities during project execution (Goldratt, 1997). CCPM is popular among project management practitioners (Herroelen & Leus, 2005; Leach, 2014; Ricketts, 2008).
5.	Startups are controlled by stakeholders (Loch & Sommer, 2019).	CCPM provides stakeholders with a protected project plan and buffer management for monitoring startup progress. CCPM simplifies project control (Steyn, 2000).

The CCPM method incorporates three buffers. The project buffer serves as a time buffer to protect the entire plan duration. The feeding buffer acts as a time buffer to prevent the non-critical chain from becoming the critical chain. The resource buffer serves as a warning to ensure that resources assigned to a critical chain activity will be available when needed.

Safety time is removed from time estimates for individual activities. Half of the safety time of the critical chain activities is placed at the end of the critical chain as a project buffer. Project duration is the sum of the critical chain activity times and the project buffer. The project buffer will be depleted when critical chain activities take longer than estimated or when a feeding buffer is depleted and some activity(s) on the associated non-critical chain need to be completed.

The following section introduces the implementation of the CCPM method for early-stage startups during a minimum viable product (MVP) design and development phase (the Appendix presents a step-by-step implementation of the CCPM method for planning, monitoring, and controlling an MVP project).

4.1.1 MVP Project Planning and Scheduling (Based on the CCPM Method)

1. Define the project activities performed by one or more resources.
2. Provide a 50% activity time estimate for each activity.
3. Create a precedence project network that includes all activity and resource dependencies.
4. Analyze the critical chain as the longest sequence of dependent events through a project network, considering activity and resource dependencies.
5. Add the project buffer at the end of the critical chain—50% of the critical chain's length (or longer due to a high uncertainty).
6. Add the feeding and resource buffers at the end of the non-critical chains, where it converges with the critical chain.
7. Present the protected critical chain project plan showing the precedence project network that includes all activity and resource dependencies based on 50% activity time estimates and project, feeding, and resource buffers.

Figure 1 presents the process of creating a protected project plan. Van de Vonder et al. (2006) noted that a project buffer equal to 50% of the critical chain length is too safe for most projects, especially those with a long duration. Since the startup project duration to reach MVP is relatively short (in many cases less than 1 year), the project buffer length will be relatively small.

The activities are subject to uncertainty that may result in numerous schedule disruptions during the project execution. Although small deviations may be acceptable, large deviations may require corrective actions. A startup team usually

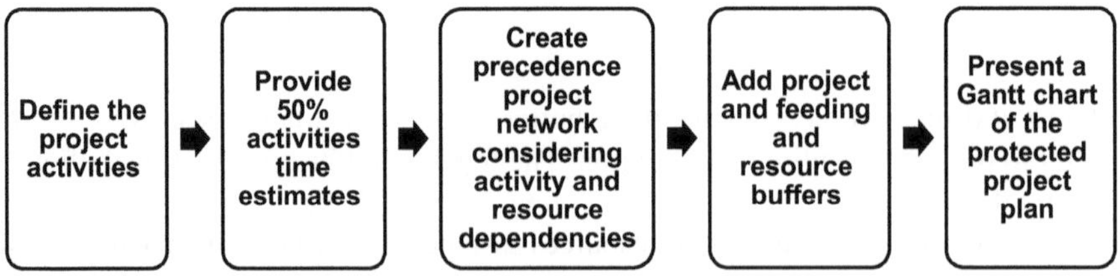

Fig. 1 The process of creating a protected project plan

discusses the development progress daily. Monitoring the status of a project is achieved by measuring its project buffer consumption (the accumulation of activity lateness on a path) to the proportion of the critical chain completed. Project buffer penetration determines how much remaining activity duration is significant. The CCPM method uses three metrics to evaluate the project execution. The metrics are according to the TOCICO Dictionary Second Edition (2012):

1. Critical chain completed (%)—The percentage of the critical chain completed. It is a measure of the project's progress to date. The percentage of the critical chain completed is calculated as follows:

$$\text{Critical chain completed}\left(\%\right) = 100\,\frac{\text{Number of days of critical chain activities completed}}{\text{Total number of days on critical chain}} \tag{1}$$

2. Project buffer burn rate—The percentage of the project buffer consumed relative to the percentage of the critical chain completed. It is a measure of the project status to date. The project buffer burn rate is calculated as follows:

$$\text{Project buffer burn rate} = \frac{\text{percentage of project buffer consumed}}{\text{percentage of critical chain completed}} \tag{2}$$

3. Project buffer consumption rate—The rate of consumption of the project buffer relative to the rate of completion of the critical chain for a single period. It is a measure of the project's progress in a period. It indicates whether the critical chain activities during the period are at risk and whether corrective actions taken at the beginning of the period were effective in returning the project to schedule. The project buffer consumption rate is calculated as follows:

$$\text{Project buffer consumption rate} = \frac{\text{Increase in \% of buffer consumed in the recent period}}{\text{Increase in \% of critical chain completed in the recent period}} \tag{3}$$

4.1.2 MVP Project Monitoring and Control (Based on the CCPM Method)

1. Measure periodically (daily or weekly) the project buffer consumption to the proportion of the critical chain completed at control points to show the relative status of the project to the remaining protection. A project buffer burn rate of more than one indicates schedule disruption during the project execution, and

immediate action is needed to bring the project back on schedule. For example, consider suspending a non-critical chain activity and reassigning its resource to a critical chain activity suffering resource constraint.
2. Measure the project buffer consumption rate for a period following the corrective action to evaluate the effectiveness of returning the project to schedule.

The critical chain may change during project execution depending on resource availability and buffer usage. For example, when a non-critical chain penetrates the critical chain, the non-critical chain becomes the new critical chain.

5 Discussion

This study indicates a lack of research on management practices for the entire startup project. One explanation may be related to the startup nature, i.e., startup projects are not prone to exact plans. Additionally, entrepreneurs may lack management knowledge and experience to plan and control the project.

This research also revealed the challenges of early-stage startups in planning long-term and controlling short-term development. Furthermore, this study exposed the regular use of short-term planning and control tools. Therefore, this study investigated the significance of the CCPM approach for the entire early-stage startup project planning, monitoring, and control. This research revealed that the CCPM method can benefit startups in their early design and development phase because it facilitates simple project management, can be learned within a short period, and may reduce project duration compared to the CPM (e.g., Ricketts, 2008; Steyn, 2000). It can also help the startup team develop a roadmap from idea to launch, see the big picture, share understanding, and synchronize activities.

A shorter development can make the difference between the success and failure of research and development projects. The primary cause of deviations in activity durations is inaccurate estimations (Hazır & Ulusoy, 2020). Focusing on critical activities and managing the project buffer can reduce uncertainty and enable early-stage startups to plan and control challenging but achievable project plans. Buffer management enables startup managers to identify schedule disruption and high-priority activities during project execution and control project milestones by looking beyond the short-term. Furthermore, the CCPM method indicates the project duration during execution.

It is essential to control the project by evaluating actual performance and resolving deviations from the plan. Furthermore, investors tighten their control by reviewing progress when startup projects face increasing risks (Loch & Sommer, 2019). Therefore, a protected project plan and buffer management can signal the startup's quality to the stakeholders (e.g., investors, incubators, and accelerators).

5.1 Practical Implications

Research results show that the CCPM method can assist startups in planning, monitoring, and controlling their operations. As the CCPM method may reduce project duration, startups benefit from reduced project cost. During the project execution, the CCPM method provides information regarding the project, activities, and buffer status. Periodically monitoring the project status facilitates making effective control decisions. For instance, identifying the activities that cause buffer penetration forms a clear priority for startup managers. A protected project plan and buffer management can also facilitate investors and venture development programs to review their startup progress.

This study focuses on MVP project management. In many cases, the duration of MVP implementation is relatively short; therefore, the length of the project buffer is relatively short. Regardless, the project buffer could be more than 50% of the critical chain's length in extreme uncertainty conditions. The Appendix illustrates the implementation of the CCPM method for early-stage startups to reach MVP. Similarly, the CCPM technique can serve intermediate milestones such as proof of concept and prototype development. Yet, the CCPM method could be employed for project replanning in case of a pivot.

6 Conclusions

This research reveals the benefits of the CCPM method for early-stage startups. Buffered projects, frequent (daily or weekly) monitoring, and control provide a structured process essential for startups in their early design and development phase. This study provides entrepreneurs with valuable insights regarding project management and the importance of a plan. Applying CCPM for the entire project planning, monitoring, and control can reduce uncertainty and improve startups' business models, management processes, and time to market. However, it is necessary to examine the implementation of the CCPM technique by considerable startups from various industries to determine its adoption and identify theoretical and practical gaps. For example, examine the combination of CCPM with agile as a hybrid project management approach. This hybrid approach could support long-term and short-term development planning and control, i.e., iterations management and buffer management of the entire project plan. Future research could also investigate handling unexpected events during the startup project execution, for example, by integrating unanticipated activities into the CCPM plan and adjusting the project buffer.

Appendix: An Illustrative Example of the CCPM Implementation for Early-Stage Startup Projects Planning, Monitoring, and Control

This study extends the Blackstone Jr et al. (2009) example to illustrate a theoretical application of the CCPM for early-stage startup project planning as well as monitoring and control. The example considers ten project activities and four human resources to reach MVP and utilizes Microsoft Project.

MVP Project Planning

Step 1: Define the project activities

Table 2 shows ten project activities, starting with market research and ending with MVP pilots.

Step 2: Provide 50% of activities' time estimates

Table 2 shows the 50% time estimates for project activities. For example, the 50% time estimate for the market research activity is six working days.

Step 3 A: Create a project network considering activity dependencies

Table 2 shows the precedence relation between project activities. For example, the market research activity precedes all other activities.

Figure 2 presents a Gantt chart considering activity dependencies. The red-colored activities are activities on the critical path, and the blue-colored activities are

Table 2 The project activities to reach MVP, the 50% time estimates, and the precedence relation between activities

	Task name	Duration	Predecessors
1	MVP project	32 days	
2	Market research	6 days	
3	Define customer value proposition	6 days	2
4	Define master plan	4 days	2
5	Define MVP requirements	4 days	2
6	Prototype development	8 days	3
7	Proof of concept	2 days	3,4
8	MVP design	6 days	4,5
9	Prototype testing	4 days	6,7
10	MVP development	6 days	7,8
11	MVP pilots	8 days	9,10

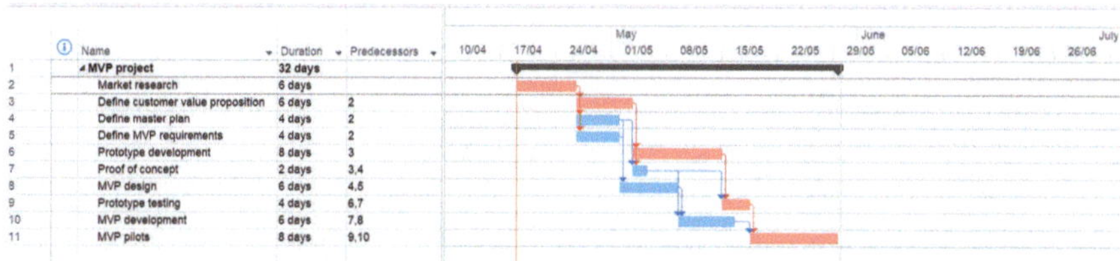

Fig. 2 Gantt chart considering activity dependencies

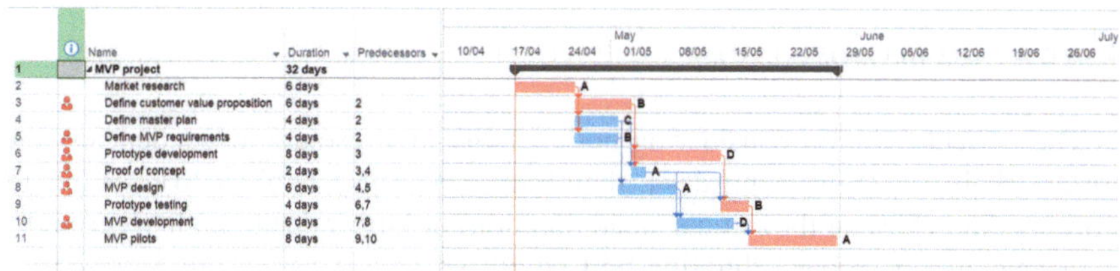

Fig. 3 Gantt chart considering activity dependencies with overlap

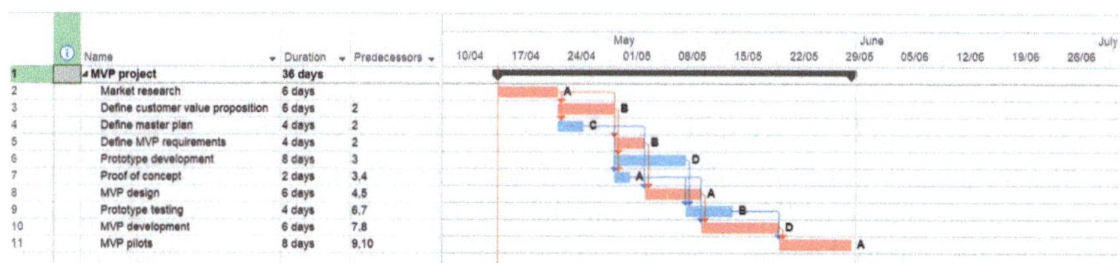

Fig. 4 Gantt chart considering activity and resource dependencies

non-critical path activities. In this case, the project duration is 32 working days (note: the Critical Path method will result in a project duration of 64 days).

Figure 3 shows how project activities are assigned to human resources: A, B, C, and D. Additionally, Fig. 3 presents an overlap in the timing of the activities assigned to the same resource. For example, proof of concept and MVP design activities are allocated to resource A and scheduled for execution simultaneously. Hence, to avoid an overlap, considering activity and resource dependencies is required (see the next step).

Step 3 B: Create a project network considering activity and resource dependencies

Figure 4 presents a Gantt chart considering both activity and resource dependencies. The activities are assigned to human resources: A, B, C, and D without overlapping. Consequently, the project duration is 36 working days.

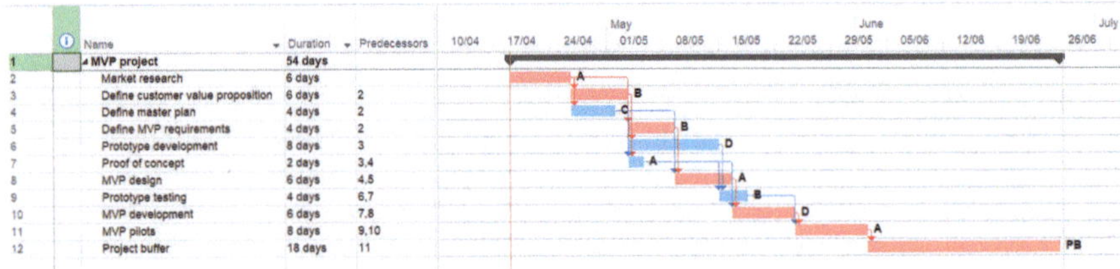

Fig. 5 Gantt chart of the project plan considering activity and resource dependencies, and the project buffer

Step 4 A: Add the project buffer

The project duration considering both activity and resource dependencies (the critical chain) is 36 working days; therefore, the project buffer (PB) will be 18 working days (50% of the critical chain duration) or longer due to high uncertainty. Consequently, the project duration will be 54 working days. Figure 5 presents a Gantt chart of the project plan considering activity and resource dependencies and the project buffer at the end of the network.

Step 4 B: Add feeding and resource buffers

Feeding buffers (FB) are added at the end of the non-critical chain activities to avoid the non-critical chain becoming a critical chain. The feeding buffer helps determine when to start the non-critical chain activity. We will analyze the project plan from the end to the start. Prototype testing is the first non-critical chain activity with a feeding buffer due to the constraint time to its following critical chain activity, the MVP pilots. The next non-critical chain activity with a feeding buffer is the define master plan activity due to the constraint time to its following critical chain activity, the MVP design. The length of this feeding buffer considers its following non-critical chain activity, the proof of concept.

Proof of concept is the first non-critical chain activity with a resource buffer due to the resource constraint with a critical chain activity, the MVP design. The next non-critical chain activity with a resource buffer is the prototype development due to the resource constraint with a critical chain activity, the MVP development. Figure 6 presents a Gantt chart of the protected project plan with parallel paths considering activity and resource dependencies, project buffer, feeding, and resource buffers. The red-colored activities are activities on the critical chain, and the blue-colored activities are non-critical chain activities. The protected project duration is 54 working days.

MVP Project Monitoring and Control

During the project execution, the CCPM method provides information regarding the project, activities, and buffer status. Monitoring of the project status periodically facilitates control decisions. For instance, identifying the activities that cause buffer penetration forms a clear priority for startup managers.

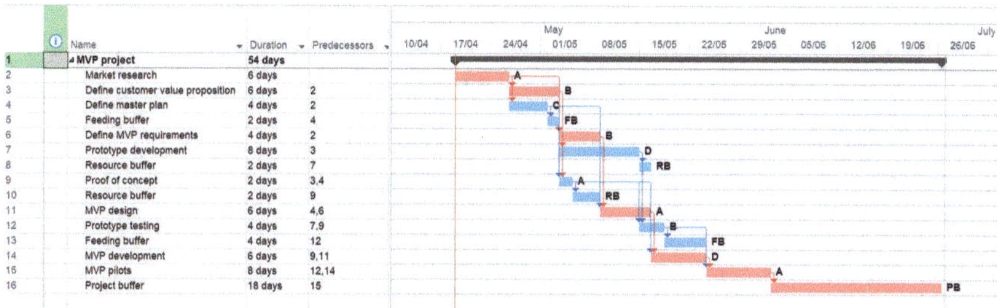

Fig. 6 Gantt chart of the protected project plan considering activity and resource dependencies, project buffer, feeding, and resource buffers

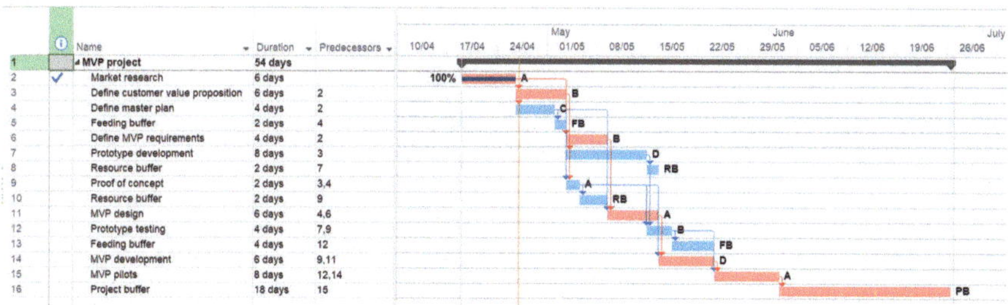

Fig. 7 Gantt chart of the protected project plan at the first control point

In this example, we monitor the project approximately weekly (at the planned finish dates of critical chain activities) and measure the project buffer consumption to the proportion of the critical chain completed during the project execution.

First control point:

Figure 7 presents a Gantt chart of the protected project plan at the first control point. Vertical lines indicate the start and planned finish dates of the project, as well as the current status. The percentage indicates the percentage of the activity completed. At the first control point, 100% of the market research activity is completed on time, meaning completion of the market research without penetrating the project buffer.

Second control point:

Figure 8 presents a Gantt chart of the protected project plan at the second control point. At this point, 100% of the master plan is defined. Additionally, 50% of the customer value proposition is defined (3 days of progress on the 6-day critical chain activity), meaning a delay in completing this activity. Moreover, that causes a delay in starting the following activities and penetrating the project buffer.

At the second control point, 25% of the critical chain is completed (9 days of 36 days of the critical chain), and 17% of the project buffer is consumed (3 days of 18 days of the project buffer). The project buffer burn rate is currently less than one,

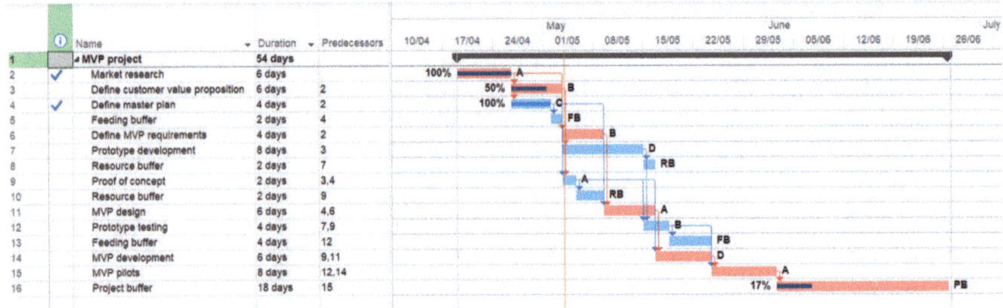

Fig. 8 Gantt chart of the protected project plan at the second control point

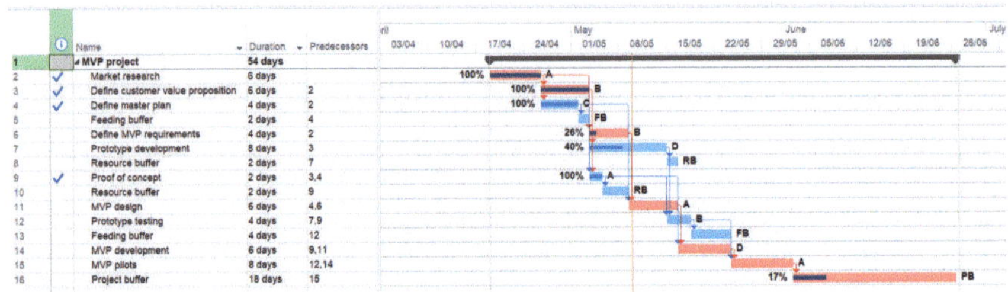

Fig. 9 Gantt chart of the protected project plan at the third control point

which means the project is on schedule; therefore, no action is required except to prioritize the defining customer value proposition, a critical chain activity.

Third control point:

Figure 9 presents a Gantt chart of the protected project plan at the third control point. At this point, 100% of the customer value proposition is defined, and 100% of the proof of concept is completed. Additionally, 25% of the MVP requirements are defined, and 40% of the prototype is developed, meaning a delay in completing these activities. As a result, the MVP design is delayed, and the project buffer is penetrated.

At the third control point, 36% of the critical chain is completed (13 days of 36 days of the critical chain), and 17% of the project buffer is consumed (3 days of 18 days of the project buffer). The project buffer burn rate is currently less than one, which means the project is on schedule; therefore, no action is required except to prioritize the defining MVP requirements, a critical chain activity.

Fourth control point:

Figure 10 presents a Gantt chart of the protected project plan at the fourth control point. At this point, 100% of the MVP requirements and 100% of the prototype development are completed. However, the MVP design and the prototype testing

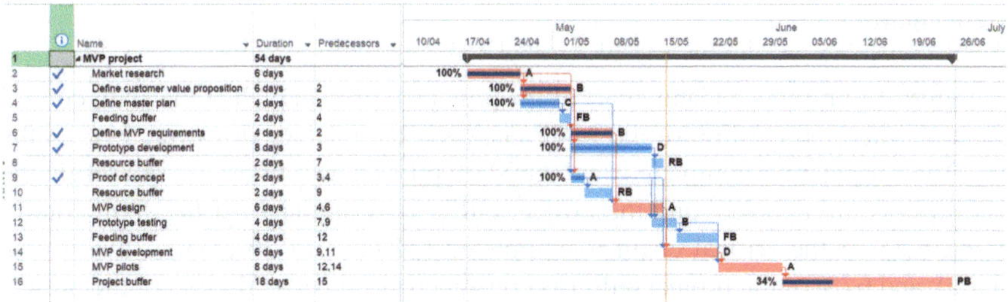

Fig. 10 Gantt chart of the protected project plan at the fourth control point

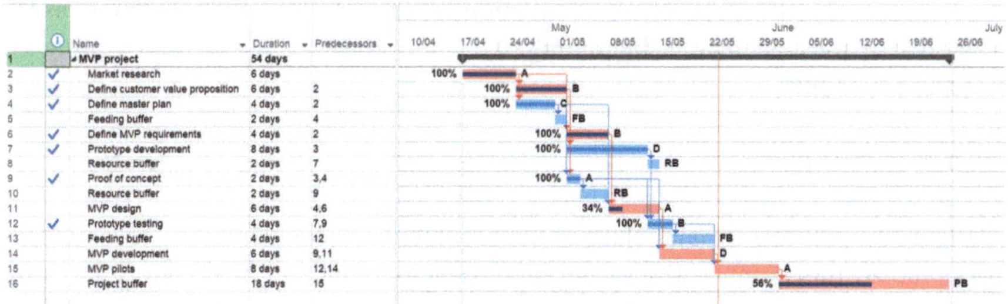

Fig. 11 Gantt chart of the protected project plan at the fifth control point

haven't started, meaning a delay in completing these activities. As a result, the MVP development is delayed, and the project buffer is penetrated. At the fourth control point, 44% of the critical chain is completed (16 days of 36 days of the critical chain), and 34% of the project buffer is consumed (6 days of 18 days of the project buffer). The project buffer burn rate is currently less than one, which means the project is on schedule; therefore, no action is required except to prioritize the MVP design, a critical chain activity.

Fifth control point:

Figure 11 presents a Gantt chart of the protected project plan at the fifth control point. At this point, 100% of the prototype testing is completed. However, 34% of the MVP design is completed, and the MVP development hasn't started, meaning a delay in completing these activities. As a result, the MVP pilots are delayed, and the project buffer is penetrated.

At the fifth control point, 50% of the critical chain is completed (18 days of 36 days of the critical chain), and 56% of the project buffer is consumed (10 days of 18 days of the project buffer). The project buffer burn rate is currently more than one, which indicates a schedule disruption and immediate action is needed to complete the MVP design and MVP development, which are critical chain activities. For example, consider reassigning available resources to the critical activities (MVP design first, followed by MVP development), dividing the activities, and assigning each part to a different resource.

Sixth control point:

Figure 12 presents a Gantt chart of the protected project plan at the sixth control point. At this point, 100% of the MVP design is completed. However, 34% of the MVP development is completed, and the MVP pilots haven't started. As a result, the MVP pilots are delayed, and the project buffer is penetrated. At the sixth control point, 67% of the critical chain is completed (24 days of 36 days of the critical chain), and 67% of the project buffer is consumed (12 days of 18 days of the project buffer). The project buffer burn rate is currently one, which means the project is on schedule; therefore, no corrective action is required. Additionally, the project buffer consumption rate is less than one (an 11% increase in buffer consumption relative to a 17% increase in critical chain completion in the recent period), which means the corrective actions taken at the beginning of the period were effective in returning the project to schedule.

Seventh control point:

Figure 13 presents a Gantt chart of the protected project plan at the seventh control point. At this point, 100% of the MVP development and MVP pilots are completed, i.e., the project finished on time (note: 10 days ahead of the Critical Path method due date).

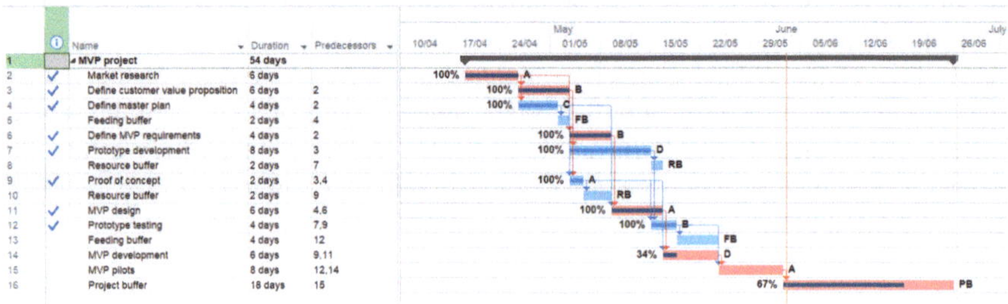

Fig. 12 Gantt chart of the protected project plan at the sixth control point

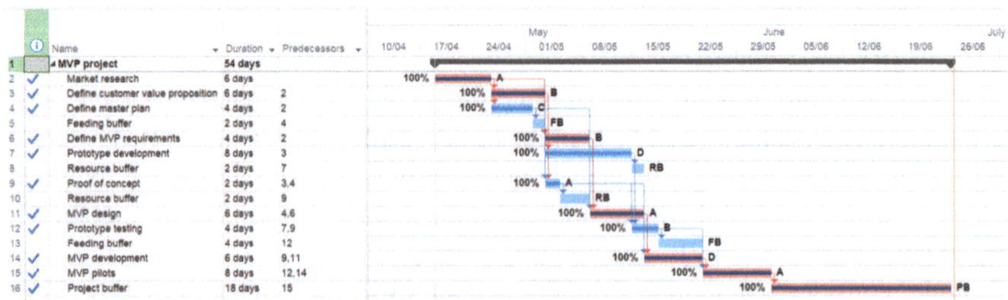

Fig. 13 Gantt chart of the protected project plan at the seventh control point

Acknowledgment The author would like to thank Eli Schragenheim, a member of TOCICO, for his valuable contribution and advice.

Declaration of Conflicting Interests The author declared no potential conflicts of interest with respect to the research, authorship, and/or publication of this article.

Funding The author received no financial support for the research, authorship, and/or publication of this article.

References

Azenha, F. C., Reis, D. A., & Fleury, A. L. (2021). The role and characteristics of hybrid approaches to project management in the development of technology-based products and services. *Project Management Journal, 52*(1), 90–110.

Blackstone, J. H., Jr., Cox, J. F., III, & Schleier, J. G., Jr. (2009). A tutorial on project management from a theory of constraints perspective. *International Journal of Production Research, 47*(24), 7029–7046.

Brucker, P., Drexl, A., Möhring, R., Neumann, K., & Pesch, E. (1999). Resource-constrained project scheduling: Notation, classification, models, and methods. *European Journal of Operational Research, 112*, 3–41.

Davila, A., Foster, G., & Ning, J. (2015). The valuation of management control systems in start-up companies: International field-based evidence. *European Accounting Review, 24*(2), 207–239.

Gemino, A., Reich, B. H., & Serrador, P. M. (2021). Agile, traditional, and hybrid approaches to project success: Is hybrid a poor second choice? *Project Management Journal, 52*(2), 161–175.

Ghaffari, M., & Emsley, M. W. (2015). Current status and future potential of the research on critical chain project management. *Surveys in Operations Research and Management Science, 20*, 43–54.

Ghezzi, A., & Cavallo, A. (2020). Agile business model innovation in digital entrepreneurship: Lean startup approaches. *Journal of Business Research, 110*, 519–537.

Goldratt, E. M. (1997). *Critical chain*. North River Press.

Hartmann, S., & Briskorn, D. (2010). A survey of variants and extensions of the resource-constrained project scheduling problem. *European Journal of Operational Research, 207*, 1–14.

Hazır, Ö., & Ulusoy, G. (2020). A classification and review of approaches and methods for modeling uncertainty in projects. *International Journal of Production Economics, 223*, 107522.

Herroelen, W., & Leus, R. (2001). On the merits and pitfalls of critical chain scheduling. *Journal of Operations Management, 19*, 559–577.

Herroelen, W., & Leus, R. (2004). Robust and reactive project scheduling: a review and classification of procedures. *International Journal of Production Research, 42*(8), 1599–1620.

Herroelen, W., & Leus, R. (2005). Project scheduling under uncertainty: Survey and research potentials. *European Journal of Operational Research, 165*, 289–306.

Herroelen, W., Leus, R., & Demeulemeester, E. (2002). Critical chain project scheduling: Do not oversimplify. *Project Management Journal, 33*(4), 48–60.

Honig, B., & Samuelsson, M. (2021). Business planning by intrapreneurs and entrepreneurs under environmental uncertainty and institutional pressure. *Technovation, 99*, 102124.

Ikeziri, L. M., de Souza, F. B., Gupta, M. C., & de Camargo Fiorini, P. (2019). Theory of constraints: Review and bibliometric analysis. *International Journal of Production Research, 57*(15–16), 5068–5102.

Leach, L. P. (2014). *Critical chain project management* (3rd ed.). Artech House.

Loch, C., & Sommer, S. (2019). The tension between flexible goals and managerial control in exploratory projects. *Project Management Journal, 50*(5), 524–537.

Mansoori, Y., & Lackéus, M. (2020). Comparing effectuation to discovery-driven planning, prescriptive entrepreneurship, business planning, lean startup, and design thinking. *Small Business Economics, 54*, 791–818.

Noelia, F.-L., & Rosalia, D.-C. (2020). A dynamic analysis of the role of entrepreneurial ecosystems in reducing innovation obstacles for startups. *Journal of Business Venturing Insights, 14*, e00192.

Ordoñez, R. E. C., Vanhoucke, M., Jose, C., Anholon, R., & Olıvio, N. (2019). A study of the critical chain project management method applied to a multiproject system. *Project Management Journal, 50*(3), 322–334.

Pellerin, R., & Perrier, N. (2019). A review of methods, techniques and tools for project planning and control. *International Journal of Production Research, 57*(7), 2160–2178.

Pinto, J. K. (1999). Some constraints on the theory of constraints: Taking a critical look at the critical chain. *The PM Network, 13*(8), 49–51.

Project Management Institute. (2021). *A Guide to the Project Management Body of Knowledge (PMBOK Guide) and The Standard for Project Management* (7th ed.). Project Management Institute.

Raz, T., Barnes, R., & Dvir, D. (2003). A critical look at critical chain project management. *Project Management Journal, 34*(4), 24–32.

Reis, E. (2011). *The lean startup: How today's entrepreneurs use continuous innovation to create radically successful businesses*. Crown Business.

Ricketts, J. A. (2008). *Reaching the goal: How managers improve a services business using Goldratt's theory of constraints*. IBM Press.

Schilling, M. A., & Hill, W. L. (1998). Managing the new product development process: Strategic imperatives. *Academy of Management Executive, 12*(3), 67–81.

Serrador, P., & Pinto, J. K. (2015). Does agile work? — A quantitative analysis of agile project success. *International Journal of Project Management, 33*, 1040–1051.

She, B., Chen, B., & Hall, N. G. (2021). Buffer sizing in critical chain project management by network decomposition. *Omega, 102*, 102382.

Shepherd, D. A., & Gruber, M. (2021). The lean startup framework: Closing the academic–practitioner divide. *Entrepreneurship Theory and Practice, 45*(5), 967–998.

Sońta-Drączkowska, E., & Mrożewski, M. (2019). Exploring the role of project management in product development of new technology-based firms. *Project Management Journal, 51*(3), 294–311.

Startup Genome. (2022). *The global startup ecosystem report 2022*. https://startupgenome.com/reports/gser2022

Steyn, H. (2000). An investigation into the fundamentals of critical chain project scheduling. *International Journal of Project Management, 19*, 363–369.

The TOCICO Dictionary – Second Edition. (2012). https://www.tocico.org/resource/resmgr/dictionary/tocico_dictionary_2nd_edition.pdf

Van de Vonder, S., Demeulemeester, E., & Herroelen, W. (2008). Proactive heuristic procedures for robust project scheduling: An experimental analysis. *European Journal of Operational Research, 189*, 723–733.

Van de Vonder, S., Demeulemeester, E., Herroelen, W., & Leus, R. (2006). The trade-off between stability and makespan in resource-constrained project scheduling. *International Journal of Production Research, 44*(2), 215–236.

Zarghami, S. A., Gunawan, I., de Zubielqui, G. C., & Baroudi, B. (2020). Incorporation of resource reliability into critical chain project management buffer sizing. *International Journal of Production Research, 58*(20), 6130–6144.

Generative AI Supporting Project Management: A Vertical Integration Using OpenAI MyGPT

Alberto Michele Felicetti, Daniele Rao, and Salvatore Ammirato

Abstract

This chapter explores the potential of Generative AI, particularly through OpenAI's ChatGPT, in the domain of project management. It highlights how project managers can leverage this technology to optimize workflows, automate routine tasks, and enhance decision-making capabilities. By integrating AI-driven tools like MyGPT, project managers can improve resource allocation, streamline project documentation, and focus on higher-level strategic activities. The chapter delves into the practical application of prompt engineering, a key concept that allows AI users to generate more precise and relevant outputs, ultimately enabling professionals without deep technical expertise to harness AI for project-specific needs. Through iterative testing and refinement, customized AI tools like MyGPT can be tailored to meet the specific demands of various industries, marking a significant shift in how technology supports project management workflows.

1 Introduction

Some years ago, the ancient Greek philosopher Heraclitus wrote: "There is nothing permanent except change". This quote is something we take for granted in the twenty-first century, as technology facilitates this reality more than ever. For

A. M. Felicetti (✉) · D. Rao · S. Ammirato
Department of Mechanical, Energy and Management Engineering, University of Calabria, Rende, Italy
e-mail: alberto.felicetti@unical.it; salvatore.ammirato@unical.it

Ö. Hazır, M. E. Bruni (eds.), *Tomorrow's Data Empowered Project Management*, Future of Business and Finance, https://doi.org/10.1007/978-3-031-84017-3_6

centuries, human curiosity and ambition have propelled the leading edge of innovation, driving life-improving developments. For the last few years, Artificial Intelligence (AI) has become a major game-changer like the invention of the internet that can create total disruption in several spaces. AI is an interdisciplinary field that blends Computer Science and large datasets, guiding machines to solve complex problems. The set of technologies that this refers to is an umbrella term for many subfields such as Machine Learning and Deep Learning (both often referred to alongside AI). The advent of AI is ushering in a new era in various domains, with project management being no exception.

The current literature mainly highlights the general use of AI in project management (Bento et al., 2022). Muller et al. (2024) provided an overview on the potential future research related to AI into Project Management both for academic and practitioner work. The Community-Led AI Report by PMI Sweden Chapter (Nilsson., 2024) informs how AI is able to improve the Project Management decision process, increase efficiency and quality of work; and the importance of ethical AI use for safety, fairness, data privacy and the ethics of AI; It gives also a possible customization of AI-generated through different components such as the cultural and the political aspect of the given region. The Report takes the AI technology used in project management a step further, showing the differences and challenges, that organizations might face if they are slow in AI adoption. In addition to the foreseen challenges, it also examines the status of companies' preparation for AI deployment that sees the human resource development as employee re-skilling and the recruitment of AI specialists as necessities alongside the demographic and spatial location of the companies AI implementation readiness.

AI has had its fair share of hype cycles, but OpenAI's ChatGPT signals a sea change in how even the skeptics are looking at artificial intelligence. Generative AI technology is progressing by leaps and bounds, improving in just a small-time range. ChatGPT from OpenAI, which was announced in November 2022 proved to be a breakthrough in Natural Language Processing (NLP), catalyzing human-like interaction with AI. Each subsequent version of the GPT series, like GPT-2, GPT-3 and GPT-4, successively improved the capabilities of the model.

An expert such as a Project Manager is rightly poised to leverage Generative AI for the multitude of use cases it has to offer. Generative AI in Project Management presents transformative potential for smarter decision-making and improves project efficiency and outcomes. Its integration in the job space could help optimize resource allocation, streamline workflows, and minimize risk. It not only increases the quality of project output but also enhances the probability of project success and becomes a key asset in the role of the project manager, enabling a move from technical to designing skills and interpersonal skills set. Project Managers could drive more efficiently in their workflow, spending less time on meticulous project documentation and investing instead in strategic decision-making with the maximum attention to stakeholder relations and innovation initiatives. The applicability of Generative AI to Project Management could be immense, if not revolutionary for business professionals. A tutorial could help in building a completely personalized chatbot leveraging the ChatGPT personalization platform, MyGPT, in creating chatbots customized to specific instructions with links to reference materials in PDFs, Excel or Word documents. These chatbots' capabilities extend beyond mere task automation; they are revolutionizing how project managers interact with team members, stakeholders, and the project environment (Felicetti et al., 2024). Project Manager role cuts across a wide landscape of fields of knowledge, in different sectors and industries, with different cultures and geographies. Although it is generally measurable in specific norms. There are methodologies, frameworks, guidelines and philosophies to help manage the project which may be effective for a specific project. In some specialized institutions of Project Management literature, these elements are formalized in standards that describe the key elements, document standards and procedures and best practices.

The chapter describes how to approach the settings such as enabling or disabling the access of chatbot to internet, maintaining control over the information a Large Language Model (LLM) can use. This will include a demonstration of creating an AI Chatbot use case for generating project management deliverables such as Project Charters, Work Breakdown Structures & Schedule. In this way, it will empower users by giving them a working understanding of how to apply generative AI technologies such as ChatGPT in their project management. The aim is to illustrate that a professional can do great things and deliver exceptional results only by doing one thing; learning how to build their skills with the right tools, no matter what experience or education they have behind them.

2 Overview of the Adoption of Generative AI in Project Management

Generative AI has demonstrated an important role in transforming industries and functions by automating tasks, augmenting human capabilities and driving innovation (McKinsey&Company, 2023).

Patel (2023) studied some of the possible applications of Generative AI in Project Management. This came up discussing implications for projects, namely Deep Learning, NLP and reinforcement learning are used to automate tasks, optimizing resource allocation, aiding decision-making and enabling forecasting and predictive analysis with risks and benefits associated with it, and illustrated it practically through some real-world use cases. For instance, Generative AI can consume data and assist in analyzing the patient profile, predict patient flow through hospitals or suggest personalized treatments; it can solve complex tasks in Construction projects (automating scheduling and predicting potential delays); it's demonstrated how Generative AI is helping automate IT Project Management repetitive tasks such as code generation, test automation and debugging. Central in this work is how AI models can be used in the context of general Project Management to generate optimized project plans with faster time frames or provide communication through automatically created project reports. The challenges in the adoption of AI are also discussed, such as data quality and availability, ethical concerns, and integration with existing company systems.

Abbas et al. (2023) discussed the benefits and challenges associated with integrating Chat-GPT into Project Management workflows. They researched the possible application of Chat-GPT in software project management to find specific fields where Chat-GPT is significantly applied like communication, risk management, resource allocation decision making. Examples referring to Chat-GPT are provided to illustrate the role of this AI technology in the process of software project management. The authors acknowledged that Chat-GPT can make project implementation much easier through improving the communication process. ChatGPT can create structured documentation, make smart replies, and offer decision support to PMs resulting in thorough handling of project constraints and unhindered issue estimation. There is indeed the issue of accuracy and sensitivity to bias as they may in theory be considered weak spots. It is, therefore, necessary to fully grasp the consequences that occur when using Chat-GPT in the environment of software project management. This, in turn, necessitates a pragmatic examination of the interconnectedness of the software project and the concomitant blend of promiscuous communication among stakeholders. As a result, the issues of underperformance and outputs prone to biased outcomes need to be addressed together with the emotional component. It is also noted that ethics and privacy issues could be a burden when using this tool so it will be better to always examine the role of this Chatbot technology in the workflows of Project Management.

In the study conducted by Vakilzadeh et al. (2023), were evaluated the potential of LLMs AI, including GPT-3.5, GPT-4 and Google-Bard, as Project Management assistants by testing their ability to answer questions like those in the PMP certification exam. A set of 400-questions was developed to attest different aspects of Project Management, such as project integration, scope, schedule, cost, quality, and stakeholder management. The correct answers were decided based on the newest version of the Project Management Body of Knowledge (PMBOK®) and the PMP exam (PMI, 2023). GPT-4 and other models were run in a test mode (non-training) so that the correctness of their responses could be checked. The use of the three models was made the subject of a comparison in the context of answering questions that bear strong resemblances to those on the certification test. In addition, Vakilzadeh et al. (2023) brought up the ethical issues of AI applications in the context of Project Management, giving one more argument that ethically AI-powered applications should be used wisely to serve humanity while successfully resolving any potential adverse effects and prejudices. The research emphasizes the necessity of following moral principles, including sincerity, transparency, and accountability, in the production and implementation of AI technology.

Prieto et al. (2023) investigated the use of ChatGPT for automating construction Project scheduling tasks evaluating the output quality and user experience. The research highlights the potential of ChatGPT in automating time-consuming tasks in the construction industry, and also acknowledges the need for further development before widespread adoption. They show how NLP can save time and improve the way projects are constructed by identifying key data and drawing from those records, minimizing human errors in data input, thus increasing the efficiency of the project. This research denotes a very promising presentation of the advanced language processing tools in construction Project Management, but at the same time, it also points out the need for further research and fine-tuning, so that their full potential can be tapped into.

Minelle and Stolfi (2023) carried out an empirical investigation on the contribution of ChatGPT as an assistant to Project Managers. They concentrated on the evaluation of the ChatGPT's quality in different project phases, the formation of a methodology, and handling challenges that might emerge in the process. The pros and cons of ChatGPT in handling these assistant tasks were assessed by asking questions concerning research methodological approaches, situational challenges, and lessons learned from project management. The responses of ChatGPT were rated according to the criteria put forward in the above questions. The researchers made use of this technique to obtain the most honest responses from ChatGPT and to evaluate its capability of guiding the projects along to success. Project simulation, a project management concept, was the strategy employed to measure the efficiency of ChatGPT in the different project phases, especially from the beginning of a project to the near end. The chatbot is asked to identify an ICT project which is about the development of a new web app for Public Administration. The state-of-art articles is summarized in Table 1.

3 Prompt Engineering for Project Management: Communicating with a Generative Large Language Model

More and more we can notice how Generative AI tools are being used as a part of the new transition that integrates them into everyday life, especially in the work environment. The utilization of these tools involves the institution of a strategic, integrative process that is typically intended to result in high standards of excellence as well as obtaining quantifiable support in a professional setting. AI users, in fact, write the first components of a dialogue which are then also the subjects for the reinforcement of AI technology in growing. The prompts produce a connection between users and AI systems, which play a leading role in presenting the AI models with the issues to be addressed, and then the technology fulfills that request. These inputs stand as welcome messages, fundamental for getting the interactions between Generative AI tools and LLMs underway. It is possible to consider a prompt as being like a text entered into the dialogue box of a sophisticated AI platform like ChatGPT or Google Bard. It represents the user's initial command, guiding the AI's response generation to be in conformance with the user's intent and the context of the query as well. The art of making the right prompt is a trick that can

Table 1 Summary of the state-of-art articles

Title	Authors	Year	Content Summary
ChatGPT, AI-generated content and engineering	Yu & Gong	2024	Investigates the integration of ChatGPT and AI-generated content in engineering management, identifying the potential for optimizing resource allocation and automating routine tasks. The study addresses the challenges of ethical considerations, reliability and robustness and suggests establishing industry-recognized databases to support AIGC applications. Key areas for AIGC impact include optimization design, engineering consulting and green engineering initiatives.
Revolutionizing Project Management with generative AI	Patel	2023	Discusses the applications of generative AI in various Project Management aspects such as healthcare, construction and IT. It showcases how AI can automate tasks, optimize resource allocation and assist in decision-making. Challenges include data, quality, ethical concerns and integration issues. The study emphasizes the transformative potential of generative AI to enhance project outcomes and efficiency.
Incorporating ChatGPT in software Project Management	Abbas et al.	2023	Examines the integration of ChatGPT in software Project Management, focusing on communication, risk management, resource allocation and decision making. The study outlines the benefits of enhanced communication and collaboration but warns of the need for customization and addressing potential biases. It stresses understanding the implications of ChatGPT in complex project environments.

(continued)

Table 1 (continued)

Title	Authors	Year	Content Summary
Evaluating the potential of large language model AI as Project Management assistants: A comparative simulation to evaluate GPT-3.5, GPT-4 and Google-bard ability to pass the PMI's PMP test	Vakilzadeh et al.	2023	Evaluates the effectiveness of AI models like GPT-3.5, GPT-4 and Google-bard in answering PMP certification exam questions. It compares their performance and discusses the application of improvement strategies such as chain of thought. The study highlights the potential of AI models to assist project managers in tasks such as scheduling and risk management, advocating for ethical considerations and responsible AI use.
Investigating the use of ChatGPT for the scheduling of construction projects	Prieto et al.	2023	Studies the use of ChatGPT to automate construction project scheduling, highlighting its potential to reduce manual errors and enhance efficiency. The research, through an experimental setup with participants, identifies limitations in accuracy and relevance of tasks generated by ChatGPT. It calls for further research and development to improve the tool's performance for real-world applicability.
AI to support PM: a ChatGPT quality assessment (ß test)	Minelle & Stolfi	2023	Provides an empirical evaluation of ChatGPT's role in supporting project managers through different project phases. It assesses ChatGPT's responses based on criteria like suitability, completeness and usability, noting its strengths in methodological aspects but limitations in situational challenges. The study suggests that detailed project information could enhance ChatGPT's performance and calls for further improvements and integration with Project Management systems.
The economic potential of generative AI	McKinsey & company	2023	Analyzes the transformative potential of generative AI across industries, projecting significant economic benefits and productivity growth. The report discusses specific use cases, workforce implications and challenges such as intellectual property and bias. It emphasizes the need for responsible deployment of generative AI to maximize societal benefits.

contribute very much to the quality and relevance of AI-generated content. This is explained by the fact that GenAI systems are designed to generate certain outputs depending on the validity of the prompts provided. The importance of high-quality input cannot be exaggerated, as it directly affects the achievement of the final goals. The development of Generative AI relies to a great extent on the iterative process of testing and improvement of various methodologies of prompt, and thus becomes the main area in the domain of Prompt Engineering (McKinsey&Company, 2024a, 2024b).

Prompt engineering is the process of designing and optimizing prompts used in NLP models to ensure accuracy, relevance and coherence in the generated output of LLMs, all by shaping the prompts effectively. Prompt Engineering can be considered as the art of refining prompts which involves the selection of the right words, phrases, symbols and formats to get the best possible result from AI models. This field is dedicated to the development and optimization of prompts, facilitating the efficient utilization of LLMs across various applications and research domains.

3.1 Prompt Engineering: Principles

Prompt engineering is emerging as a relevant skill in maximizing the effectiveness of LLMs like ChatGPT. As these models are trained on vast and diverse datasets, the quality and relevance of their responses heavily depend on how the prompts are constructed. Crafting precise, informative, and contextually relevant prompts is essential for extracting accurate and useful information from the model. This process is not merely about formulating questions: it involves understanding the model's underlying capabilities, limitations, and the nuances required to guide the output towards a desired goal. As such, prompt engineering directly influences the outcomes generated by LLMs.

The iterative nature of prompt engineering demands ongoing refinement and correction, adapting to the responses generated by the LLM; with every repetition, the prompt can change to give more hints or correct misinterpretations as the LLM produces results (Parmar & Patel, 2024). Experimenting with various prompt iterations can substantially enhance the quality of generated output (Ekin, 2023).

A prompt can be a set of instructions, context, input data and output indicators, but not all the four elements. Selection of the appropriate prompt basically depends on several factors:

- *User intent*: catching the user's objective and expected outcome aids in tailoring a prompt that resonates with their goals. Whether it's seeking information, generating content, or solving a problem, understanding the purpose of the interaction is crucial.
- *Model comprehension*: despite being innovative, ChatGPT may encounter challenges with certain tasks or provide inaccurate information, so it is important to understand the model's capabilities and limitations.
- *Domain specificity*: in specialized fields, should be considered to incorporate domain-specific terminology or context guides the model towards desired responses. Offering additional context or examples enhances the accuracy and relevance of generated outputs.

- *Clarity and specificity*: crafting prompts that are unambiguous and precise mitigates the appearance of suboptimal responses. Ambiguity often arises from unclear instructions, vague queries, or insufficient context.
- *Constraints*: identifying necessary constraints, such as response length or format, ensures the attainment of desired outputs. Explicitly defining constraints assists the model in generating responses that meet specific requirements, such as character limits or structured formats.

3.2 Basic Recommendations for Prompting

It is possible to identify some basics tips and best practice in the iterative process of creating useful prompts to enable language models to execute tasks. Giving clear and explicit instructions is necessary to avoid ambiguous guidance. Concurrently, specifications regarding style and tone shape the desired flavor of the output, whether formal, informal, or poetic and imbue it with the appropriate emotional resonance, be it humorous, serious or informative. Additionally, information retrieval is meant to supplement the prompt with external knowledge, enriching context and guiding the LLMs understanding. Context amplification emphasizes crucial aspects within the prompt, directing the LLM's attention to essential elements. Then feedback and experimentation drive continuous learning and improvement, identifying effective techniques and refining the prompt engineering process. In essence, prompt engineering is a dynamic and holistic approach that orchestrates the interplay of various strategies to steer LLM responses towards desired outcomes and being specific; giving the right context with as useful information as possible, is part of a recipe to the right responses from these tools (Parmar & Patel, 2024).

There are three important aspects of good prompt creation: what it is based on (domain knowledge), how it is done (critical thinking) and the need for changes over time (iterative design).

- The term content knowledge implies that one must have a profound understanding of the topic to steer an AI's answers towards user objectives. Hence, it goes beyond mere knowing of facts; rather it encompasses comprehension of their implications and contexts. Thus, the specificity of a prompt has an influence on its relevance and correctness as far as AI's answer is concerned. This means that formulation of prompts requires thoughtful language usage along with innovative engagement with content which turns how we evaluate knowledge upside down.
- On the other hand, critical thinking indicates the ability to analyze and think critically about AI implemented in important jobs. This involves identifying hallucinations, biases, inaccuracies or any other unfit output of an AI system. It is important especially because errors are known to happen with AI output. Therefore, this ability comes in handy in addressing possible mistakes made by comparing the outputs from AIs with what was intended. Some examples include

detecting bias and relevance judgment that help scrutinize AI responses to enhance their quality while encouraging cognitive plus social skills.
- Iterative design process leads to a cycle that starts again and again. After making an input prompt, one evaluates its accuracy, relevance and appropriateness then improves it. The iterative process is not just a technique; it is the way to get the best LLM AI outputs. (Cain, 2023).

Several prompting techniques have been recently developed (Sahoo et al., 2024)

- **Zero-shot prompting**. This technique involves crafting prompts that allow LLMs to perform tasks without prior examples or labeled data. It leverages the general training of LLMs to follow instructions, which can be enhanced by providing multiple task datasets, improving their zero-shot performance.
- **Few-shot prompting**. When zero-shot prompting is insufficient, few-shot prompting introduces specific examples to guide the LLM. This method improves task performance but may still be influenced by biases, such as favoring frequent words.
- **Role-play prompting**. This technique assigns a role to LLM (e.g., "act like a detective") to control the style and accuracy of the output. It typically involves two stages: setting the role and generating feedback, which together guide the LLM's response to a task.
- **Chain-of-thought prompting**. Designed for complex reasoning tasks, this method breaks down problems into intermediate steps, enabling the LLM to generate clearer, step-by-step rationales. This improves interpretability and accuracy, particularly in tasks like solving math problems.
- **Zero-shot-CoT prompting**. A recent approach that adds simple instruction like "Let's think step by step" to the prompt, encouraging the LLM to generate reasoning chains without examples. This method is easy to implement and has shown excellent results.
- **Auto-CoT prompting**. To automate the generation of reasoning chains, this technique uses Zero-Shot-CoT and involves clustering questions and sampling diverse demonstrations. It reduces the manual effort involved in creating examples but must ensure the generated chains are accurate.

4 Creating and Managing a Customized MyGPT for Project Management

4.1 A Brief Introduction to ChatGPT

ChatGPT, which is opened by AI, is an advanced conversation AI that carries out several tasks. These tasks include but are not limited to translating languages, debugging codes, telling stories and keeping conversations going. As part of OpenAI's Artificial Intelligence Generated Content (AIGC) initiative, ChatGPT marks a major step in understanding and creating human language by AI. One of its main attributes is the ability to recollect what has been said earlier in the conversation, making it give clearer and contextually relevant responses. Thus, this capability enhances user-experience as interactions with the robot seem more realistic and flowing.

ChatGPT is an evolution of the Generative Pre-trained Transformer (GPT) model that is based on several versions since its earliest application. The GPT series started with GPT-1 which was launched in June 2018. Although it had certain limitations relative to subsequent editions, GPT-1 was the first transformer based large scale language model showcasing what such models could do when properly trained. Later came along OpenAI's release of GPT-2 in February 2019 marking a great leap forward in terms of machine learning technology. It had a total of 1.5 billion parameters and an important advancement made by it was multi-task learning allowing for generalizations across multiple tasks without needing extra fine tuning for every task separately put on it as indicated above. However, due to fears concerning its probable abuse or misuse Open AI chose not to release the complete version at first citing these reasons but later did so after evaluating it more deeply between then and November 2019.

The GPT series continued to evolve with the release of GPT-3, which introduced the concept of in-context learning. This enabled the model to generalize better over different tasks by considering the context given within the prompt. It is also worth noting that GPT-3 was a big step in terms of size and offered over 100 billion parameters, thus positioning it among the best language models at that time. Due to its capacity to perform many tasks without minimum extra training, GPT-3 became a multipurpose operational software within various applications.

In March 2023, OpenAI launched GPT-4, which marked an important point in AI development. At the same time, ChatGPT went through a significant update and gained new features that allowed it to do more things than before. Now users can enter both text and images so that ChatGPT can do even more tasks than before. This allows for more complex multimodal tasks such as image captioning, chart reasoning and paper summary making thus creating wider avenues of interaction and usage for end-users. Such a powerful tool must be very useful as in project management sector.

An implementation of Freemium business model was adopted by OpenAI which consists of two plans: Standard Plan and Plus Plan. The Standard Plan is offered free of charge but allows the use of GPT-3.5 model for ordinary applications. However, it should be noted that Standard users may sometimes find their responses delayed or inaccessible because they are competing with other people over the same limited resources.

On the other hand, paying more under the Plus Plan gives access to GPT-4 model that is larger, more advanced and powerful when compared to its predecessor. This means that the output provided by GPT-4 can give much more accurate information besides having a tone that suits various situations besides being multilingual (over 25 languages) since it can also take images as inputs together with texts. In addition to this faster response times are guaranteed even during times when there is high traffic on the network for Plus Plan subscribers while advanced tools like plugins and authentications with third parties help in expanding ChatGPT's capabilities are also made available through the Plus Plan subscription. Such plugs can be used in various areas like travel planning or data analysis among others making it very essential for professionals and businesses. In addition, OpenAI MyGPT, a revolutionary feature enabling users to create personalized chatbots suited for specific applications without needing programming skills or deep understanding of LLMs has been launched. With MyGPT subscription, available for ChatGPT Plus and Enterprise users only; one can design tailored versions of ChatGPT using either a combination of GPT-3.5 or GPT-4 with more functionalities. The creation of custom GPTs in professional contexts could be used to create highly accurate and autonomous support tools. Project Management, for instance, would face its disruption from this ability thereby changing the role, workflows as well as daily objectives of a Project Manager. There's no doubt that every aspect of Project Management will be disrupted starting from the core processes employed by project managers to those specific industries in which they operate such as construction, manufacturing or even logistics. A person without any coding background and no expertise on LLMs can make use of ChatGPT; hence enabling total colonization by Project Management professionals without data science training whatsoever. This aspect is an advantage to the complete appropriation of those Project Management professionals not having a data science formation. By creating custom GPTs, Project Managers can leverage this technology to build powerful, practical tools that offer technical support and streamline various Project Management processes, tailoring to Industry-specific needs, enhancing decision-making and improving collaboration and communication.

4.2 How to Customize a MyGPT for Project Management

The chatbot customization process must be iterative and can be stopped when a version considered suitable for subsequent demonstrations is reached. Note that further iterations and further attempts at study and analysis, possibly exploring other prompting techniques, are certainly useful to obtain better performance in response to user requests. This process must be accompanied by complete direct tests, aimed at evaluating the consequent evolution of the responses generated by the NLP model. Particular attention must be paid to understanding the chatbot response patterns in relation to the implemented changes, with the aim of obtaining progressive and incremental improvements.

Initially, the hypotheses focused on improving the application of ChatGPT in a certain setting in Project Management. The aim was to achieve greater detail, more accuracy, and consistency with knowledge sources, as well as to ensure clarity and usability in the workplace. To attain this objective, it was necessary to have a gradual understanding of ChatGPT's behavior and use an iterative approach that would end after enough attempts.

The goal is to produce a tool that can generate useful documents for Project Management concerning various stages of Project Integration, Scope Management, and Schedule Management along with their respective users. This selection is made especially based on the literature review which illustrates how such fields and topics could be highly influenced by AI technologies (Muller et al., 2024).

The GPT Builder's interface, used for creating customized chatbots, is divided into three key sections, each designed to facilitate the development and refinement of these AI tools.

Create Tab. It is the initial step where users specify the desired functionalities of their chatbot. It is particularly useful for those unfamiliar with the design process. Users can input commands like "Create a creative assistant" or "Create a Project Management expert," setting the foundation for the chatbot's capabilities. Users can also upload files to provide additional context, ensuing the chatbot aligns with their specific needs.

Configure Tab. In this section users can name and assign profile images to GPTs which helps in defining their purpose and identity. A description of the chatbot's role, as well as its ideal use cases, is provided to guide future users. In the Knowledge section, users may upload files for building a specialized knowledge base for any profession or business context that they want the chatbot to be tailored to. Different file types are supported by the platform, although this comes with restrictions on file size and token usage so that processing remains efficient. Thus, simple text formats are recommended for optimal performance. Customization of the chatbot involved uploading several key documents on the MyGPT platform in the dedicated file upload section. These documents provided foundational knowledge necessary for generating accurate and relevant outputs by the chatbot within project management as requested.

Training a MyGPT model for project management would involve using a diverse set of documents that cover various aspects of project management. Here's a possible list of the types of documents that could be beneficial:

- *Project Management Standards and Guidelines*. Formalized guides and frameworks that outline the best practices, methodologies, and standards in project management. They serve as the foundational knowledge for managing projects effectively, covering everything from initiation to closing. For example, PMBOK® (Project Management Body of Knowledge), PRINCE2 (Projects IN Controlled Environments) manuals and guides, ISO 21500: Guidance on project management standards, or Agile Guides like Scrum Guides, Agile Practice Guide (from PMI), and other agile frameworks.
- *Project Templates and Tools*. Templates provide standard formats for common project management documents, ensuring consistency and efficiency. They include forms, checklists, and outlines for project plans, charters, WBS, WBS dictionary and other essential documents.
- *Reports on Past Company Projects*. These are internal documents that offer detailed overviews of completed projects within the organization. They include information on progress, outcomes, challenges encountered, solutions implemented, costs, timelines, and lessons learned. These reports are valuable for

improving the management of future projects by providing a concrete reference on how past projects were handled and which practices were effective or not.

- *Case Studies and Academic Papers.* Case studies offer real-world examples of how projects are managed, highlighting successes and failures. Academic papers provide in-depth research and analysis on various aspects of project management, offering insights into emerging trends and methodologies.
- *Industry-Specific Project Management Documents.* These documents are tailored to the unique requirements of specific industries, such as construction, IT, or healthcare. They include industry-specific regulations, compliance documents, and specialized project plans that address the nuances of projects within those sectors.
- *Scientific Papers on Prompt Engineering.* These documents include research papers and academic articles focused on the study and development of prompt engineering techniques. These documents are extremely useful for training a MyGPT model towards specific forms of interaction with the user. For example, (Wei et al., 2022)**:** Discussing the Chain of Thought approach, (Wang et al., 2022)**:** Examining Auto-CoT prompting techniques, (Zhang et al., 2022)**:** Providing CoT reasoning insights into advanced prompting methods.

The Conversation Starters section enables the setup of prompts that guide users in interacting with the chatbot. For example, a set of conversation starters tailored for a MyGPT supporting project management may include "*Can you help me create a Project Charter?*", "*Create a WBS*", "*Please, help me to develop a risk management plan*" and so on.

The *Instructions* section allows users to precisely develop the characteristics of the chatbot and steer its actions towards users. Here, it is possible to decide the tone of communication, detail the instructions and outline the approach to task execution. During the editing phase of this section, employing methods and principles of prompt construction is beneficial to develop a chatbot capable of delivering high-quality outputs that effectively meet user requests. This setup enables the chatbot to guide users optimally, providing responses that can be tailored in length and format, whether it be images, text, code strings, spreadsheets or tables. The Instructions section functions like the backstage or backend of functionality definition, with the advantage of requiring no programming code. Adhering to correct prompt construction frameworks can enhance the level and utility of this product for professionals, facilitating the integration of technology into everyday use.

Below, are presented some prompts that could be used in the Instructions section.

[*Welcome the user with a message, something like: "Hello there, I'm here to help you with your projects"].*

[*Act as a specialist in Project Management. As an expert in this field, you will support Project Managers in creating Project Management documents. Specifically, you specialize in creating Project Charters, Work Breakdown Structures, Scheduling.]*

[The purpose is to streamline the scope management process, making it more efficient and effective based on the guidelines provided in the attached documents ("guide_1.pdf"; "guide_2.pdf")]

[If the user presses the "Create a WBS" Conversation Starter, prompt them to upload the project charter input document as the conversation begins. First and foremost, refer to the documents I uploaded ("guide_1.pdf"; "guide_2.pdf") during the creation of the final WBS. Use a Waterfall approach to build the WBS. If the user uploads a document, such as the Project Charter, analyze it carefully. Before delivering the WBS, review and correct it on your own, continuously improving it by considering the PMBOK® guidelines. This will help you decide whether to split or reduce a Work Package as needed. Deliver the Work Breakdown Structure as a detailed Word document. Ask the user if they would like to include the Project Management Work Packages.]

[If the user requests the development of a WBS Dictionary, first ask them to provide or upload the WBS and, if possible, a project description (including any relevant project documents or reports). Refer primarily to the documents I uploaded ("guide_1.pdf"; "guide_2.pdf") when creating the Dictionary. Use a traditional Project Management approach, specifically the Waterfall methodology. If a document such as the Project Charter is uploaded, analyze it carefully. Before delivering the WBS Dictionary, review and refine it independently. Deliver the Work Breakdown Structure in a detailed Word document. Do not include the Project Management Work Packages.]

[If the user requests assistance in developing a WBS Dictionary, first ask them to provide or upload the WBS and, if possible, a description of the project, including any relevant documents or reports].

[Interact with the user by outlining the necessary requirements to achieve the desired output. When the user uploads documents, descriptions, images, or charts as inputs, analyzes them thoroughly before proceeding with the reasoning process. Remind the user that the more information they provide, the better the result will be.]

[The formats of the outputs I have indicated should be:

- *Table format in Excel for scheduling, filling out the uploaded template "template_01.xlsx"*
- *Word format for the Work Breakdown Structure, filling out the uploaded template "template_02.docx"*
- *Word format for the Project Charter, filling out the uploaded template " filling out the uploaded template "template_03.docx"]*

[Use a professional tone. You must be brief and concise, providing only the strictly necessary information and the examples only if explicitly requested by the user.]

The Capabilities section offers advanced functionalities, including web browsing, image generation via DALL·E, and code execution through a Code Interpreter. These features expand the chatbot's ability to handle complex tasks, such as real-time data analysis or generating visual content.

Table 2 Presentation of customization settings

Customization Setting	Details
Web browsing	Disabled
Purpose	Limits references to user-provided knowledge and original training data.
DALL-E image generation	Enabled
Purpose	Allows generation of images for projects and presentations.
Code interpreter	Enabled
Purpose	Supports creating charts, performing calculations, and other coding tasks.
APIs and external connections	Not included
Purpose	Focuses on core functionalities without external integrations; potential for future enhancements like Zapier.
NLP model settings	GPT-4
Purpose	Focus on the most performing model at that time

In terms of other customization options, Web Browsing feature is disabled as such references should only be based on user's knowledge and OpenAI's training dataset at the beginning level. DALL-E Image Generation checkbox and Code Interpreter checkbox are both enabled for users who want images or graphs for their work and make good use of them. If APIs and external application connections were included, it would be great for professionals who want their aid to automated tools: for example, Zapier ensures that you can have Gmail connected to it at any point. Table 2 presents the customization settings.

Actions allow the GPT to connect to the internet and interact with external applications, enabling it to perform tasks like scheduling events or accessing specific websites. Developers can define these interactions using schemas, ensuring the GPT handles requests securely and effectively.

Preview This part has an open chatbot where users can converse with the bot to test and improve its answers. To increase effectiveness, it is important to do multiple rounds of testing. The collaboration between multiple GPTs through "@" tagging in GPT Builder helps too, sharing knowledge across diverse models for better solutions provision. The team works like a multi-disciplinary team, where different expertise come together to find solutions to intricate issues quickly.

The overall design of the GPT Builder's interface makes it accessible for users without technical expertise, enabling the creation of powerful, customized chatbots. These tools can be tailored to specific industries or professional needs, making them valuable assets in various fields. The ability to integrate advanced features like web browsing and code execution further enhances the chatbot's utility, allowing it to perform a wide range of tasks. Through real-time collaboration among multiple

GPTs, the system becomes more robust and versatile, capable of delivering precise solutions across different domains.

5 Concluding Remarks

Research is currently being conducted on the convergence of this technology with Project Management, and this study draws on a range of references from the scientific literature to understand how LLMs can be used by Project Managers for generating content that is powered by AI. According to the reviewed literature, AI is also making headway to optimize work, automate tedious tasks that do not contribute much value, as well as help in decision-making processes in various sectors. The trend applies across diverse disciplines including Information Technology (IT), Health care and Construction Industry which basically supports Project Management, more particularly risk management issues, project time management and scheduling concerns, data reporting processes plus performance monitoring mechanisms. The use of Generative AI can contribute to adding value and generating significant economic benefits to industries. However, several challenges have been identified regarding the adoption and integration of Generative AI in professional settings, such as the need for high-quality data to train the models and the development of necessary skills for full integration into processes and workflows.

In this chapter, project management and one of the fastest growing technologies of recent years were mixed. Given its increasing acceptance, this technology is expected to become a critical component in our lives. The main aim was to demonstrate in practice what this emergent technology could mean for a meaningful tool, not depending on one's Data Science and AI engineering knowledge or expertise. Specifically, the chapter examined how to access and utilize a Generative AI tool including customization features like MyGPT.

The advent of ChatGPT marked a significant shift in the mass market and a systematic move towards Generative AI—a subset of AI that includes Deep Learning models capable of generating high-quality text, images, and other content, all trained on specific datasets. The chapter offered insights into how to customize Generative AI from a Project Management perspective, with a specific focus on co-creating key project documents related to Integration Management (Project Charter), Scope Management (Work Breakdown Structure), and Schedule Management (Project Scheduling). Part of the chapter introduced basic concepts of Prompt Engineering; an emerging research field focused on designing instructions that optimize the performance of NLP models like those underpinning ChatGPT. The technical issues encompassing Deep Learning and augmenting the performance of chatbot NLP models were not part of the chapter's ambit. The practical implementation made use of tools and techniques that are supposed to be available to all practitioners, even those who do not have degrees in Computer Science or Data Science. The aim is to affirm and ease utilization of this technology with a view towards adoption in Project Management activities where it would serve as a value addition.

Once MyGPT got rolled out, it is proposed that users compare its functionality with that of standard ChatGPT through qualitative comparative analysis of three key documents' generation on real project cases.

As a final remark, it is important to outline a roadmap for using and customizing these chatbots, demonstrating how they could be effectively adopted and adapted across various industrial sectors. Key benefits include increased productivity, enhanced decision-making support, large-volume data analysis, and the provision of insights that can elevate professional work through tailored solutions for specific workflows. However, it is important to note that further improvements can be achieved primarily through continuous chatbot use, as it progressively learns more about user needs, requests, expectations, project types, and by leveraging user feedback mechanisms.

Future work should explore existing tools more thoroughly and seek improvements to make chatbot customizations more consistent and reliable in the field of Project Management, integrating them into existing work frameworks with the intent of providing customizable yet universally applicable tools. Achieving a higher level of customization and performance requires expertise, as familiarity with Data Science, Deep Learning models, and programming are necessary.

It is crucial to use such tools responsibly and with a critical mindset, as this technology has limitations and technical issues that can lead to errors or knowledge biases. Therefore, sound judgment is essential to make these tools a strength rather than a weakness. It is also important to be aware of how data is handled on such platforms, how privacy regulations are respected, and to always evaluate whether the use of these tools may conflict with company policies, potentially risking sensitive data or even competitive advantages. Organizations and professionals should be aware of the social and labor market impact that an emerging technology like Generative AI can have. Strategic planning for training and learning in the use of such technologies would be beneficial to facilitate their adoption and full integration into Project Management processes.

References

Abbas, Q., Younus, W., Malik, S., & Hassan, M. H. (2023). Incorporating ChatGPT in software project management. *IEEE-SEM Issue, 9*, 11.

Bento, S., Pereira, L., Goncalves, R., Dias, A., & Costa, R. L. D. (2022). Artificial intelligence in project management: Systematic literature review. *International Journal of Technology Intelligence and Planning, 13*(2), 143–163. https://doi.org/10.1504/IJTIP.2022.10050400

Cain, W. (2023). *Prompting change: Exploring prompt engineering in large language model AI and its potential to transform education.*

Ekin, S. (2023). *Prompt engineering for ChatGPT a quick guide to techniques, tips and best practices*. Texas A&M University.

Felicetti, A. M., Cimino, A., Mazzoleni, A., & Ammirato, S. (2024). Artificial intelligence and project management: An empirical investigation on the appropriation of generative Chatbots by project managers. *Journal of Innovation & Knowledge, 9*(3), 100545.

McKinsey & Company. (2023). *The economic potential of generative AI.*

McKinsey & Company. (2024a). *What is generative AI?*

McKinsey & Company. (2024b). *What is prompt engineering.* Tratto da https://www.mckinsey.com/featured-insights/mckinsey-explainers/what-is-prompt-engineering

Minelle, F., & Stolfi, F. (2023). AI to support PM: A ChatGPT quality assessment (ß test). *PM World Journal, 12*(5).

Muller, L., Holzmann, N., & Sagay. (2024). Artificial intelligence and Project Management: State of art, and guidelines for future research. *Project Management Journal, 55*(I), 9–15.

Nilsson. (2024). *Artificial intelligence and project management: A global chapter-led survey.* Project Management Institute: Sweden Chapter.

Parmar & Patel. (2024). *Prompt engineering for large language model.*

Patel, D. (2023). Revolutionizing Project Management with generative AI. *International Scientific Journal of Engineering and Management, 02*(05).

Prieto, S. A., Mengiste, E. T., & García de Soto, B. (2023). Investigating the use of ChatGPT for the scheduling of construction projects. *Buildings, 13*(4), 857.

Project Management Institute Germany. (2023). *PMI Infinity.* Accessed Oct 4, 2024, from https://pmi-gc.de/en/news-eng/1044-pmi-infinity-your-new-project-assistant

Sahoo, P., Singh, A. K., Saha, S., Jain, V., Mondal, S., & Chadha, A. (2024). A systematic survey of prompt engineering in large language models: Techniques and applications. *arXiv preprint arXiv:2402.07927.*

Vakilzadeh, A., Pourahmad Ghalejoogh, S., & Hatami, M. (2023). Evaluating the potential of large language model AI as Project Management assistants: A comparative simulation to evaluate GPT-3.5, GPT-4, and Google-bard ability to pass the PMI's PMP test. In *Mohsen, evaluating the potential of large language model AI as project management assistants: A comparative simulation to evaluate GPT-3.5, GPT-4, and Google-bard ability to pass the PMI's PMP test (August 1, 2023).*

Wang, B., Min, S., Deng, X., Shen, J., Wu, Y., Zettlemoyer, L., & Sun, H. (2022). Towards understanding chain-of-thought prompting: An empirical study of what matters. *arXiv preprint arXiv:2212.10001.*

Wei, J., Wang, X., Schuurmans, D., Bosma, M., Xia, F., Chi, E., et al. (2022). Chain-of-thought prompting elicits reasoning in large language models. *Advances in Neural Information Processing Systems, 35*, 24824–24837.

Yu, Z., & Gong, Y. (2024). ChatGPT, AI-generated content, and engineering. *Frontiers of Engineering Management (FEM), 66*(1), 159–166.

Zhang, Z., Zhang, A., Li, M., & Smola, A. (2022). Automatic chain of thought prompting in large language models. *arXiv preprint arXiv:2210.03493.*

Part II

Recent Developments and Challenges in the Organization of Projects

Stakeholder Engagement and the Mindset Open to Innovate in the Digital Era

Elisabetta Bracci and Maria Elena Bruni

Abstract

This chapter discusses the role and importance of stakeholder management and engagement in a complex innovation ecosystem from multiple theoretical and practical perspectives. The contribution theorizes on the connections between stakeholder engagement and project managers in the digital era, offers novel concepts to broaden the discussion, and raises critical questions. We extend current stakeholder engagement models from static to active engagement, particularly for high-impact innovation projects. We discuss five central ideas of the construct of the stakeholder engagement pathway in complex innovation ecosystems, showcased through a real case study based on the "Open to Innovate Manifesto".

1 Introduction

In contemporary management theory and practice, the rise and role of stakeholders as significant players in organizational dynamics are widely recognized and recorded. Freeman's stakeholder theory (Freeman, 1984) is the first and foremost theory for stakeholders, having valuable implications in project management regarding stakeholder identification, analysis, alignment, and building relationships. This approach emerged in sharp contrast to the previous one, the so-called shareholder

E. Bracci (✉)
Cluster Manager Clust-ER Innovate of Emilia-Romagna Region, Bologna, Italy
e-mail: elisabetta.bracci@innovate.clust-er.it

M. E. Bruni
University of Calabria, Rende, Italy
e-mail: mariaelena.bruni@unical.it

Ö. Hazır, M. E. Bruni (eds.), *Tomorrow's Data Empowered Project Management*, Future of Business and Finance, https://doi.org/10.1007/978-3-031-84017-3_7

theory developed by Milton Friedman (1970 "A Friedman Doctrine: The Social Responsibility of Business is to Increase Its Profits') and later reinforced by Michael C. Jensen (1976 'Theory of the Firm: Managerial Behaviour, Agency Costs, and Ownership Structure'). This shareholder theory, which had an impact on the corporate business from the 1980s to the 2000s, assumed that a company has no social responsibility to society but that its only responsibility is to its shareholders, as the economic engine of the organization and the only entity to which the company is socially responsible. Unlike the previous approach, Freeman first introduced the concept of stakeholders, defined as any individual or group beyond the groups of shareholders, clients, and customers who can affect or be affected by the project process or the project outcomes. This pluralistic view extends well beyond the traditional concept of shareholders to include employees, suppliers, customers, trade unions, communities, etc. The engagement of stakeholders in projects is claimed to be crucial to value creation as well as project success (Bayiley & Teklu, 2016; Freeman et al., 2010; Oppong et al., 2017). Various strategies for project stakeholder engagement have been proposed. Several researchers have extended the stakeholder theory to bring out the social network theory lens for identifying and assessing key stakeholders in terms of power, legitimacy, urgency, and influence (Assudani & Kloppenborg, 2010). Strategies for appropriately managing roles, responsibilities and activities have been developed, including various forms of dialogue (Di Maddaloni & Davis, 2018; Lehtinen et al., 2019), using visualization strategies (Walker et al., 2008).

Achieving project stakeholder engagement, however, has proven difficult, for the wide range of expectations, interests, culture, priorities and feelings of stakeholders and conflicts are not rare. Moreover, in an ever-changing competitive VUCA—Volatile, Uncertain, Complex, Ambiguity—environment, pressure on existing project management strategies and initiatives is increasing, opening-up plethora of global project opportunities and challenges (Elkington et al., 2017). Project managers worldwide can be essential to accompany the "big transitions" era, but they are being called upon to address emerging societal and business challenges. The fast growth of digital technologies, big data, cloud computing and the vast amount of data that devices and applications collect daily drive organisations to transform their business models radically. Algorithms and technologies with increasing computing power disrupt the social and relational fabric, influencing for-profit and not-for-profit public and private organizations. Increasing connectivity, rapid changes in technical capabilities, and ever-improving technical solutions are upsetting the logical progression of a traditional project. The overwhelming presence of technology calls for new, emerging capabilities, new forms of structures, new ways of cooperation, and the capacity to obtain benefits from digital technologies to name but a few.

On the other hand, competitive pressure to innovate drives companies to seek new ideas well beyond their own walls. Innovation is not only about successfully translating a new idea into practice, but it involves the creation of value for all stakeholders in various ways. Projects should be developed and managed with people (and not only for people) to address their interlaced needs in the complex modern landscape. This new orientation challenges engaging, co-designing, or co-creating projects with different stakeholders (Patricio et al., 2020), exploring the wide-ranging emerging issues mentioned above. That is why stakeholders' commitment and active involvement are key to innovation. We must adapt our approach to stakeholder management and engagement to a new reality: enabling technologies and methodologies are taking us to a higher level.

While research has offered many promising starting points for understanding the role of stakeholders, how and why organizations engage with various stakeholders, and what kinds of outcomes this provides to the participants in these processes (Kujala et al., 2022), the impact of drivers as digitalization, pervasive technology and innovation on stakeholder engagement have been mostly neglected. From the perspective of practitioners and academia, what is not known is how digitalization and new technologies impact project management strategic choices, including approaches to open innovation. In the following sections, we will elaborate on the topic and provide best practices and recommendations to foster a proactive and dynamic role for stakeholders to be collaboratively engaged in the innovation process.

2 Stakeholder Engagement in Complex Innovation Ecosystems

The innovation ecosystem concept first appeared in a publication of a Harvard Business Review article by Adner (2006), which also provides the probably most widely used definition of innovation ecosystems as "the collaborative arrangements through which firms combine their offerings into a coherent, customer-facing solution". In broad terms, it can be defined as systems with a specific purpose (core value proposition), often characterised by openness to external influences (Oh et al., 2016) and consists of actors, activities, products and services, institutions, along with a network of various relationships that span collaborative, complementary, and competitive interactions (Granstrand & Holgersson, 2020; Ostapenko et al., 2024). The system exhibits complexity due to the interconnectedness, interactions, and interdependencies among these actors and the frequent presence of conflicting goals.

Since the innovation ecosystem involves many actors and has no clear hierarchical structure, engaging and managing the stakeholders can become an issue. Engagement is an effort to build trust and persuade actors without a formal mandate, focusing on knowledge and relationships rather than economic returns or normative relationships. To implement this intricate process, a structured approach is needed. It is, therefore, essential to create a sequential method for profiling and guiding stakeholders through becoming aware of technologies and understanding and using digital transformation tools in complex projects.

We propose a five-step approach, depicted in Fig. 1, that provides a clear roadmap for stakeholder engagement but requires an empowerment of the role of the project manager. Although the pathway is quite general and flexible, it must be navigated carefully, ensuring the approach is adapted to fit the project's unique context. This acknowledgment of challenges underlines the importance of a tailored,

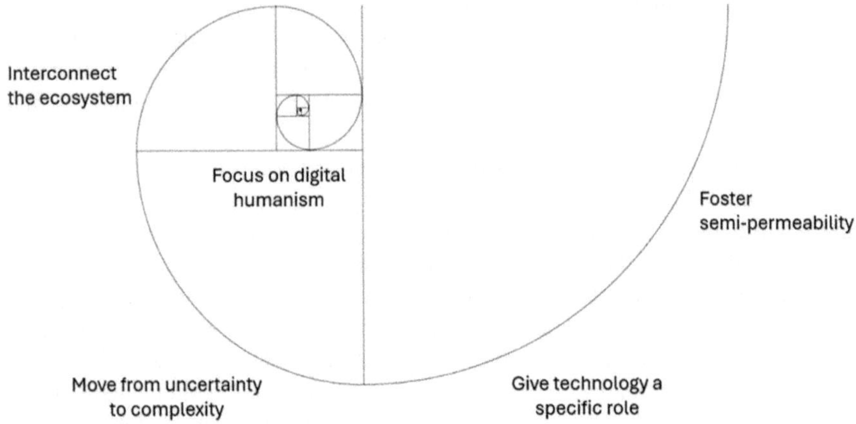

Fig. 1 Engagement pathway in complex innovation ecosystem

context-sensitive application in achieving effective stakeholder engagement and management. Figure 1 summarises the key points of this model. This figure provides a clear roadmap for understanding our study's focus and findings.

3 Focus on Digital Humanism

> Technology profoundly shapes the world we live in, and the stakes are high. Digital humanism deals with digital technology development and policies based on human rights, democracy, inclusion, and diversity. (Vienna Manifesto, 2023).

Digital humanism (Werthner et al., 2023) is an emerging interdisciplinary field addressing the complex relationships between humans, society, and digital technologies and it advocates for human-centered technology development. Digital humanism is an approach that aims to create a society that fully respects universal human rights by describing, analysing, and attempting to influence the interaction between enabling technologies and humanity. This approach helps us better understand the technological potential for sustainable growth in terms of human capability to use technologies for their well-being in everyday life. The same emphasis is also present in the emergent paradigm of Industry 5.0, which, unlike the purely efficiency-driven and technology-centric approach of Industry 4.0, introduces a more holistic perspective, integrating human-centricity, environmental sustainability, and socio-economic considerations into the fabric of industrial innovation. At the core of Industry 5.0 is the recognition that technological advancements and sustainability, in broader sense, are not mutually exclusive indeed complementary. It emphasizes the critical role of various stakeholders, including governments, companies, and consumers, and underscores the importance of human-centered design principles in shaping a sustainable industrial future.

In every project dealing with innovation, it is strategic to start from people's needs, instead of technology's capabilities, because we use technology and develop innovation projects to improve people's lives, promoting a sustainable and harmonious future (Agrawal et al., 2023). Project managers need to shape stakeholders' experience in the project's development and to support them in the human-centred design of project impacts.

3.1 Experience and Human-Centred Design as Crucial Success Factors

Sometimes, when there is a leak, we focus too much on creating a new type of wrench instead of focusing on the needs of the plumber. Perhaps we confuse the plumber and the wrench. The plumber is the main character in the story, the wrench is a tool that's worth nothing if it's useless to the plumber. An effective project manager tries to make the plumber's job easier through the innovation project. If the project team focuses too much on technology tools and not on human needs, they will create an unnecessary wrench, not an innovative wrench.

That's why stakeholders must be involved at every stage of the project putting in place a system of feedback and co-design phases that enables the creation of an excellent user experiences. The more the stakeholders don't fully understand the technology that can be applied for the deliverables, the more the project team must be supportive in every project stage.

A process model that was explicitly created to achieve these objectives of continuous comparison and verification is Human Centred Design (HCD). HCD involves stakeholders considering their specific psycho-physical characteristics and incorporating their needs, desires, and ways of working into the project.

HCD allows users to be involved from the earliest stages of analysis to design and implementation. This model allows project specifications to be reviewed and modified at every stage. This makes the workflow fluid and constantly evolving. As these changes are made early, before the project moves into the implementation phase, the cost is also much lower than in the cascade process models.

However, moving to a highly iterative process model managed by a multidisciplinary team requires a significant change in project management actors' mindset.

There are many types of applications of this iterative process, which has its roots in the 1980s, thanks to Donald Arthur Norman, an American psychologist and engineer who, among other prestigious positions, headed the Department of Cognitive Science at the University of California (San Diego), was Vice-President of Apple and an executive at Hewlett Packard.

The most formalized approach is currently ISO 9241-210, 'User-centred design for interactive systems,' which defines the four main phases of user-centered design.

1. Understand and specify the context of use
2. Specify user requirements
3. Create design solutions based on requirements
4. Iteratively evaluate and modify design solutions

It is important to stress how the first two phases constitute what is known as "user research", which serves to understand and specify the context of use and the desired result. As many as two of the four phases are related to the analysis that precedes the actual design, but it is essential to confront the users, even before imagining what the final product will look like.

The third phase is the actual "design", and the fourth and final phase is the "evaluation" of both the technical-functional and user experience evaluations. That's one of the most common approaches to reaching a user experience design that will assure stakeholders' satisfaction.

3.2 Project Managers as Designers and Advisors

In the early stage of the project definition, during project charter drafting, the project manager creates value by supporting the stakeholders in focusing on the real impact of the project deliveries. It means that the project manager can lead stakeholders, with both a maieutical and a generative approach, in creating the overall picture of project impacts. There are four main impact areas:

- People: evaluate the impact of the project delivery inside and outside the organisation. Some simple questions could be: Does the project foster well-being and equality? Does the project include upskilling/reskilling to ensure its valuable application? Does the project phases involve co-design techniques?
- Society: evaluate the impact of the project delivery on social mechanisms and balance. Some simple questions could be: Does the project have an impact on local or global social balance? Does the project promote democracy and inclusion? Is the project pervasive and agentive in social mechanisms like behaviours and decision-making?
- Environment: Evaluate the impact of the project delivery on the environment with a "total cost of ownership approach." Some simple questions could be: Is it possible to foresee the project footprint and the deliverable's lifetime footprint? How can we mitigate the project impact by design?
- Economics: Evaluate the project's impact on economics for each stakeholder, not only for clients and sponsors, because the project interconnects customers, suppliers, employees, investors, communities, and others who have a stake in the organization (Freeman, 1984). Some simple questions could be: Does the project create value for all stakeholders, and not just shareholders? How the created value matches the stakeholders' expectations? (Fig. 2).

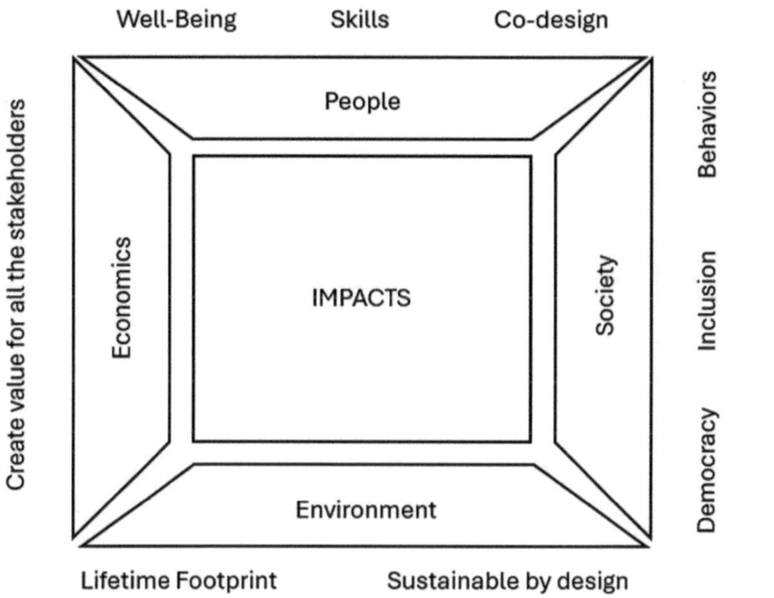

Fig. 2 Project impacts dimensions

4 Interconnect the Ecosystem

Innovation ecosystems form a complex network of interrelationships involving links, complementary elements, and alternatives. They operate at multiple levels (e.g. city, regional, national) and within multiple sectors (e.g. agriculture, health, education), but they all are made up of different actors, interacting with each other, including customers that generate the demand, companies, that provide the innovative service/product, facility, and physical infrastructure managers, investors, that provide explicitly or implicitly the resources needed, institutional authorities, that regulate the system through tax, incentives, regulations, laws, citizens, caring about emissions, safety, and sustainability in the broad sense, and that can influence the institutional authorities through their votes. All the stakeholders play a role in taking a great idea to transformative impact at scale. The actors above have their own goals, make their own decisions, and are linked with others through many interconnections, interactions, and interdependencies.

All contribute to making the ecosystem a complex system. Decisions and interrelations in the ecosystem, may be affected by uncertainty from many different sources (Bruni et al., 2011, 2017), require coordination and fast information flows among several actors, interoperability among the different actors' activities, and cannot neglect behavioural aspects. We illustrate this situation and complexity through the Social Business Network (The GUEST initiative, 2017) shown in Fig. 3, where nodes are groups of stakeholders and links are interactions between them. The study of these networks allows understanding of the rules governing the

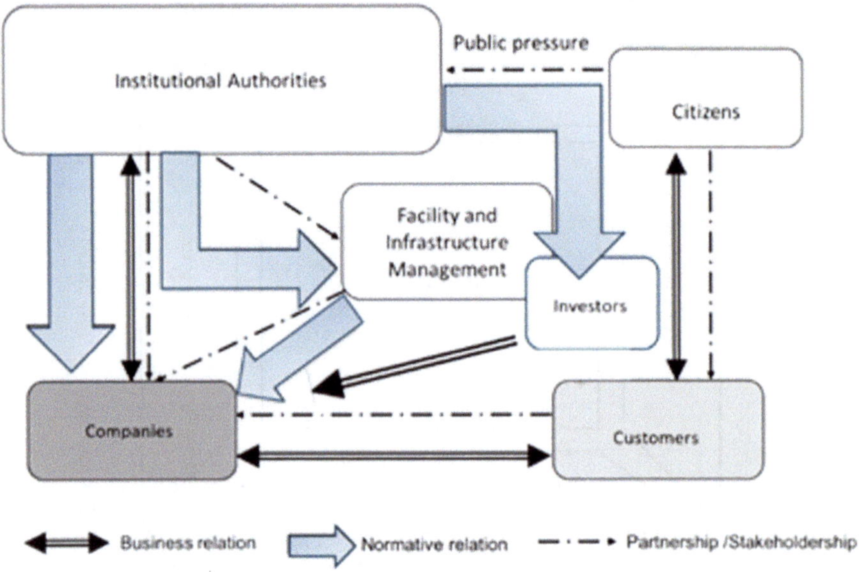

Fig. 3 Social Business Network of a complex ecosystem

topology of their links and assessing how network structure drives the network dynamics and resilience to perturbations. The arcs represent different types of relationships between nodes (i.e., commercial, normative, or stakeholdership).

These connections should be fostered through exchanging information and knowledge value co-creation systems: Which role actors play and how dominant they are depending on their motivation, position, and resources. Their power basis may vary between legal, expertise-based, financial or support-based. Depending on the situation, project managers may choose to create new networks or to use the existing ones.

4.1 Innovation Ecosystem Network

The networks of an innovation ecosystem are a nested adaptive multi-layered network. Multi-layered networks are used to model systems with multiple interacting components, each being represented by a network layer, where each layer stands for a particular component of the system, the components interacting in multiple types of relationships. In our case, the network is nested, meaning that each layer comprises several layers. Therefore, new complexities in those systems emerge, highlighting the need for a new body of knowledge in project management: There is still a limited number of models and tools that can capture, describe, and understand the dynamics of these systems, where each layer affects, and is affected, by each other. By using this view, many questions may be posed: Where do the interaction rules come from? Are they evolving in time and space? What type of interaction arises between different layers? Is there any leverage that can be used to foster new connections in the network? These questions have caused hot philosophical debates among biologists, economists, social scientists and other theorists concerning who controls the "invisible hand" of ecosystems (Hodgson, 1997), still far from being resolved, especially when the network infrastructure is heavily dependent on human actions and interactions and individual perceptions. These complex phenomena are spatial and temporal; they never reach stable equilibrium states, and one individual action might cause a local change that might also trigger changes in the global state of the system. The so-called complexity science deals with phenomena that present such characteristics (Arthur, 2014).

We can devise at least four essential layers in any innovation ecosystem besides the physical and economical ones: the communication layer (with nested layers of communication), the knowledge layer, the legal layer, and the decision layer.

4.1.1 Communication Layer

The different types of actors in systems (e.g., individuals, groups, organizations, with different configurations and reach) and the different temporal scales of change underline the importance of distinguishing among different layers of communications: intrapersonal communication, interpersonal communication, group communication, and cultural communication. Understanding the differences of these layers is necessary for an effective stakeholder engagement strategy. Each of these different levels of communication has a different purpose and is used in different situations.

4.1.2 Knowledge Layer

Knowledge in this context is composed of the explicit knowledge of the individual system constituents and the tacit knowledge that ensues from interactions between the system actors. Explicit knowledge is the most basic form of knowledge, accessible and easily recorded, communicated, and (most notably in knowledge management) stored and shared. Tacit knowledge is our knowledge garnered from personal experience, context, background, and individual characteristics. It isn't easy to articulate or present in a tangible form.

4.1.3 Legal Layer

The complex restrictions on legal products and services amount to extraordinary protection regulation for business entities. This extensive regulation has substantial economic costs, it brings risks, and it builds additional intra- and inter-layers links. The obvious effect of strict regulation is reduced innovation in legal products and services. The greater impact on innovation ecosystems, however, probably comes from an indirect obstacle framed by the homogeneity of the population of potential innovators, since very often the shared knowledge is very standardized and communicated in a standardized way.

4.1.4 Decision Layer

The decision layer is the most simplified layer of the stakeholder network. Very often, decisions follow unilaterally oriented arcs, from the decision maker to the stakeholders. A participatory decision-making process where several stakeholders exchange opinions to find a shared and transitive collective decision might be desirable and beneficial to decision-making contexts with widespread collective impact. Moreover, involving all the actors in decision-making leads to decisions that reflect the real needs and opinions of the interested parties.

4.2 Project Managers as Connectors

Project managers must foster connectivity within the stakeholder network (see also Chap. 2 of Ulusoy & Hazır, 2021). Structural and functional connectivity (describing the dynamical processes operating within the structurally connected network) are important (Turnbull et al., 2018). While the network topology influences structural connectivity, functional connectivity is inferred from the system's dynamics represented by fluxes along and between the network's layers. The challenge is avoiding the separation between structural and functional connectivity and carefully and explicitly considering the reciprocal interactions at different timescales. The structural-functional evolution of a system may lead to emergent behaviour that leads to the formation of patterns; simple and complex patterns at the larger scale can be formed by very simple interactions at the local level.

Project managers need to stimulate interactions and connections in the ecosystem network in different layers:

Communication: Effective communication is paramount to the success of stakeholder engagement since it helps align towards common goals and objectives, facilitating consensus-building. Effective communication helps build trust, credibility, and transparency, enhancing reputation, facilitating conflict resolution, and fostering constructive dialogue and collaboration. Understanding communication barriers, however, is necessary to implement the process correctly. Differences in cultures, perspectives, interests, and language diversity can lead to conflicts, misunderstandings, misinterpretations, and communication breakdowns. For example, some cultures may prioritize direct and assertive communication, while others may always seek harmony and indirect communication styles. Nonverbal communication, including facial expressions and body language, can differ significantly across cultures, and the same gestures can be considered appropriate, acceptable, or offensive in different countries. Differences in norms, values, and social customs can impact communication dynamics: in some cultures, strict hierarchical structures may inhibit open communication. Infrastructure disparities, such as unreliable internet connectivity and inadequate telecommunications networks, can hinder communication, particularly in remote or developing regions. Disparities in access to technology and digital literacy skills contribute to the digital divide, exacerbating communication challenges and leading to inequities in information exchange and participation. Navigating cultural differences effectively is a proactive approach to overcoming communication barriers: learning about cultural norms, values, communication styles, and etiquette relevant to the regions and communities involved in the project encourages open-mindedness and flexibility. Clear communication protocols, guidelines, procedures, and expectations regarding communication channels, formats, and frequency are essential for consistency and transparency. To enable seamless communication and collaboration across geographic boundaries, stakeholders can leverage various digital tools and platforms to facilitate real-time communication and information exchange. The metaverse holds tremendous potential to impact the entire innovation ecosystem, seamlessly bridging the gap between the real and virtual worlds, making meaningful connections, and maximizing the value for all participating stakeholders.

Knowledge: Implementing organizational mechanisms on knowledge processes, i.e., knowledge creation, retention, and sharing, facilitates stakeholder engagement, improving project outcomes. The definition of policies, procedures, and systems to create, store, retrieve, and share knowledge assets ensures that knowledge is harnessed, utilized, stored, organized, and accessible to others and provides mechanisms and tools for knowledge sharing, such as regular team meetings, cross-functional collaboration, and communities of practice, also capturing tacit knowledge. This involves establishing clear processes, structures, and mechanisms for managing knowledge within projects. For example, project managers can establish knowledge repositories, conduct interviews, or encourage storytelling sessions to capture and document tacit knowledge. Stakeholder interrelationships can be categorized into four types (Yu et al., 2024): mutual interaction, where both stakeholders benefit from their interaction; exploitation, when one stakeholder benefits more from the interaction than the other stakeholder; neutral, where both stakeholders are unaffected by the interaction; competitive, where both stakeholders and are negatively impacted. The type of interaction affects the role the Project manager should have. Only interactions of the first type should be fostered, while the others may undermine long-term collaboration by reducing the willingness to share valuable information.

4.2.1 Legal Network

Legal-specific networks, like the International Lawyers Network, have become invaluable resources for legal professionals and will become an essential part of every innovation system. As technologies develop, novel and complex legal issues involving data and consumer privacy, intellectual property, antitrust, and financial and ESG regulatory compliance will become increasingly important. Retaining a user's identity or ownership of digital assets will pose novel legal issues. However, the adoption of tech is not the most profound change. What matters is the complete rethinking of how legal work is handled. Legal education needs to change, and the project manager must support this change. The project manager should connect the law firm with the client to work together or at least grow the relationship around shared innovation goals and give feedback to each other. These connections, especially if carried out multiple times, may lead to changes in the law firm, (or even the legal sector as a whole), will raise the awareness of the importance of the legal aspects, and will highlight the need to invest in forming experts in legal innovation. This will serve as a fertilizer for different parts of the legal innovation landscape and lower the barriers to the actual application of technology innovation.

4.2.2 Decision Making

The shift from a hierarchical decision-making paradigm to one that values empowerment and collaboration represents a profound cultural realignment within organisations and projects. Decision making is now increasingly seen as the product of collective intelligence, starting from the exploitation of diverse perspectives and expertise of the stakeholders. This democratization of the decision-making process does not mean the absence of leadership but rather an evolution of the role of project managers from directors to facilitators of a process that leverages the collective capabilities of the ecosystem and fosters a sense of ownership and accountability. This transition calls for meticulously crafted strategies to ensure its successful implementation. One cornerstone is the empowerment of the stakeholders and strengthening the connections between them in such a way that each stakeholder feels trusted and capable of making significant contributions. Empowerment comes through training: informed and trained stakeholders can make decisions swiftly. Of course, transparency is a critical strategy in this evolution. This layer and the communication layer are tightly interlaced. Project managers should connect the stakeholders through communication channels to form the backbone of decentralised decision-making. Regular check-ins and meetings, whether in person or virtual, help to maintain a seamless flow of information and serve as platforms for feedback, enabling continuous improvement and adaptation.

5 Move from Uncertainty to Complexity

As helping stakeholders to reduce uncertainty and understand complexity is a crucial point in the stakeholder engagement process, we will devote some space to this step of the pathway.

However, what is complexity? Alberto Felice De Toni (De Toni, 2024), one of Italy's leading experts on complexity, defines complexity as the inherent characteristic of systems comprising many interrelated and interdependent elements. Understanding the inherent complexity of projects is particularly important now, in an age of grand transitions, where the convergence of multiple system pressures, such as unprecedented expectancies, extreme innovation rates, and awareness about sustainability issues, are testing the resilience of projects worldwide.

According to De Toni, complexity has a light side and a dark side. When we face complexity, we feel the dark side; when we generate complexity, someone else feels the dark side. A prime example of this is the behaviour of midges and frogs. Midges, whose flight pattern is unpredictable, evolved this discontinuous movement as a survival mechanism because frogs—their predators—quickly learn to anticipate straightforward movements. If mosquitoes flew in a simple, predictable way, it would likely lead to their death. The complexity of their flight is not just an advantage; it is crucial to their survival. From the frogs' point of view, however, this complexity is a challenge because they must adapt as fast as they can to survive. So, complexity has two sides: the 'friendly complexity' or light side (as seen in the midges perspective) and the 'hostile complexity' or dark side (as experienced by the frogs). Whenever someone else changes the environment, we perceive a hostile complexity and must start adapting and changing how we behave to meet new challenges and increase the chances of winning.

The complex ecosystem, nested or embedded within one another interdependencies, should also be adaptive, a characteristic that increases dynamism and, therefore, complexity. "An adaptive complex system is an open system made up of several elements that interact with each other in a non-linear way, forming a single, dynamically organised entity that adapts to the environment" (Paoli, 2006). We can think, for example, of the human body and its systemic hierarchy: the body is made up of organs, which are made up of cells, which are made up of nucellus, cytoplasm, membrane, and so on. Each subsystem influences and is influenced by the others in the context of cross-contamination. This involves continuous adaptation, creating a reorganization that changes as each individual node in the network learns through interaction with others.

The dynamic nature implies that a certain amount of "irreducible uncertainty" will persist within the system. According to De Toni, the interaction between these elements produces unpredictable and non-deterministic behaviour, making it difficult to predict the system's overall behaviour from its parts. This is a never-ending process. Just as there are no closed systems in nature, it is in high-tech contexts where non-linearity makes the system difficult to predict: by varying the input, the output may behave nonlinearly to the input variation, making the context uncertain.

5.1 Project Managers as Complexity Surfers

How can a project manager deal with uncertainty while the stakeholders require precise time, cost, and quality outputs? That is one of the leading project delivery issues in high technology projects. It shapes a new role for the project manager in a complexity perspective, that can be defined as a complexity leadership. We argue that embracing complexity requires embracing irreducible uncertainty—given that uncertainty elimination cannot exist in a complex system with no finite and simple solutions. Managing uncertainty may require minimizing the emphasis on standardized processes and enabling the exploration of multiple potential solutions.

The project manager must be able to design and facilitate participative processes for organisational transformation and change management, in an environment of adaptive innovation development that considers uncertainty, adaptability and the continuous evolution of the system. Leadership is no longer predicated on hierarchy and formal roles but becomes an entrepreneurial effort to ensure that the ecosystem remains adaptive and can face uncertainty. Complexity leaders also stimulate innovative ideas and ensure adequate space, time, and resources to allow innovations to materialize.

The involvement of stakeholders' values and voices is increasingly embraced in leadership, aligning with a complexity perspective, but underscores the tension between uncertainty reduction and uncertainty absorption (i.e., acknowledging the extent of interdependencies and the importance of numerous potential solutions). Often, to reduce uncertainty, project managers may (unintentionally) minimize the numerous interdependencies, resulting in more significant uncertainty reduction and less uncertainty absorption. The project manager needs to guide how to respond to pressures in innovative, collaborative, and action-oriented ways, increasing the stakeholder participation in decision-making as an effective approach to uncertainty absorption.

One of the possible approaches is a different organizational model that can be used to reshape the team collaboration model. The concept of adhocracy, for example, can be used as a starting point for redesigning the organisation of the project team. Adhocracy is an organization that can be seen as the antithesis of bureaucracy. This term was coined in 1971 by Alvin Toffler in his book "Future Shock" and reworked and popularised by Henry Mintzberg in "The Structuring of Organisations" (1979) and "Strategy formation in an adhocracy", Administrative Science Quarterly (1985).

In his extensive work and reading on organisations, Mintzberg has identified five complex models, that is five forms of organisational coordination. He argues that they can only be considered a priori to be valid. He believes that the form of coordination must be chosen according to the organization's characteristics and the environment in which it operates. Therefore, there are contingencies that cannot be ignored in the design: to be effective, organizations must achieve a certain internal harmony and coherence while being consistent with external situational or contingent factors. To create optimal configurations, the parameters of organisational design and situational factors must be combined. Here the five Mintzberg structural models:

- Simple structure: centralised and often autocratic
- Machine bureaucracy: relies heavily on a robust technostructure
- Professional bureaucracy: based on clear lines of authority and standards set by law, regulations or independent external bodies, including professional bodies.
- Divisionalised structure: A small central core provides guidelines for business units with a high autonomy level.
- Adhocracy structure: a task or project-based structure that responds quickly and flexibly to changing demands.

An Adhocracy structure is a non-hierarchical coordination mechanism in which interpersonal communication is informal and immediate, thanks to its horizontal nature. There is little formality, so direct supervision and defined processes are less important than in other organization structures. Research and development can be a primary driver of adhocracies, as typified by new technology industries. This form of coordination is more frequent in organisations that have been operating in the specific project area for a long time, with people who have a strong background in the subject matter and an equally strong work management autonomy. In an adhocracy environment, the project team becomes a group that facilitates and synthesizes complex contexts. Increasingly, they will need to call on external consultants to do the same for them, to help them understand emerging technologies and methodologies, and to guide them in making strategic choices.

6 Give Technology a Specific Role

Emerging technologies make big promises and create hype, but there is often a huge gap between their maturity and their applicability to the real needs of projects. We need to understand if it makes sense to use a specific technology in a specific field and, most importantly, how to choose well (see Chap. 15 of Ulusoy & Hazır, 2021). Building on the work of Rip (2006), we differentiate between enactors and selectors. Enactors are those stakeholders that 'enact' a technological option, whereas selectors assess the different expectations and promises. Every stakeholder can perform both roles sequentially and even simultaneously. A practical starting point is analysing the balance between expectations and feasibility.

On the one hand, expectations play a central role in stakeholder satisfaction and are fundamental to every individual's life. They manifest themselves automatically in everyone's mind and play a vital role in the actions and behaviours, characterizing how projects are developed and evaluated. Expectations are formed due to a complex combination of past experiences, the environment, and one's desires. For this reason, a misperception of the relationship between needs and technological solutions, or the presence of cognitive biases, influences stakeholders' expectations, creating a mismatch between ideas and reality and generating negative emotions such as disappointment, dissatisfaction, and frustration.

On the other hand, implementing a complex project with a strong potential impact on one's own organization, requires a complete feasibility analysis to create an awareness of the results. This is why feasibility analysis is essential for assessing the real possibility of project success. It must be developed along several dimensions:

- Skills and technology: make-or-buy analysis of the technical and scientific skills present in the team and the availability of technology.
- Economic sustainability: cost-benefit analysis of the project, economic risk analysis, financial analysis. In the case of for-profit organizations, it is always important to include a market analysis, a competitor analysis, and a sales projection.
- Environmental sustainability: impact of the project on the environment regarding emissions, lifecycle, and footprint.
- Process sustainability over time: impact on organisational structure and value generated by processes with time projection.

Awareness of the maturity level of a technology is crucial to undertake a feasibility analysis and we can use as a reference the Gartner Hype Cycle, a widely recognized framework that positions emerging technologies on a timescale and gives a picture

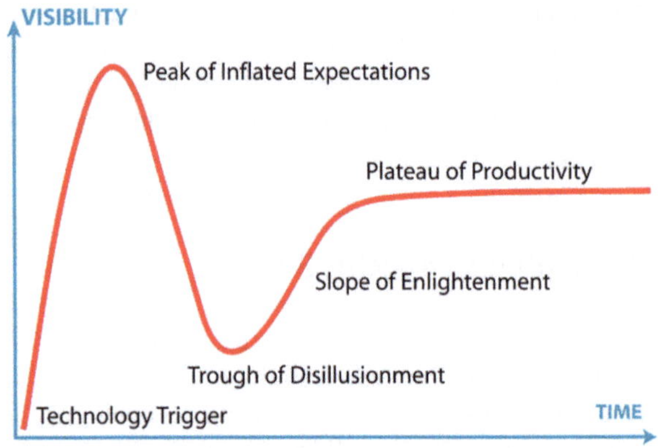

Fig. 4 Gartner Hype Cycle Jeremykemp Wikipedia, CC BY-SA 3.0

of the maturity and adoption of technologies over time. An archetypal illustration of the timeline is presented in Fig. 4. The graph shows how an enabling technology evolves through different stages, from initial excitement to eventual mainstream adoption. After the innovation trigger, expectations rise sharply and culminate into a hype. The peak is thus a period in which the enactors successfully communicate their positive expectations (and promises), as others share or acknowledge them. As the so-called peak of inflated expectations is reached. Since early success stories may lead to unrealistic expectations, disappointment starts to surface. When this disappointment becomes stronger, expectations drop rapidly, resulting in the trough of disillusionment. The market may show frustration, and some projects may be abandoned. After some time, the technology might recover, the understanding of benefits becomes more apparent, and practical applications emerge. In the final stage, the technology becomes widely accepted and its benefits are well understood. The technology reaches mainstream adoption, establishing its place in the market. During these phases, the capability of the application evolves from the highest to the lowest level of affordability in terms of effort: cost, knowledge, process redesign, and effectiveness. But does technological innovation increase the satisfaction of our project managers? And does it encourage them to make good decisions?

This is a critical question to understanding whether there are cognitive biases underlying project managers' use of enabling technologies and how the abundance of technology choice is a crucial factor in its application in project management.

6.1 Technology Abundance and the Paradox of Choice

Every time a new technological development comes to market, emerges the need to understand a new enabling technology, the associated methodology and skills, and to act as quickly as possible to achieve a new goal. Decision fatigue and cognitive load inevitably increase in this environment. These are two of the most potent enemies of quality in project development. Reducing the stress-related sensation can be a strategic action by the project manager to engage and retain stakeholders. The abundance of available enabling technologies and methodologies may appear to be a sign of freedom and opportunity, but the abundance of choice hides decision fatigue. More often than we expect, technological complexity inhibits decision-making and drives the project team to inaction. Let's get help from the "Paradox of Choice", an inspiring thought introduced by American psychologist Barry Schwartz in his 2004 book The Paradox of Choice: Why More Is Less. It highlights a counterintuitive idea: having some choices is generally positive, but having too many choices can lead to negative consequences. Rather than increasing our happiness, too many choices increase the difficulty of knowing what is best and can lead to stress, anxiety, and dissatisfaction. Instead of increasing our freedom to have what we want, the paradox of choice suggests that having too many choices limits our freedom.

Learning to choose takes a lot of work. Learning to choose well is more brutal.

When we're faced with a vast array of options, the process of making a decision can become overwhelming. Instead of feeling liberated by the ability to choose, we can feel bogged down by the sheer volume of possibilities. This can lead to what is known as "decision fatigue," where the mental effort required to choose becomes exhausting.

6.2 Project Managers as Technology Enablers

Project managers should become facilitators to make technology sustainable in terms of efforts. This sounds obvious, but it is not. Integrating technology into a project's deliverables requires much effort from stakeholders in terms of skills, redesigning and consolidating new processes, and patience to see results. The "last mile" of a project is increasingly becoming a critical phase, as we observe too many organizations willing to embrace technology but unable to use it at the end of the implementation project. The hype generated by new technologies leads to the misconception that their introduction alone. In reality, new technologies require people who can use them to their full potential by adapting their potential to specific and sectorial needs. This requires continuous review of skills and processes to ensure that organizations create value, not entropy.

The new role of the project manager is to understand the context and to ensure that stakeholders feel genuinely involved and guided in the project choices, as they will be able to understand the technological implications for the project outcomes and the impact of innovation. Their cognitive fatigue will decrease, their sense of engagement will increase, and their ownership of the project outcomes will be assured. This approach ensures possible co-design and shared responsibility even in a complex environment. The project team must guide the stakeholders in integrating the technology into the intended deliverables once the issue of technology complexity has been resolved.

Without the proper support, stakeholders could face three main issues, as shown in Fig. 5:

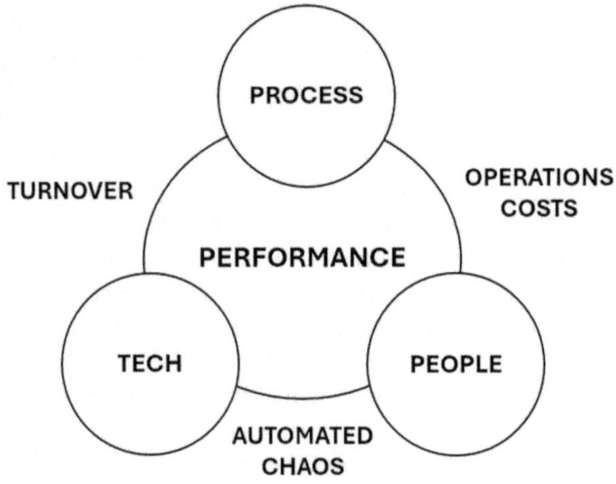

Fig. 5 Relationship between People, process and Technology

1. People turnover and talent loss if they will reinforce processes inserting enabling technologies without engaging people and supporting new skills development
2. Automated chaos, if they focus on people and technologies without redesigning and reinforcing processes
3. Increase operational costs if they insert technology but cannot use it, so they continue developing value "manually".

Technology can be seen as a booster and a decoder for the interaction and decision-making in complex ecosystems. Indeed, the ability to collect, normalize, store, and correlate vast amounts of data through high computational power is one of the most important features of technology. On the other hand, the ability to provide a competitive perspective and to think outside the box are human skills.

If we can help our stakeholders combine these two key capabilities, we can engage them in the project purpose and lead them to success (Fig. 6).

7 Foster Semi-Permeability

Anyone who claims to be innovating is talking about open innovation. The term was coined by US economist Henry Chesbrough, who, in his essay The Era of Open Innovation (2003), reflected that globalization had made research and development processes increasingly expensive and risky as the life cycle of products had become shorter. In closed innovation, an organization generates and develops its ideas. This philosophy of self-reliance dominated the R&D operations of many leading industrial corporations for most of the twentieth century. In the new open innovation model, an organization works on its ideas and other organizations' innovations, seeking ways to bring its ideas to market through routes outside its current business.

Let us take some innovation principles and compare them:

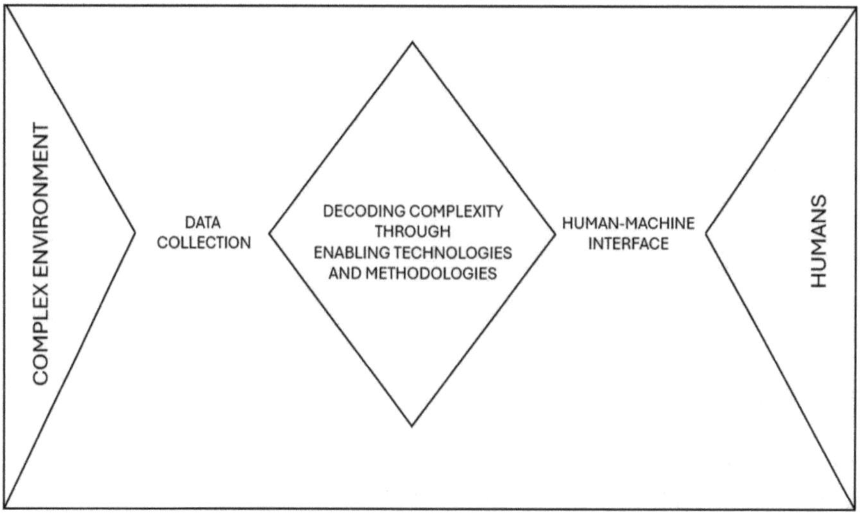

Fig. 6 Human—Environment relationship through enabling technologies and methodologies application

About talents: In closed innovation models, it is thought that the smartest people in our fieldwork for us. In an open innovation approach, we know that not all of the smartest people in our fieldwork for us, so we must connect talents inside and outside our organization to maximize knowledge and expertise.

About timing and idea generation: In closed innovation models, it is thought that if we discover it ourselves, we will get it to market first because if we create the best ideas in the industry, we will win. In an open innovation approach, we understand that we do not have to originate the research to profit from it. In fact, instead of getting to market first, it is often better to learn from others' goals and mistakes to build a stronger value proposition and generate a more competitive business model.

About intellectual property: In closed innovation models, it is thought that we must control our intellectual property (IP) so that our competitors don't profit from our ideas. In open innovation approaches, our IP becomes an asset: we should profit from others' use of our IP and buy others'.

7.1 Project Managers as Open to Innovate Coaches

The boundary between the organization and its environment is porous in open innovation environments, allowing innovations to move more easily between the two. Organisations cannot be completely open to all contaminants, so there must be barriers. The porosity, i.e., the semi-permeability, must be weighed, and the width of the holes calibrated. If the ports are too narrow, there will not be enough contamination. If the ports are narrow enough, there will be more fragmented impulses for the organizations, which will then spend too much time and energy in an unfocused

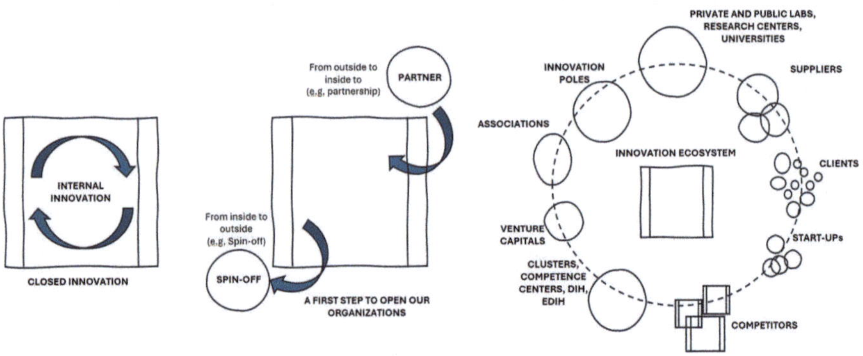

Fig. 7 From closed innovation to open ecosystem

way. Therefore, rather than talking about open innovation as a tool, the project manager needs to adopt the mindset of the innovator: the open-to-innovate mindset.

This cultural approach to innovation is based on a few fundamental principles, including:

- Definition of the level of permeability and the size of the pores that connect the project to the outside world.
- Definition of the best stakeholders for the project in order to maximize its success through contamination
- Dialogue engagement with clients in order to support them in the development of their permeability.

The mindset of being open to innovation is the one that is needed in innovation environments, and the project manager needs to adopt it and pass it on to his team (Fig. 7).

8 Conclusions and Manifesto "O2I: open to innovate"

This chapter highlights the urgency for project managers to take decisive actions toward integrating stakeholder engagement principles with the open to innovate framework. It is essential to foster an innovative collaborative landscape that promotes stakeholder engagement in project practices. Equally important is the use and development of enabling technologies that are not merely efficient but are also inclusive. We have offered insights into how to incorporate stakeholders in every aspect of a complex innovation ecosystem. An important theme here is the multidimensionality of stakeholder value. We argue that we need both a broader understanding of the concept of stakeholder value and a deeper understanding of the value they are producing. This refers to values beyond the economic or financial performance toward broader sustainability principles, offering a blueprint for a more equitable future. The perspective of this research holds the strong understanding that stakeholders are a piece of a symbiotic wider system co-sustaining projects in all its forms. On this basis then, project managers need to re-orient their initiatives into holistic engaging directions, bringing project teams, stakeholders, shareholders, and society towards meaningful and successful innovation experiences. Distinctively, the framework showed evidence of its potential in the Open to Innovate Manifesto,[1] designed during a 2 years pathway and developed by more than 120 stakeholders of the digital innovation ecosystem of the Emilia Romagna Region, members of Clust-ER Innovate. It started with an in-depth study of the values of the Innovate Clust-ER Community and a focus on the characteristics of an ecosystem that is able to produce value for the entire community. The group decided to represented their mindset, passion and believes in an open manifesto, aiming to voice a territory rich in opportunities and prospects, the Emilia-Romagna Region, and all those who embrace this approach. The manifesto's statements follow the five-step method:

Focus on digital humanism

1. The future belongs to people, not to technology.
2. Good inventions leave a sustainable footprint.
3. A project has a future if its development is ethical and inclusive.
4. Digital humanism is about relationships, not only business.

Interconnect the ecosystem

5. Networking is our ecosystem. Without it, you cannot innovate.
6. Living as a part of a network sharing ideas, values, and enormous challenges.
7. The local area is our soil. People and skills are our sap.

Move from uncertainty to complexity

8. Complexity is the driving force behind evolution.
9. Uncertainty is an opportunity. Curiosity drives discovery.

Give technology a specific role

10. Technology is the key to innovation.
11. Connecting different disciplines generates value.

Foster semi-permeability

[1] Manifesto credits: you can find manifesto at this link https://innovate.clust-er.it/manifesto-open-to-innovate/The manifesto was delivered in 2023 by Clust-ER Innovate Members and was sponsored by Clust-ER Innovate President, Prof. Antonio Corradi and by the Board of Directors. Special thanks go to *Filippo Bosi, Vice President of Clust-ER Innovate and CEO of Imola Informatica, that supported the creation process of the Manifesto and to Gino Corbolante and Daniela Malavolti, Co-Founder and Communication Specialist of Pidiprogetto, who supported the manifesto definition and design, distilling the concepts in sentences and images.*

12. Open innovation is a game changer.
13. Experimenting together brings common benefits.
14. Open minds change the world.

The last sentence keeps the manifesto open to future scenarios and ideas integration.

9 The World Evolves and our Narrative is Open

In this manifesto, the network becomes the most effective tool for evolution, the source of cross-pollination. Complexity becomes the engine of discovery. The territory becomes the cradle of ideas. The well-being of people and respect for the future become the purpose of innovation. Shared culture and values are needed to ensure widespread and sustainable innovation from an ethical, economic, and environmental perspective.

Looking to this approach, we highlight several challenges arising to address the existing gaps in understanding the role of stakeholder engagement in promoting innovation objectives. Among these, a particularly pertinent and constructive avenue for further exploration would be to investigate the collaborative mechanisms and partnerships that should be established among diverse stakeholders. Examining successes, and lessons learned in building and maintaining such partnerships, also considering different approaches to govern the development and utilization of enabling technologies like chatbots, social media platform, virtual/augemented reality, online collaboration tools, would also be an interesting avenue for future studies. Moreover, data platforms, providing support for effective data sharing and exchange, should ensure data sovereignty, i.e., the ability for each stakeholder to control how digital processes, infrastructures, and flows of data are structured, built, and managed. Understanding how these disruptive technologies impact stakeholder engagement and projects is vital.

The common assumption that stakeholder engagement brings only benefits and no risks needs to be thoroughly examined: cybersecurity and data space vulnerabilities, ethical issues, risks that are related to biases, impacts on project team, and disruptions to established business processes should be considered to develop rigorous strategies to deal with these risks.

References

Adner, R. (2006). Match your innovation strategy to your innovation ecosystem. *Harvard Business Review, 84*(4), 98–107.

Agrawal, S., Sharma, N., Bruni, M. E., & Iazzolino, G. (2023). Happiness economics: Discovering future research trends through a systematic literature review. *Journal of Cleaner Production, 416*, 137860.

Arthur, W. B. (2014). *Complexity and the economy*. Oxford University Press.

Assudani, R., & Kloppenborg, T. J. (2010). Managing stakeholders for project management success: An emergent model of stakeholders. *Journal of General Management, 35*(3), 67–80.

Bayiley, Y. T., & Teklu, G. K. (2016). Success factors and criteria in the management of international development projects: Evidence from projects funded by the European Union in Ethiopia. *International Journal of Managing Projects in Business, 9*(3), 562–582.
Bruni, M. E., Beraldi, P., Guerriero, F., & Pinto, E. (2011). A scheduling methodology for dealing with uncertainty in construction projects. *Engineering Computations (Swansea, Wales), 28*(8), 1064–1078.
Bruni, M. E., Beraldi, P., & Guerriero, F. (2017). The stochastic resource-constrained project scheduling problem. *Handbook on Project Management and Scheduling, 2*, 811–835.
Chesbrough, H. (2003). *"The era of open innovation", in open innovation: The new imperative for creating and profiting from technology*. Harvard Business School Press.
De Toni, A. F. (2024). *Decalogo della complessità*. Franco Angeli.
Di Maddaloni, F., & Davis, K. (2018). Project manager's perception of the local communities stakeholder in megaprojects. An empirical investigation in the UK. *International Journal of Project Management, 36*(3), 542–565.
Elkington, R., Pearse, N. J., Moss, J., Van der Steege, M., & Martin, S. (2017). Global leaders' perceptions of elements required for effective leadership development in the twenty-first century. *Leadership & Organization Development Journal, 38*(8), 1038–1056.
Freeman, R. E. (1984). *Strategic management: A stakeholder approach*. Pitman.
Freeman, R. E., Harrison, J. S., Wicks, A. C., Parmar, B. L., & de Colle, S. (2010). Stakeholder theory: The state of the art. *Academy of Management Annals, 4*(1), 403–445.
Friedman, M. (1970). A Friedman doctrine: The social responsibility of business is to increase its profits. *The New York Times Magazine*.
Granstrand, O., & Holgersson, M. (2020). Innovation ecosystems: A conceptual review and a new definition. *Technovation, 90-91*, 102098.
Hodgson, G. M. (1997). *Economics and evolution: Bringing life back into economics*. University of Michigan Press.
Jensen, M. C. (1976). Theory of the firm: Managerial behaviour, agency costs and ownership structure. *Journal of Financial Economics, 3*(4), 305–360.
Kujala, J., Sachs, S., Leinonen, H., Heikkinen, A., & Laude, D. (2022). Stakeholder engagement: Past, present, and future. *Business & Society, 61*(5), 1136–1196.
Lehtinen, J., Aaltonen, K., & Rajala, R. (2019). Stakeholder management in complex product systems: Practices and rationales for engagement and disengagement. *Industrial Marketing Management, 79*, 58–70.
Mintzberg, H. (1979). *The structuring of Organisations: A synthesis of the research*. Prentice Hall.
Mintzberg, H., & McHugh, A. (1985). Strategy formation in an adhocracy. *Administrative Science Quarterly, 30*(2), 160–197.
Oh, D.-S., Phillips, F., Park, S., & Lee, E. (2016). Innovation ecosystems: A critical examination. *Technovation, 54*, 1–6.
Oppong, G. D., Chan, A. P., & Dansoh, A. (2017). A review of stakeholder management performance attributes in construction projects. *International Journal of Project Management, 35*(6), 1037–1051.
Ostapenko, V., Tyshchenko, V., Rats, O., & Brusentseva, O. (2024). Structuring and determining the influence of stakeholders on the innovation ecosystem. *Journal of Governance & Regulation, 13*(1), 123–134.
Patricio, R., Moreira, A., Zurlo, F., & Melazzini, M. (2020). Co-creation of new solutions through gamification: A collaborative innovation practice. *Creativity and Innovation Management, 29*(1), 146–160.
Paoli, M. (2006). *Management della complessità, complessità del management*. Franco Angeli.
Rip, A. (2006). Folk theories of nanotechnologists. *Science as Culture, 15*(4), 349–365.
Schwartz, B. (2004). *The paradox of choice*. HarperCollins.
The GUEST Initiative. (2017). http://www.theguestmethod.com
Toffler, A. (1971). *Future shock*. Bantam Books.
Turnbull, L., Hütt, M. T., Ioannides, A. A., et al. (2018). "Connectivity and complex systems: Learning from a multi-disciplinary perspective", applied network. *Science, 3*(11).

Ulusoy, G., & Hazır, Ö. (2021). *An introduction to project modeling and planning*. Springer International Publishing.

Vienna Manifesto on Digital Humanism. (2023). Technische Universität Wien. https://caiml.org/dighum/dighum-manifesto/

Werthner, H., Stanger, A., Schiaffonati, V., Knees, P., Hardman, L., & Ghezzi, C. (2023). *Digital humanism: The time is now* (Vol. 56, pp. 138–142).

Walker, D. H., Bourne, L. M., & Shelley, A. (2008). Influence, stakeholder mapping and visualization. *Construction Management and Economics, 26*(6), 645–658.

Yu, L., Zhu, P., Mlecnik, E., Qian, Q. K., & Visscher, H. J. (2024). *Dissemination, manipulation or monopolization? Understanding the influence of stakeholder information sharing on resident participation in neighborhood rehabilitation of urban China*. Land Use.

Digital Technologies and Sustainability in Project Management: Current Trends and Future Perspectives

Leila Moslemi Naeni and Roksana Jahan Tumpa

Abstract

The increasing global focus on sustainability has promoted a paradigm shift in project management methodologies. This chapter explores the recent advancements and trends of digital technologies that enhance the sustainability performances of projects and reshape the project management approaches to align with sustainability goals. Through an analysis of recent studies, this chapter identifies Building Information Modeling (BIM), blockchain, and cloud computing as key digital technologies employed in project settings to contribute to more sustainable outcomes. Additionally, the chapter provides insights into the evolving landscape of project management, examines the challenges and opportunities associated with integrating digital technologies to enhance project sustainability, and highlights emerging trends in sustainable project management. By addressing these aspects, the research offers a comprehensive understanding of the current landscape of digitalization of project management in the context of sustainability and provides key future opportunities.

L. M. Naeni (✉)
University of Technology Sydney, Sydney, NSW, Australia
e-mail: Leila.mosleminaeni@uts.edu.au

R. J. Tumpa
Central Queensland University, Sydney, NSW, Australia
e-mail: r.tumpa@cqu.edu.au

Ö. Hazır, M. E. Bruni (eds.), *Tomorrow's Data Empowered Project Management*, Future of Business and Finance, https://doi.org/10.1007/978-3-031-84017-3_8

1 Introduction

Sustainability and sustainable practices have long been key areas of interest for project management scholars and practitioners, especially in recent decades. The connections between sustainability and project management have been extensively explored (Moehler et al., 2018; Sabini et al., 2019), with numerous studies investigating how sustainable practices can be integrated into project management (Banihashemi et al., 2017; Sánchez, 2015; Silvius & Schipper, 2010). Project management has even been identified as an important vehicle for delivering sustainability (Kivilä et al., 2017; Marcelino-Sádaba et al., 2015), with sustainability targets being incorporated into traditional project goals of time, cost, and quality. Consequently, project performance is now evaluated not only on these traditional criteria but also on environmental, social and economic impacts, often referred to as the triple bottom line (Fernández-Sánchez & Rodríguez-López, 2010; Stanitsas et al., 2021). Additionally, the concept of "sustainability sublime" has been introduced as a driving motivation for creating megaprojects that contribute to the United Nations's sustainable development goals (SDGs) (Sankaran et al., 2020).

Guandalini (2022) defined sustainability as "meeting the needs of the present without compromising the ability of future generations to meet their own needs". While the definitions of "project" and "project management" are well-established, the concept of "sustainable project management" (SPM) is still in the development stage and not fully standardized (Moehler et al., 2018). In a broad sense, the intersection of sustainability and project management can be referred to as SPM. According to Silvius and Schipper (2014) "Sustainable Project Management is the planning, monitoring, and controlling of project delivery and support processes, with consideration of the environmental, economic and social aspects of the life cycle of the project's resources, processes, deliverables and effects, aimed at realizing benefits for stakeholders, and performed in a transparent, fair, and ethical way that includes proactive stakeholder participation." However, in a recent book, Silvius and Huemann (2024) identified SPM as "still a relatively 'young' research stream", which involves a combination of considerations for sustainability requirements of the project as well as the project contributions to broader sustainability goals (Huemann & Silvius, 2017).

Concerns about sustainability have led to many challenges and changes in the project management profession (Schipper & Silvius, 2017; Toljaga-Nikolić et al., 2020), contributing to a growing body of academic knowledge on sustainability and project management, as highlighted in recent reviews (Kiani Mavi et al., 2021; Sabini et al., 2019; Zhang et al., 2023). Digital technologies are recognized as a catalyst for advancing sustainable goals (Camodeca & Almici, 2021; George et al., 2021) and play significant role in advancing the concept of SPM and ensuring that project management practices align more closely with sustainability guidelines.

Digital technologies offer numerous opportunities for project managers to transform their processes, methods, and practices. They enhance productivity and performance and enable the setting and achieving new goals. While project management software and data analytics have been around for decades, streamlining workflows, enhancing communications, and improving project performance and efficiency (Marnewick, 2016), emerging digital technologies are taking these capabilities to a new level. Innovations such as artificial intelligence, machine learning, and big data are significantly advancing these functionalities, transforming the traditional ways of working (Li et al., 2022). These technologies improve the prediction of project outcomes, enabling more accurate forecasting and better decision-making (Bakici et al., 2021; Fridgeirsson et al., 2021; Narbaev et al., 2024).

Digital technology is recognized as a crucial enabler for enhancing sustainability performance across social, economic, and environmental dimensions (Fukawa et al., 2021; Robertsone & Lapiņa, 2023). It drives digital transformation by enhancing business operations, organizational capabilities, and work processes (Rachinger et al., 2018), and it also improves value creation and benefits stakeholders (Grunwald, 2022; Lähteenmäki et al., 2022). Acknowledging the impact of digital transformation on sustainability, George et al. (2021) coined the term "digital sustainability" to describe "organizational activities aimed at advancing sustainable development goals through the innovative use of technologies that create, utilize, transmit, or source electronic data."

There are several review papers on the general impact of digital technologies on project management (Kozak-Holland & Procter, 2019; Simion et al., 2018; Swart et al., 2022; Wu, 2022). However, very few review papers focused specifically on the effects of digitalization on project sustainability. Therefore, this study employs a systematic literature review to synthesize the existing academic literature to identify the key digital technologies utilized in project environments to enhance project sustainability.

The remainder of the chapter is organized as follows. Next section details the research methodology and the steps taken to gather relevant literature. We then present the findings and discussion, focusing on the key digital technologies used in projects to enhance sustainability and the enablers and challenges identified in this context. Finally, we provide the conclusions and suggest future directions based on this review.

2 Research Method

A systematic literature review (SLR) was adopted to identify recent trends in digitization in improving the sustainable performance of projects. SLR aims to search, retrieve, and analyze the literature identified through preset inclusion and exclusion criteria to address research questions (Akomea-Frimpong, Jin, et al., 2024a; Ghamarimajd et al., 2024). SLR has widely been used to explore extant literature in many disciplines, including construction, project management, education, business, management, and accounting (Figueiredo et al., 2024; Kukah et al., 2023; Tumpa et al., 2024; Yarnold et al., 2023). To investigate the potential application of digital technologies in achieving sustainability in projects, the SLR was performed in three stages: (1) retrieval of articles, (2) identification of relevant articles, and (3) data analysis. Figure 1 illustrates the research method.

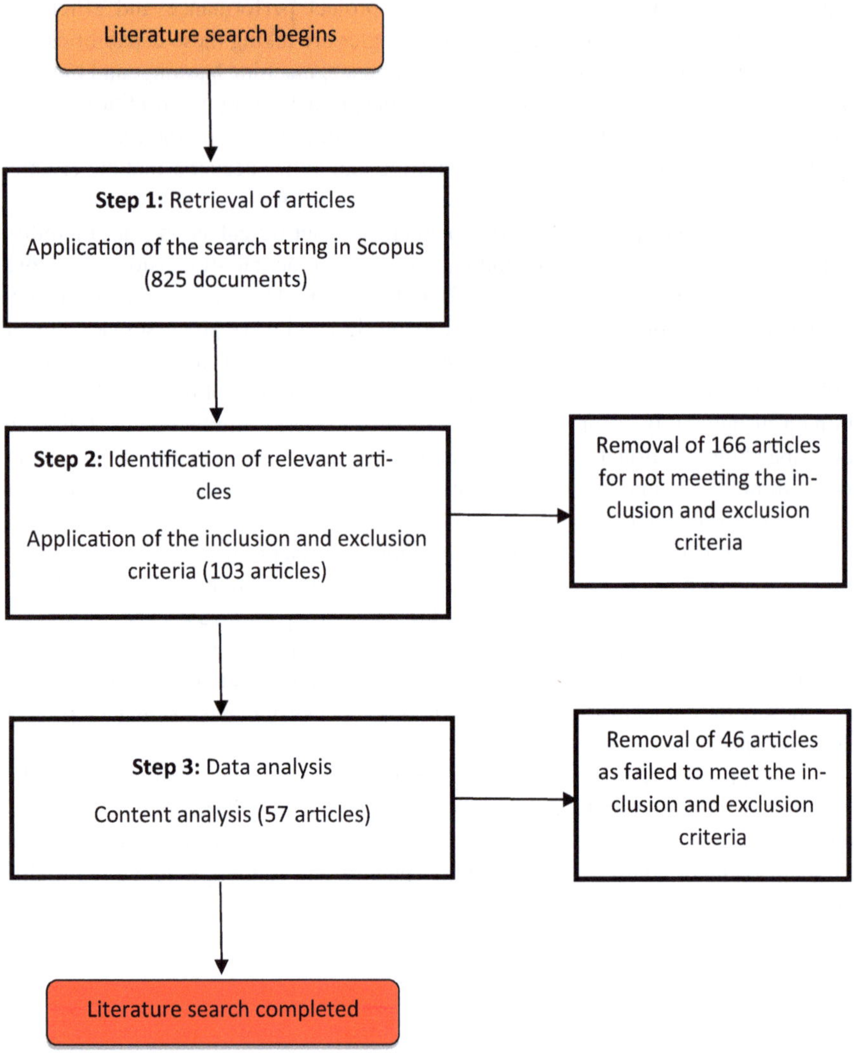

Fig. 1 Steps of the SLR method

Step 1: Retrieval of Articles

Scopus was utilized as the main search engine to identify the relevant studies and unveil the potential application of digital technologies in sustainable project management. Scopus has been identified as one of the main search engines for indexing transdisciplinary research (Afzal & Tumpa, 2024; Akomea-Frimpong, Tetteh, et al., 2024b; Cui et al., 2018; Meho & Rogers, 2008) due to the following reasons: (1) Scopus contains more recent and leading journals than any other search engines (Faruk et al., 2021); (2) Scopus is one of the most frequently used databases to index sustainable and digital technologies related studies (3) it is the most updated and expanded search engine for comprehensive searchable citations and abstracts (Baier-Fuentes et al., 2019; Joshi, 2016). Furthermore, Scopus is known to be comparatively a better search engine than Web of Science, Google Scholar and PubMed (Meho & Rogers, 2008). A comprehensive search string was used to extract all relevant studies published on digitization, sustainability, and project management. The search string below was applied to Scopus. The search was performed in August 2024. The initial search in Scopus resulted in 825 documents.

"Sustainability" OR "Sustainable practices" OR "sustainable" OR "green".*

AND

"drone" OR "mixed reality" OR "augmented reality" OR "big data" OR "cloud computing" OR "machine learning" OR "machine learning" OR "digital technologies" OR "artificial intelligence" OR "digitization" OR "digital technology" OR "Digital Transformation" OR "ICT" OR "industry 4.0" OR "industry 5.0" OR "disruptive technology" OR "blockchain" OR "IoT" OR "BIM" OR "AI" OR "digital twin".

AND

"Project management".

Step 2: Identification of Relevant Articles

A set of inclusion and exclusion criteria were set to select relevant articles for analysis to reveal the potential application of digital technologies in achieving sustainability criteria in projects. The following inclusion and exclusion criteria were applied to the 825 documents retrieved through Step 1.

1. Articles comprehensively cover digital technologies' application in advancing sustainability or SDGs in projects.
2. Articles focused on projects ranging from construction and infrastructure to IT and manufacturing projects.
3. Peer-reviewed journal articles were included. Conference papers, book chapters, editorials, or any other grey literature were excluded.
4. Only empirical research was included. All reviews were excluded for further analysis.
5. Articles only written in English was included.

269 articles were identified after applying the inclusion and exclusion criteria mentioned above. The 269 articles were screened to ensure they fulfilled the inclusion and exclusion criteria. First, the titles and abstracts of the 269 articles were reviewed, which resulted in a reduction of 166 articles. Many articles were removed at this stage because (1) articles did not examine sustainability and digitization in combination; (2) articles discussed digital technologies but were not linked to any sustainability or SDGs; (3) the main focus of the articles was not entirely on digital technologies or digitization and sustainability. The terms were merely used in the abstracts.

Second, the full text of the remaining 103 articles was read to be considered for further analysis. At this stage, another 46 articles were removed for not closely discussing applications of digital technologies in enhancing sustainability performance in a project environment. Finally, 57 articles were selected for data analysis in Step 3. Before the data analysis commenced, both authors independently went through the articles to ensure that the articles were eligible to be included in the data analysis.

Step 3: Data Analysis
A content analysis was employed to review the 57 articles critically. The content analysis aimed to investigate the relationship between digital technologies and sustainability and how digital technologies were applied to achieve sustainable project performance. Content analysis is a 'systematic, rigorous approach to analyzing documents obtained or generated during research' (White & Marsh, 2006). The articles were read entirely and coded using NVIvo (Akomea-Frimpong et al., 2023; Jayasena et al., 2021). Finally, themes were generated based on the extracted code to address the research aim.

3 Results and Discussion

3.1 Digital Technologies and Sustainability

There is a consensus among researchers and industry experts that the successful adoption of digital technologies is key to improving the sustainable performance of projects (Kumar & Padala, 2024; Maqbool et al., 2023). The successful utilization of Industry 4.0 and various implementations of the Internet of Things (IoT) can potentially improve projects' environmental, social, and economic sustainability. Numerous ICT tools have been developed and implemented in small to large-scale projects to gain sustainable advantages in projects (Hosseini et al., 2017). A range of digital technologies have been implemented in different kinds of projects, including Building Information Modelling (BIM), Blockchain, Big Data, Cloud Computing, Drones, Robots, Machine Learning, Internet of Things (IoT), Artificial Intelligence (AI) and Digital Twin. Although all of these digital technologies have been prominently employed in projects to shift to digitization in project operation, the review of the selected literature suggests that BIM, Blockchain, and Cloud Computing are mostly widely used to improve the sustainability performance of projects. Therefore, these digital technologies are discussed based on the reviewed literature, and how they can be leveraged to advance sustainable project performance, thus contributing to addressing SDGs and net-zero targets, are explored.

3.2 Building Information Modeling (BIM)

In the reviewed articles, the most widely adopted digital technology for improving the sustainability performance of projects was BIM (Dervishaj & Gudmundsson, 2024; Kumar & Padala, 2024; Oke, Aliu, et al., 2023a; Tabejamaat et al., 2024;

Wang, 2022). Paolini et al. (2019) state that "a Building Information Model is a comprehensive digital representation of a building that contains geometric and semantic data such as building element types and material properties."The literature suggests that BIM is predominantly utilized for advancing economic and environmental sustainability (Dervishaj & Gudmundsson, 2024; Mandičák et al., 2024; Wang, 2022). On the other hand, Abdel-Tawab et al. (2023) demonstrated that BIM contributes to the overall success of sustainability. However, construction projects have been the main area of application for BIM.

BIM enables project professionals to plan and manage resources meticulously throughout the project lifecycle by developing accurate models. These models help identify areas for waste reduction and promote recycling, thus facilitating resource optimization (Mandičák et al., 2024). Through BIM, resource optimization can contribute to both environmental and economic sustainability. For example, generating less waste, reusing materials, and recycling all contribute to environmental sustainability. By providing detailed models and designs, BIM can also identify inefficient resource use, which helps eliminate rework and modifications, improving projects' economic sustainability (Mandičák et al., 2024). Furthermore, economic sustainability is achieved through cost reduction associated with recycling and waste management (Fonseca et al., 2024).

Additionally, digital data obtained from BIM can help analyze energy-related data and improve planning, thus reducing CO2 emissions (Kumar & Padala, 2024; Tabejamaat et al., 2024). The "Green BIM" concept is also highlighted, offering an integrated design, construction, and maintenance of Net Zero Energy buildings (Maltese et al., 2017). Many projects worldwide use BIM to manage data during design, construction, and operation, enhancing sustainability performance. For instance, implementing BIM in Sydney's Northwest Metro project reduced costs (economic sustainability) by optimizing raw materials and minimizing on site labor through prefabricated elements (BIMCommunity, 2020).

BIM has been widely discussed in the reviewed literature as a tool for improving stakeholder engagement and facilitating informed decision-making (Abdel-Tawab et al., 2023; Babatunde et al., 2020; Gong et al., 2019; Kumar & Padala, 2024; Oke, Aliu, et al., 2023a). Digital technologies like BIM facilitate and enhance stakeholder engagement, crucial for making informed decisions that lead to more sustainable solutions (Kumar & Padala, 2024). Gong et al. (2019) identified that BIM can improve stakeholder collaboration by enabling the sharing of critical project information among multiple stakeholders. Sharing key information and collaborating effectively is essential for making decisions that enhance the sustainability performance of projects (Abdel-Tawab et al., 2023; Babatunde et al., 2020; Oke et al., 2024). BIM provides project professionals with detailed data on design, resources, costs, and even emissions, assisting them in making decisions that support improved sustainability performance.

A significant amount of data is generated during project operation and shared with different stakeholders through digital technologies like BIM. Information sharing fosters effective collaboration among stakeholders, improving transparency throughout a project's different phases (Oke et al., 2024). BIM facilitates real-time data collection and management throughout the project lifecycle (Fonseca et al., 2024). The availability of real-time data helps reduce risks and enhance time, cost, and quality management, leading to better project outcomes (Fonseca et al., 2024). By continuously monitoring and optimizing resources through BIM, project professionals gain a deeper understanding of sustainability-related data, allowing them to make informed decisions that align with sustainability goals. Real-time information offers insights into project operations, helping professionals assess whether sustainability goals are being met and take corrective actions if needed. Furthermore, the availability of real-time information through BIM ensures that sustainability reports are accurate and substantiated (Anjomshoa, 2024), which reduces the likelihood of greenwashing behavior and enhances the credibility of sustainability efforts.

BIM plays a crucial role in project monitoring and tracking the supply chain. In projects, many suppliers are involved throughout the supply chain. Managing and tracking these suppliers and their associated activities can be challenging for contractors. BIM enhances this process by visualizing suppliers' and construction activities, improving comprehension and oversight (Gong et al., 2019). BIM can also improve social procurement practices by integrating detailed information about materials and resources used in a project and its supply chain. It allows for better tracking of the supply chain and detailed analysis of materials, offering insights into the ethical procurement of resources. This detailed information also illustrates the ethical labor practices within the supply chain. It helps identify instances of labor exploitation, thereby enhancing the detection of modern slavery in the supply chain (Alhusban et al., 2024).

Despite these benefits, the utilization of BIM to achieve social sustainability is less developed than its application for environmental sustainability. Implementing BIM for enhancing social sustainability requires a comprehensive overhaul of the procurement system, which poses additional risks and complexities (Chong et al., 2017). Consequently, more empirical research is required to unpack the relationship between BIM and social sustainability fully.

3.3 Blockchain

A few articles in the reviewed literature discussed how blockchain can be applied to improve the sustainability performance of projects. Blockchain is a disruptive technology that stores and distributes data in real-time among stakeholders in the network (Crosby et al., 2016; Weking et al., 2020). With the advancement of Blockchain, relevant stakeholders can access transaction information in real-time. Traditionally, transaction data was stored in the centralized hub and shared with the stakeholders on demand. Blockchain technology has transformed this process by decentralizing the transaction system, allowing relevant stakeholders to access information directly and instantly (Treiblmaier, 2018; Wamba et al., 2020).

In the age of sustainability, the reviewed literature suggests that blockchain can contribute to the environmental, social, and economic aspects of sustainability within the supply chain (Yoon & Pishdad-Bozorgi, 2022; Sadeghi et al., 2024).

Environmental sustainability in the supply chain refers to the optimum management of natural resources in alignment with environmental policies (Qorri et al., 2021). Sarkis (2003) developed a strategic decision framework for green supply chain management, highlighting the dynamic relationship between businesses and the natural environment. This dynamic nature necessitates a real-time monitoring system to keep all relevant stakeholders informed.

Blockchain supports environmental sustainability in two ways: (1) through environmental emission reduction and (2) by improving resource management (Park & Li, 2021). In the first case, blockchain technology enables project professionals to track the location of materials, carbon emissions, wastewater, and toxic pollutants, allowing them to take immediate action if environmental policies are violated (Saberi et al., 2019). In the second case, blockchain can monitor raw materials' origins, helping avoid excessive extraction and overuse of natural resources and managing waste, thereby promoting environmental sustainability (Kouhizadeh et al., 2021).

Unlike environmental sustainability, the impact of blockchain on social and economic aspects of sustainability has received less attention in the reviewed literature. Social sustainability refers to the impact of projects on employees, customers, and local communities to support a healthy society (Mani et al., 2016). In the supply chain context, social sustainability involves ensuring that procurement decisions do not result in any negative consequences on human rights or labor practices (D'Eusanio et al., 2019). For example, Helo and Hao (2019) discuss a socially unsustainable supply chain in the case of "blood diamonds," highlighting the exploitation of child labor and unethical practices in diamond sourcing. In recent years, there has been growing criticism of modern slavery, which is defined as "the exploitation of a person who is deprived of individual liberty anywhere along the supply chain from raw material extraction to the final customer for service provision or production" (Gold et al., 2015, p. 5).

Blockchain technology can potentially advance social sustainability significantly, particularly by promoting ethical procurement practices. One key focus in the reviewed literature is the reduction of unethical procurement and promoting sustainable procurement, aligning with SDG 12 (Responsible Consumption and Production). Blockchain can make procurement processes more transparent and ensure ethical practices are followed (Oyedijo, 2024).

E-procurement, driven by blockchain, automates and standardizes steps within the procurement cycle, reducing administrative burdens, cutting costs, and improving efficiency (Govindan et al., 2024). Blockchain technology securely maintains records, allowing only authorized personnel to modify critical information within the blockchain-based supply chain. It logs all transactions, capturing and recording any unexpected changes to enhance transparency. If any unethical sources are introduced into the supply chain, blockchain makes it visible, enabling prompt action to address the issue (Deloitte, 2023).

Managing an ethical supply chain to achieve social sustainability can be cumbersome without digital tools like blockchain. Unethical sourcing in projects can ruin the reputation of contractors, while ethical and trustworthy subcontracting fosters a healthy business environment and builds trust (Pishdad-Bozorgi & Yoon, 2022). Blockchain can also help address the misuse of power by supply chain partners (Oyedijo et al., 2022). Therefore, blockchain can be a powerful tool to address ethical issues in the supply chain, providing project professionals an excellent level of transparency and visibility.

Another prominent application of blockchain technology is smart contracts, which are indispensable components for controlling purchasing throughout the project lifecycle value chain (Lakkakula et al., 2020). Khalfan et al. (2022) explored how smart contracts can address procurement-related issues by enabling automated operations, controlling flexibility, providing flexible monitoring, troubleshooting, and ensuring on-time tendering systems. Smart contracts also enhance transparency, allow for equipment and materials tracking, expedite inspections, streamline communication, and facilitate secure, automatic fund transfers. Smart contracts can improve project sustainability across environmental, social, and economic dimensions (Cheng et al., 2023).

Economic sustainability in projects can be enhanced through smart contracts by automating procurement transactions, which reduces exchange and transaction costs. Smart contracts have been shown to lower costs, enhance time efficiency, and improve quality and productivity. In terms of social sustainability, smart contracts can track employees' safety and satisfaction levels and foster effective collaboration among stakeholders (Cheng et al., 2023; Moosavi et al., 2021) through workforce monitoring and performance evaluation. Additionally, smart contracts contribute to environmental sustainability by tracking the consumption of green and recycled materials, managing resource usage, and monitoring pollution indicators (Cheng et al., 2023).

3.4 Cloud Computing

Cloud computing is "on-demand access of computing resources —physical or virtual, data storage, networking capabilities, application development tools, software, AI-powered analytic tools and more—over the internet with pay-per-use pricing" (Susnjara & Smalley, 2024). As demand for computing sources grows, cloud computing continues to evolve to meet these needs. This technology enables clients to purchase the required resources and pay for the actual usage (Jain et al., 2013).

Although not yet widely adopted, cloud computing holds significant potential for addressing project sustainability challenges. The reviewed articles discuss its role in enhancing sustainability, particularly in environmental and economic aspects (Afolabi et al., 2017; Kineber et al., 2022; Oke, Kineber, et al., 2023b). Project-based organizations can benefit from cloud computing by avoiding the substantial costs associated with purchasing, installing, configuring, and managing their infrastructure. Instead, they can improve resource availability, productivity, and administrative control (Alzakholi et al., 2020; Fernando et al., 2016; Kumar et al., 2010). Cloud computing allows project-based organizations to pay for cloud-based infrastructure and other computing resources as they use them. This can bring economic sustainability to project-based organizations. Oke, Kineber, et al. (2023b) note that cloud computing supports sustainable economic activities through its scalability, pay-per-use model, and accessibility. Additionally, by automating many manual tasks, cloud computing optimizes resource utilization, reduces waste, and advances economic sustainability.

Transferring data infrastructure to cloud computing can significantly contribute to environmental sustainability. Traditional large-scale data infrastructure often consumes substantial energy for cooling systems and optimizing hardware usage, resulting in high carbon emissions. To mitigate these impacts, energy-efficient strategies are essential for minimizing the environmental footprint of cloud computing. By leveraging cloud computing, project-based organizations can avoid needing individual data centers, reducing overall energy consumption and enhancing environmental sustainability. Additionally, cloud computing enables remote access to applications and data, significantly decreasing travel and commuting. Collectively, these factors make cloud computing a valuable tool for improving environmental sustainability in projects.

Based on the reviewed literature, the potential of cloud computing has not been fully explored. Future research should investigate how cloud computing can be leveraged to enhance the sustainability performance of projects across various sectors.

3.5 Enablers for Advancing Digital Technologies in Sustainability

Several key factors must be considered to successfully adopt digital technologies in projects and leverage their benefits. One critical factor is the need for innovative leadership styles or competencies among project managers (Bag et al., 2021; Lee et al., 2015; Schneider, 2018). Project managers with an innovative mindset are better equipped to manage project complexity and appreciate the importance of integrating digital technologies into sustainable projects (Al Amri et al., 2021).

Traditional leadership styles may not effectively address the challenges of digital transformation in achieving SDGs (Afzal & Tumpa, 2024; Mittal & Dhar, 2015). Project managers with the right leadership approach can navigate technological challenges and other disruptions (Schneider, 2018). Transforming to digitization requires collaboration with internal and external stakeholders, which requires novel skills and ideas (Al Amri et al., 2021). Therefore, project managers must possess open innovation skills to foster effective collaboration and drive successful digital transformation.

Shifting project delivery from traditional methods to sustainable approaches while integrating digital technologies is a complex challenge. This transition requires moving beyond a purely "technocentric" focus on technology, products, and processes to address "soft" dimensions such as policy alignment, value orientation, and vision through a systematic change management process (Lozano et al., 2016). Tabassi et al. (2016) highlighted that sustainability achievement is closely linked to project managers' behavior, knowledge, skills, and abilities. Therefore, efforts should be directed towards enhancing these aspects of project managers.

Al Amri et al. (2021) emphasize the need for new skill sets essential for embracing digital technologies and managing internal and external changes. These skills include talent management, digital receptivity, marketing orientation, complexity management, and open innovation. Among these, digital receptivity is crucial for effectively integrating digital technologies and achieving sustainability.

As digital technologies offer huge potential to improve the sustainability performance of projects, organizations should push this initiative and motivate project professionals to embrace digital technologies (Bag et al., 2021). To achieve this, stringent policies should be established to enforce the use of digital technologies to improve sustainability. These policies should include initiatives that motivate individuals at various levels—project, team, industry, and individual. A comprehensive approach to adopting digital technologies should integrate both top-down and bottom-up management models to ensure a holistic strategy for improving project sustainability performance (Tian et al., 2023). Furthermore, support from the senior management level is critical to effectively implement the policies on the project level (Bag et al., 2021).

Another success criterion for incorporating digital technologies in sustainability projects is stakeholder engagement. Stakeholders should maintain effective collaboration and communication to make informed decisions regarding environmental, social, and economic sustainability (Tian et al., 2023). Adopting technology is not only a mere change in technology but also a holistic change in work practices and processes. This necessitates relevant stakeholders to come forward and embrace the changes with open mindset (Tian et al., 2023). Waqar et al. (2023) also highlight that stakeholder participation, coordination, and a willingness to transition from traditional methods to digital transformation are essential. This complex task requires key actors' involvement across the entire value chain (Bang & Andersen, 2022). Moreover, to be effectively integrated, digital technology must be embedded throughout the entire project lifecycle.

To ensure the successful integration of digital technology, project professionals must possess sufficient knowledge and technical expertise (Longo et al., 2017). Without the necessary competencies and familiarity with digital technologies, it becomes challenging to effectively meet sustainability goals through their application (Al Amri et al., 2021). With the emergence of digital technologies, training programs for cross-field specialists in smart and sustainable initiatives should be offered to project professionals (Al Amri et al., 2021; Benešová & Tupa, 2017; Olawumi & Chan, 2022). Al Amri et al. (2021) emphasize that project managers with comprehensive training and qualifications better understand digital transformation, highlighting the importance of providing ongoing training. Ideally, training should occur independently of individual projects, but if this is not possible, it is crucial to initiate training as soon as all subcontractors and suppliers are engaged.

Lastly, previous research has shown that project management plays a significant role in facilitating the implementation of digital technologies in sustainable project delivery (Bag et al., 2021; Piyathanavong et al., 2024; Tian et al., 2023; Waqar et al.,

2023). Effective project management ensures alignment between organizational goals, the mindset of project professionals, and directives from senior management, all of which contribute to the successful adoption of digital technologies and the advancement of sustainability (Piyathanavong et al., 2024).

3.6 Challenges for Advancing Digital Technologies in Sustainability

The literature identifies several key barriers to implementing digital technologies to achieve sustainable projects. Oke et al. (2024) highlighted a range of barriers, such as organizational, management, technical, regulatory, and economic barriers. One of the most widely mentioned barriers was the need for more technical expertise among project professionals and the awareness of the importance of digital transformation (Oke et al., 2024; Olawumi & Chan, 2022; Piyathanavong et al., 2024). To overcome this challenge, cross-disciplinary training should be incorporated into the professional development of project teams. Such training should cover knowledge management, data sharing, data and information ownership, and data security and protection (Oke et al., 2024; Piyathanavong et al., 2024).

Lack of senior management and organizational support are additional prominent barriers (Oke et al., 2024). Operational shifts become challenging without financial and motivational support from organizations and senior leadership (Piyathanavong et al., 2024). Oke et al. (2024) underscored that the most critical barriers are lack of management support, hesitation to shift away from legacy software, and budget constraints. This finding is aligned with the results of Agyekum et al. (2022); Alam et al. (2019); and Iqbal et al. (2021). Government enforcement to achieve SDGs can catalyze such changes (Oke et al., 2024). Industrial behavior and attitude may also hinder the adoption of digital technologies in sustainable project delivery.

Additionally, Oke et al. (2024) identified some technical and regulatory barriers that can impede digital technology integration in sustainable projects. Technical barriers encompass interconnectivity issues, network limitations, device compatibility, feasibility, complexities of technological applications, compatibility with existing software, and system challenges. Identified regulatory barriers include challenges associated with compliance, legal obligations, contractual ambiguities, and a dearth of standards and reference architectures.

4 Conclusion and Future Recommendations

This chapter explored the landscapes of sustainability and how digital technologies enhance the sustainability performance of projects. Following a systematic literature review, existing literature was critically reviewed to identify the prominent digital technologies applied to improve the sustainability performance of projects. BIM, blockchain, and cloud computing were identified as leading digital technologies advancing projects' sustainability performance and playing key roles in improving the triple bottom line of projects. These technologies significantly contribute to real-time data collection, analysis, decision making and stakeholder engagement. Additionally, the chapter highlighted key enablers and challenges in advancing the application of digital technologies. Competencies of project professionals, technical expertise, support from senior management, an open and innovative mindset, and stakeholder engagement are critical for the successful implementation of digital technologies. However, despite these advancements, various barriers, including technical, organizational, and regulatory challenges, still need to be addressed to fully leverage the potential of digital technologies in promoting sustainable projects.

Based on the critical review, several key trends and future opportunities in the application of digital technologies for sustainability in projects have been identified:

4.1 Integration of Digital Technologies

BIM has the potential to significantly enhance its capabilities by leveraging cloud computing technologies. By integrating with cloud platforms, BIM can improve data accessibility and facilitate seamless collaboration among project stakeholders. This integration enables project professionals to access real-time data from various platforms, including IoT sensors, carbon monitoring tools, and resource allocation systems. The enhanced visibility and accessibility of the synergy between BIM and cloud computing supports more informed and timely decision-making processes. Moreover, the combination of blockchain, BIM, and cloud computing will develop a powerful platform, and their seamless integration in project settings will ensure a robust improvement in the sustainability performance of projects.

4.2 Advancements in Digital Technologies

The rapid advancement of digital technologies is creating exciting new opportunities across various fields, and sustainability and project management are no exception. Emerging technologies are continually evolving, offering enhanced capabilities and efficiencies. For example, expanding cloud computing allows more computational power to process vast amounts of data, enabling more sophisticated simulations and analytics. These advancements open new possibilities for improving project management processes, enhancing decision making, and fostering greater sustainability.

4.3 The Promise of Artificial Intelligence (AI) and Machine Learning (ML)

Although the use of AI and ML has not been prominent in the reviewed articles, the future applications of these technologies are promising for improving the sustainability performance of projects. For instance, AI algorithms may predict waste consumption patterns and adjust systems like Heating, ventilation, and air conditioning to minimize waste. Additionally, ML can detect patterns in air and water quality, analyzing data collected through sensors, satellites, and drones. ML can also forecast waste generation by analyzing historical data. Moreover, AI can suggest modifications in design to reduce waste, further enhancing sustainability performance.

4.4 Focus on Social Sustainability

The use of digital technologies in improving social sustainability is set to be a major focus in the future. Social sustainability has started gaining momentum, and digital technologies can play a crucial role. Specifically, these technologies can help eradicate modern slavery, detect unethical work practices, promote diversity, improve work and safety practices, and ensure the well-being of project team members is an area of future growth.

4.5 Wider Adoption across Industries

Digital technologies are discussed more widely in the construction, building, energy, and manufacturing sectors. To keep up with the pace of Industry 5.0, other sectors should also embrace digital technologies, leverage its advantages, and gain competitive advantages in the dynamic market conditions.

4.6 Development of Robust Frameworks

Future research can develop comprehensive and robust frameworks for implementing digital technologies to enhance the sustainability performance of projects. These frameworks need to be tailored to each technology's unique contributions and operating systems. Another promising avenue for exploration could be using generative AI (GenAI) chatbots to analyze sustainability data and suggest corrective actions. However, many challenges still need to be addressed with regard to the accuracy and reliability of GenAI, like ChatGPT.

Although this research offers a comprehensive understanding of the use of digital technologies in project sustainability, it has certain limitations. While both authors performed data screening, cognitive biases may still exist. The review was limited to peer-reviewed journal articles indexed in Scopus, excluding studies from other databases. Additionally, studies written in languages other than English were not considered. Future research may address these limitations.

References

Abdel-Tawab, M., Kineber, A. F., Chileshe, N., Abanda, H., Ali, A. H., & Almukhtar, A. (2023). Building information modelling implementation model for sustainable building projects in developing countries: A PLS-SEM approach. *Sustainability, 15*(12), 9242.

Afolabi, A., Ojelabi, R., Fagbenle, O., & Mosaku, T. (2017). The economics of cloud-based computing technologies in construction project delivery. *Technology, 8*(12), 233–242.

Afzal, F., & Tumpa, R. J. (2024). Exploring leadership styles to Foster sustainability in construction projects: A systematic literature review. *Sustainability, 16*(3), 971.

Agyekum, K., Opoku, A., Oppon, A. J., & Opoku, D.-G. J. (2022). Obstacles to green building project financing: An empirical study in Ghana. *International Journal of Construction Management, 22*(15), 2922–2930.

Akomea-Frimpong, I., Jin, X., Osei-Kyei, R., & Tumpa, R. J. (2023). A critical review of public–private partnerships in the COVID-19 pandemic: Key themes and future research agenda. *Smart and Sustainable Built Environment, 12*(4), 701–720.

Akomea-Frimpong, I., Jin, X., Osei Kyei, R., Tetteh, P. A., Tumpa, R. J., Ofori, J. N. A., & Pariafsai, F. (2024a). A review of circular economy models and success factors on public-private partnership infrastructure development. *Built Environment Project and Asset Management, 14*(1), 109–126.

Akomea-Frimpong, I., Tetteh, P. A., Ofori, J. N. A., Tumpa, R. J., Pariafsai, F., Tenakwah, E. S., Asogwa, I. E., Vanapalli, K. R., Adu-Gyamfi, G., & Kukah, A. S. (2024b). A bibliometric review of barriers to circular economy implementation in solid waste management. *Discover Environment, 2*(1), 20.

Al Amri, T., Puskas Khetani, K., & Marey-Perez, M. (2021). Towards sustainable I4. 0: Key skill areas for project managers in GCC construction industry. *Sustainability, 13*(15), 8121.

Alam, M., Zou, P. X., Stewart, R. A., Bertone, E., Sahin, O., Buntine, C., & Marshall, C. (2019). Government championed strategies to overcome the barriers to public building energy efficiency retrofit projects. *Sustainable Cities and Society, 44*, 56–69.

Alhusban, M., Elghaish, F., Hosseini, M. R., & Mayouf, M. (2024). Revamping established project procurement approaches to support BIM implementation. *Smart and Sustainable Built Environment.*

Alzakholi, O., Shukur, H., Zebari, R., Abas, S., & Sadeeq, M. (2020). Comparison among cloud technologies and cloud performance. *Journal of Applied Science and Technology Trends, 1*(1), 40–47.

Anjomshoa, E. (2024). *The application of building information modeling (BIM) system in the smartification of green and sustainable buildings*. Engineering, Construction and Architectural Management.

Babatunde, S. O., Perera, S., Ekundayo, D., & Adeleye, T. E. (2019). An investigation into BIM-based detailed cost estimating and drivers to the adoption of BIM in quantity surveying practices. *Journal of Financial Management of Property and Construction, 25*(1), 61–81.

Babatunde, S. O., Ekundayo, D., Adekunle, A. O., & Bello, W. (2020). Comparative analysis of drivers to BIM adoption among AEC firms in developing countries: A case of Nigeria. *Journal of Engineering, Design and Technology, 18*(6), 1425–1447.

Bag, S., Yadav, G., Dhamija, P., & Kataria, K. K. (2021). Key resources for industry 4.0 adoption and its effect on sustainable production and circular economy: An empirical study. *Journal of Cleaner Production, 281*, 125233.

Baier-Fuentes, H., Merigó, J. M., Amorós, J. E., & Gaviria-Marín, M. (2019). International entrepreneurship: A bibliometric overview. *International Entrepreneurship and Management Journal, 15*, 385–429.

Bakici, T., Nemeh, A., & Hazir, Ö. (2021). Big data adoption in project management: Insights from French organizations. *IEEE Transactions on Engineering Management, 70*(10), 3358–3372.

Bang, S., & Andersen, B. S. (2022). *Utilising artificial intelligence in construction site waste reduction.*

Banihashemi, S., Hosseini, M. R., Golizadeh, H., & Sankaran, S. (2017). Critical success factors (CSFs) for integration of sustainability into construction project management practices in developing countries. *International Journal of Project Management, 35*(6), 1103–1119. https://doi.org/10.1016/j.ijproman.2017.01.014

Benešová, A., & Tupa, J. (2017). Requirements for education and qualification of people in industry 4.0. *Procedia Manufacturing, 11*, 2195–2202.

BIMCommunity. (2020). *Sydney's North West Metro Project with BIM wins global ENR award.* BIMCommunity. Retrieved 25 August from https://www.bimcommunity.com/news/load/1288/sydney-s-north-west-metro-project-with-bim-wins-global-enr-award

Camodeca, R., & Almici, A. (2021). Digital transformation and convergence toward the 2030 Agenda's sustainability development goals: Evidence from Italian listed firms. *Sustainability (Switzerland), 13*(21), 11831. https://www.mdpi.com/2071-1050/13/21/11831

Cheng, J. C., Liu, H., Gan, V. J., Das, M., Tao, X., & Zhou, S. (2023). Construction cost management using blockchain and encryption. *Automation in Construction, 152*, 104841.

Chong, H.-Y., Lee, C.-Y., & Wang, X. (2017). A mixed review of the adoption of building information modelling (BIM) for sustainability. *Journal of Cleaner Production, 142*, 4114–4126.

Crosby, M., Pattanayak, P., Verma, S., & Kalyanaraman, V. (2016). Blockchain technology: Beyond bitcoin. *Applied Innovation, 2*(6–10), 71.

Cui, C., Liu, Y., Hope, A., & Wang, J. (2018). Review of studies on the public–private partnerships (PPP) for infrastructure projects. *International Journal of Project Management, 36*(5), 773–794. https://doi.org/10.1016/j.ijproman.2018.03.004

D'Eusanio, M., Zamagni, A., & Petti, L. (2019). Social sustainability and supply chain management: Methods and tools. *Journal of Cleaner Production, 235*, 178–189.

Deloitte. (2023). *Using blockchain to drive supply chain transparency.* Deloitte. Retrieved 4 September from https://www2.deloitte.com/us/en/pages/operations/articles/blockchain-supply-chain-innovation.html

Dervishaj, A., & Gudmundsson, K. (2024). From LCA to circular design: A comparative study of digital tools for the built environment. *Resources, Conservation and Recycling, 200*, 107291.

Faruk, M., Rahman, M., & Hasan, S. (2021). How digital marketing evolved over time: A bibliometric analysis on scopus database. *Heliyon, e08603*, e08603.

Fernández-Sánchez, G., & Rodríguez-López, F. (2010). A methodology to identify sustainability indicators in construction project management—Application to infrastructure projects in Spain. *Ecological Indicators, 10*(6), 1193–1201. https://doi.org/10.1016/j.ecolind.2010.04.009

Fernando, Y., Wah, W. X., & Shaharudin, M. S. (2016). Does a firm's innovation category matter in practising eco-innovation? Evidence from the lens of Malaysia companies practicing green technology. *Journal of Manufacturing Technology Management, 27*(2), 208–233.

Figueiredo, N., Abrantes, J. L., & Costa, S. (2024). Mapping the sustainable development in health tourism: A systematic literature review. *Sustainability, 16*(5), 1901.

Fonseca, S. S., Benito, P. A., & Piña Ramírez, C. (2024). Digital horizons in construction: A comprehensive system for excellence in Project Management. *Buildings, 14*(7), 2228.

Fridgeirsson, T. V., Ingason, H. T., Jonasson, H. I., & Jonsdottir, H. (2021). An authoritative study on the near future effect of artificial intelligence on project management knowledge areas. *Sustainability (Switzerland), 13*(4).

Fukawa, N., Zhang, Y., & Erevelles, S. (2021). Dynamic capability and open-source strategy in the age of digital transformation. *Journal of Open Innovation: Technology, Market, and Complexity, 7*(3), 175. https://doi.org/10.3390/joitmc7030175

George, G., Merrill, R. K., & Schillebeeckx, S. J. D. (2021). Digital sustainability and entrepreneurship: How digital innovations are helping tackle climate change and sustainable development. *Entrepreneurship Theory and Practice, 45*(5), 999–1027. https://doi.org/10.1177/1042258719899425

Ghamarimajd, Z., Ghanbaripour, A., Tumpa, R. J., Watanabe, T., Mbachu, J., & Skitmore, M. (2024). *Application of systems thinking and system dynamics in managing risks and stakeholders in construction projects: A systematic literature review.* Systems Research and Behavioral Science.

Gold, S., Trautrims, A., & Trodd, Z. (2015). Modern slavery challenges to supply chain management. *Supply Chain Management: An International Journal, 20*(5), 485–494.

Gong, P., Zeng, N., Ye, K., & König, M. (2019). An empirical study on the acceptance of 4D BIM in EPC projects in China. *Sustainability, 11*(5), 1316.

Govindan, K., Jain, P., Singh, R. K., & Mishra, R. (2024). Blockchain technology as a strategic weapon to bring procurement 4.0 truly alive: Literature review and future research agenda. *Transportation Research Part E: Logistics and Transportation Review, 181*, 103352.

Grunwald, G. (2022). Sustainability co-creation in digitalized global value chains. *Strategic Change, 31*(1), 19–29. https://doi.org/10.1002/jsc.2477

Guandalini, I. (2022). Sustainability through digital transformation: A systematic literature review for research guidance. *Journal of Business Research, 148*, 456–471. https://doi.org/10.1016/j.jbusres.2022.05.003

Helo, P., & Hao, Y. (2019). Blockchains in operations and supply chains: A model and reference implementation. *Computers & Industrial Engineering, 136*, 242–251.

Hosseini, M. R., Banihashemi, S., Rameezdeen, R., Golizadeh, H., Arashpour, M., & Ma, L. (2017). Sustainability by information and communication technology: A paradigm shift for construction projects in Iran. *Journal of Cleaner Production, 168*, 1–13.

Huemann, M., & Silvius, G. (2017). Projects to create the future: Managing projects meets sustainable development. *International Journal of Project Management, 35*(6), 1066–1070. https://doi.org/10.1016/j.ijproman.2017.04.014

Iqbal, M., Ma, J., Ahmad, N., Ullah, Z., & Ahmed, R. I. (2021). Uptake and adoption of sustainable energy technologies: Prioritizing strategies to overcome barriers in the construction industry by using an integrated AHP-TOPSIS approach. *Advanced Sustainable Systems, 5*(7), 2100026.

Jain, A., Mishra, M., Peddoju, S. K., & Jain, N. (2013). *Energy efficient computing-green cloud computing*. 2013 international conference on energy efficient technologies for sustainability,

Jayasena, N. S., Waidyasekara, K., Mallawaarachchi, H., & Peiris, S. (2021). Ensuring engagement of stakeholders in smart city projects: Case study in Sri Lanka. *Journal of Urban Planning and Development, 147*(4), 05021045.

Joshi, A. (2016). Comparison between Scopus and ISI web of science. *Journal Global Values, 7*(1), 1–11.

Khalfan, M., Azizi, N., Haass, O., Maqsood, T., & Ahmed, I. (2022). Blockchain technology: Potential applications for public sector E-procurement and project management. *Sustainability, 14*(10), 5791. https://doi.org/10.3390/su14105791

Kiani Mavi, R., Gengatharen, D., Kiani Mavi, N., Hughes, R., Campbell, A., & Yates, R. (2021). Sustainability in construction projects: A systematic literature review. *Sustainability (Switzerland), 13*(4), 1932.

Kineber, A. F., Oke, A. E., Alyanbaawi, A., Abubakar, A. S., & Hamed, M. M. (2022). Exploring the cloud computing implementation drivers for sustainable construction projects—A structural equation modeling approach. *Sustainability, 14*(22), 14789.

Kivilä, J., Martinsuo, M., & Vuorinen, L. (2017). Sustainable project management through project control in infrastructure projects. *International Journal of Project Management, 35*(6), 1167–1183.

Kouhizadeh, M., Saberi, S., & Sarkis, J. (2021). Blockchain technology and the sustainable supply chain: Theoretically exploring adoption barriers. *International Journal of Production Economics, 231*, 107831.

Kozak-Holland, M., & Procter, C. (2019). *Managing transformation projects: Tracing lessons from the industrial to the digital revolution* [Book]. *Springer International Publishing*. https://doi.org/10.1007/978-3-030-33035-4

Kukah, A. S. K., Owusu-Manu, D.-G., & Edwards, D. (2023). Critical review of emotional intelligence research studies in the construction industry. *Journal of Engineering, Design and Technology, 21*(6), 1925–1947.

Kumar, B., Cheng, J. C., & McGibbney, L. (2010). Cloud computing and its implications for construction IT. In *Computing in civil and building engineering, Proceedings of the International Conference*.

Kumar, H., & Padala, S. S. (2024). A BIM-integrated multi objective optimization model for sustainable building construction management. *Construction Innovation.* (ahead-of-print).
Lähteenmäki, I., Nätti, S., & Saraniemi, S. (2022). Digitalization-enabled evolution of customer value creation: An executive view in financial services. *Journal of Business Research, 146*, 504–517.
Lakkakula, P., Bullock, D., & Wilson, W. (2020). Blockchain technology in international commodity trading. *The Journal of private enterprise, 35*(2), 23–46.
Lee, J., Bagheri, B., & Kao, H.-A. (2015). A cyber-physical systems architecture for industry 4.0-based manufacturing systems. *Manufacturing Letters, 3*, 18–23.
Li, Y., Sun, H., Li, D., Song, J., & Ding, R. (2022). Effects of digital technology adoption on sustainability performance in construction projects: The mediating role of stakeholder collaboration. *Journal of Management in Engineering, 38*(3), 04022016.
Longo, F., Nicoletti, L., & Padovano, A. (2017). Smart operators in industry 4.0: A human-centered approach to enhance operators' capabilities and competencies within the new smart factory context. *Computers & Industrial Engineering, 113*, 144–159.
Lozano, R., Nummert, B., & Ceulemans, K. (2016). Elucidating the relationship between sustainability reporting and organisational change management for sustainability. *Journal of Cleaner Production, 125*, 168–188.
Maltese, S., Tagliabue, L. C., Cecconi, F. R., Pasini, D., Manfren, M., & Ciribini, A. L. (2017). Sustainability assessment through green BIM for environmental, social and economic efficiency. *Procedia Engineering, 180*, 520–530.
Mandičák, T., Spišáková, M., & Mésároš, P. (2024). Sustainable design and building information modeling of construction Project Management towards a circular economy. *Sustainability, 16*(11), 4376.
Mani, V., Gunasekaran, A., Papadopoulos, T., Hazen, B., & Dubey, R. (2016). Supply chain social sustainability for developing nations: Evidence from India. *Resources, Conservation and Recycling, 111*, 42–52.
Maqbool, R., Saiba, M. R., Altuwaim, A., Rashid, Y., & Ashfaq, S. (2023). The influence of industrial attitudes and behaviours in adopting sustainable construction practices. *Sustainable Development (Bradford, West Yorkshire, England), 31*(2), 893–907. https://doi.org/10.1002/sd.2428
Marcelino-Sádaba, S., González-Jaen, L. F., & Pérez-Ezcurdia, A. (2015). Using project management as a way to sustainability. From a comprehensive review to a framework definition. *Journal of Cleaner Production, 99*, 1–16.
Marnewick, C. (2016). Benefits of information system projects: The tale of two countries. *International Journal of Project Management, 34*(4), 748–760.
Meho, L. I., & Rogers, Y. (2008). Citation counting, citation ranking, and h-index of human-computer interaction researchers: A comparison of Scopus and web of science. *Journal of the American Society for Information Science and Technology, 59*(11), 1711–1726. https://doi.org/10.1002/asi.20874
Mittal, S., & Dhar, R. L. (2015). Transformational leadership and employee creativity: Mediating role of creative self-efficacy and moderating role of knowledge sharing. *Management Decision, 53*(5), 894–910.
Moehler, R., Hope, A., & Algeo, C. (2018). *Sustainable project management: Revolution or evolution? Academy of management proceedings.*
Moosavi, J., Naeni, L. M., Fathollahi-Fard, A. M., & Fiore, U. (2021). Blockchain in supply chain management: A review, bibliometric, and network analysis. *Environmental Science and Pollution Research*, 1–15.
Narbaev, T., Hazir, Ö., Khamitova, B., & Talgat, S. (2024). A machine learning study to improve the reliability of project cost estimates. *International Journal of Production Research, 62*(12), 4372–4388.
Oke, A. E., Aliu, J., Jamir Singh, P. S., Onajite, S. A., Kineber, A. F., & Samsurijan, M. S. (2023a). Application of digital technologies tools for social and sustainable construction in a developing economy. *Sustainability, 15*(23), 16378.

Oke, A. E., Aliu, J., & Onajite, S. A. (2024). Barriers to the adoption of digital technologies for sustainable construction in a developing economy. *Architectural Engineering and Design Management, 20*(3), 431–447.

Oke, A. E., Kineber, A. F., Alsolami, B., & Kingsley, C. (2023b). Adoption of cloud computing tools for sustainable construction: A structural equation modelling approach. *Journal of Facilities Management, 21*(3), 334–351.

Olawumi, T. O., & Chan, D. W. (2022). Developing project evaluation models for smart sustainable practices implementation in construction projects: A comparative study between Nigeria and Hong Kong. *Engineering, Construction and Architectural Management, 29*(3), 1522–1552.

Oyedijo, A. (2024). Relationships between disruptions and unethical procurement and supply chain practices: Insights from the covid-19 pandemic. In *The Palgrave handbook of supply chain management* (pp. 1009–1034). Springer.

Oyedijo, A., Francois Koukpaki, A. S., Kusi-Sarpong, S., Alfarsi, F., & Yang, Y. (2022). Restraining forces and drivers of supply chain collaboration: Evidence from an emerging market. *Supply Chain Management: An International Journal, 27*(3), 409–430.

Paolini, A., Kollmannsberger, S., & Rank, E. (2019). Additive manufacturing in construction: A review on processes, applications, and digital planning methods. *Additive Manufacturing, 30*, 100894. https://doi.org/10.1016/j.addma.2019.100894

Park, A., & Li, H. (2021). The effect of blockchain technology on supply chain sustainability performances. *Sustainability, 13*(4), 1726.

Pishdad-Bozorgi, P., & Yoon, J. H. (2022). Transformational approach to subcontractor selection using blockchain-enabled smart contract as trust-enhancing technology. *Automation in Construction, 142*, 104538.

Piyathanavong, V., Huynh, V.-N., Karnjana, J., & Olapiriyakul, S. (2024). Role of project management on sustainable supply chain development through industry 4.0 technologies and circular economy during the COVID-19 pandemic: A multiple case study of Thai metals industry. *Operations Management Research, 17*(1), 13–37.

Qorri, A., Gashi, S., & Kraslawski, A. (2021). Performance outcomes of supply chain practices for sustainable development: A meta-analysis of moderators. *Sustainable Development, 29*(1), 194–216.

Rachinger, M., Rauter, R., Müller, C., Vorraber, W., & Schirgi, E. (2018). Digitalization and its influence on business model innovation. *Journal of Manufacturing Technology Management, 30*(8), 1143–1160.

Robertsone, G., & Lapiņa, I. (2023). Digital transformation as a catalyst for sustainability and open innovation. *Journal of Open Innovation: Technology, Market, and Complexity, 9*(1), 100017. https://doi.org/10.1016/j.joitmc.2023.100017

Saberi, S., Kouhizadeh, M., Sarkis, J., & Shen, L. (2019). Blockchain technology and its relationships to sustainable supply chain management. *International Journal of Production Research, 57*(7), 2117–2135.

Sabini, L., Muzio, D., & Alderman, N. (2019). 25 years of 'sustainable projects'. What we know and what the literature says. *International Journal of Project Management, 37*(6), 820–838.

Sadeghi, M., Mahmoudi, A., Deng, X., & Moslemi Naeni, L. (2024). Enterprise blockchain solutions for vibrant construction ecosystem: Grey Ordinal Priority Approach. *Grey Systems: Theory and Application, 14*(1), 115–143.

Sánchez, M. A. (2015). Integrating sustainability issues into project management. *Journal of Cleaner Production, 96*, 319–330.

Sankaran, S., Müller, R., & Drouin, N. (2020). Creating a 'sustainability sublime' to enable megaprojects to meet the United Nations sustainable development goals. *Systems Research and Behavioral Science, 37*(5), 813–826. https://doi.org/10.1002/sres.2744

Sarkis, J. (2003). A strategic decision framework for green supply chain management. *Journal of Cleaner Production, 11*(4), 397–409.

Schipper, R., & Silvius, G. (2017). The sustainable project management canvas. *The Journal of Modern Project Management, 4*(3).

Schneider, P. (2018). Managerial challenges of industry 4.0: An empirically backed research agenda for a nascent field. *Review of Managerial Science, 12*(3), 803–848.

Silvius, A., & Schipper, R. P. (2014). Sustainability in project management: A literature review and impact analysis. *Social business, 4*(1), 63–96.

Silvius, A. G., & Schipper, R. (2010). A maturity model for integrating sustainability in projects and project management. In *24th world congress of the international project management association (IPMA)*.

Silvius, G., & Huemann, M. (2024). Introduction: Shaping society through sustainable project management. In *Research handbook on sustainable Project Management* (pp. 1–10). Edward Elgar Publishing.

Simion, C.-P., Popa, S.-C., & Albu, C. (2018). *Project management 4.0–project management in the digital era*. Proceedings of 12th International Conference on Project Management

Stanitsas, M., Kirytopoulos, K., & Leopoulos, V. (2021). Integrating sustainability indicators into project management: The case of construction industry. *Journal of Cleaner Production, 279*, 123774.

Susnjara, S., & Smalley, I. (2024). *What is cloud computing?* IBM. Retrieved 30 August from https://www.ibm.com/topics/cloud-computing

Swart, K., Bond-Barnard, T., & Chugh, R. (2022). Challenges and critical success factors of digital communication, collaboration and knowledge sharing in project management virtual teams: A review. *International Journal of Information Systems and Project Management, 10*(4), 84–103.

Tabassi, A. A., Argyropoulou, M., Roufechaei, K. M., & Argyropoulou, R. (2016). Leadership behavior of project managers in sustainable construction projects. *Procedia Computer Science, 100*, 724–730. https://doi.org/10.1016/j.procs.2016.09.217

Tabejamaat, S., Ahmadi, H., & Barmayehvar, B. (2024). Boosting large-scale construction project risk management: Application of the impact of building information modeling, knowledge management, and sustainable practices for optimal productivity. *Energy Science & Engineering, 12*(5), 2284–2296.

Tian, L., Wright, A., Painter, B., & Pazhoohesh, M. (2023). Factors influencing BIM use in green building construction project management in the UK and China. *Building Research & Information, 51*(7), 853–870.

Toljaga-Nikolić, D., Todorović, M., Dobrota, M., Obradović, T., & Obradović, V. (2020). Project management and sustainability: Playing trick or treat with the planet. *Sustainability (Switzerland), 12*(20), 8619. https://www.mdpi.com/2071-1050/12/20/8619

Treiblmaier, H. (2018). The impact of the blockchain on the supply chain: A theory-based research framework and a call for action. *Supply Chain Management: An International Journal, 23*(6), 545–559.

Tumpa, R. J., Ahmad, T., Naeni, L. M., & Kujala, J. (2024). Computer-based games in project management education: A review. *Project Leadership and Society, 100130*, 100130.

Wamba, S. F., Queiroz, M. M., & Trinchera, L. (2020). Dynamics between blockchain adoption determinants and supply chain performance: An empirical investigation. *International Journal of Production Economics, 229*, 107791.

Wang, W. (2022). Automatic system design of assembly building components for sustainable building projects based on BIM technology. *Mathematical Problems in Engineering, 2022*(1), 4902862–4902811.

Waqar, A., Othman, I., Hayat, S., Radu, D., Khan, M. B., Galatanu, T. F., Almujibah, H. R., Hadzima-Nyarko, M., & Benjeddou, O. (2023). Building information modeling—Empowering construction projects with end-to-end life cycle management. *Buildings, 13*(8), 2041.

Weking, J., Mandalenakis, M., Hein, A., Hermes, S., Böhm, M., & Krcmar, H. (2020). The impact of blockchain technology on business models–a taxonomy and archetypal patterns. *Electronic Markets, 30*, 285–305.

White, M. D., & Marsh, E. E. (2006). Content analysis: A flexible methodology. *Library Trends, 55*(1), 22–45.

Wu, T. (2022). Digital project management: Rapid changes define new working environments. *Journal of Business Strategy, 43*(5), 323–331.

Yarnold, J., Banihashemi, S., Lemckert, C., & Golizadeh, H. (2023). Building and construction quality: Systematic literature review, thematic and gap analysis. *International Journal of Building Pathology and Adaptation, 41*(5), 942–964.

Yoon, J. H., & Pishdad-Bozorgi, P. (2022). State-of-the-art review of blockchain-enabled construction supply chain. *Journal of Construction Engineering and Management, 148*(2), 03121008.

Zhang, L., Mohandes, S. R., Tong, Y., Cheung, C., Banihashemi, S., & Shan, M. (2023). Sustainability and digital transformation within the project management area: A science mapping approach. *Buildings, 13*(5), 1355.

Exploring the Agile Project Management in the Software as a Service Sector

Lauriane Saint-Denis

Abstract

Software as a Service startup operating in the software development business has broadly adopted Agile frameworks to maintain a competitive advantage. This adoption supports continuous innovation and customer-centric development. This chapter intends to explain the multifaceted benefits of Agile methodology in driving business growth. We uncover the great value of automation, allowing a stream of tasks to be handled across teams and leading to scalability. It investigates how customer growth and retention are linked to product improvement. This chapter serves as a guide for project managers who plan to apply Agile methodologies in the business-to-business landscape.

1 Introduction

Software as a service (SaaS) companies within the ecosystem of specialized software are paving the way with emerging solutions to answer current challenges driven by the growth of niche markets. According to market forecasts, SaaS companies reached a market size of nearly USD 297 billion in 2023 and are expected to reach USD 829 billion in 2031 (Skyquest, 2024).

Niche start-ups span into sectors where precision and creativity are needed to gain the attention and trust needed to exist by the side of generalists. In their definition and evolution, they will face unique challenges, from the demand for specialized functionalities to the constant adaptation to trends. They often need help with the dilemma of innovating rapidly with limited resources. This resource shortage often blocks the knowledge transfer from similar structures to help them overcome

L. Saint-Denis (✉)
Barcelona, Spain

Ö. Hazır, M. E. Bruni (eds.), *Tomorrow's Data Empowered Project Management*, Future of Business and Finance, https://doi.org/10.1007/978-3-031-84017-3_9

common errors. Solving the issues adds pressure to deliver innovative solutions while managing tight budgets. The detailed examination of data scattered around distinct teams and platforms is complex, and the inefficiency from the lack of analysis impacts productivity.

Agile Project Management (APM) is a flexible, iterative approach rooted in the Agile Manifesto (2001). It emphasizes collaboration of teams, taking feedback from clients continuously, and re-engineering the "rigid" processes towards higher adaptability. While Agile refers to a broad management framework, some specific methodologies have been commonly used within this framework. They support technical development and ensure product development aligns with clients' demands.

While much literature on Agile in software development has existed since 2015, a study that investigates its application in business-to-business (B2B) SaaS startups to improve operational efficiency, customer engagement, and scalability is needed. We will examine APM as a framework and discuss the implications of Agile adoption in SaaS startups. We present Scrum and Kanban as specific methodologies. The focus will be on how to improve operational efficiency and customer relationship management. This part will highlight data enrichment's role in boosting sales and retaining customers by using tailored communication strategies. It then explores the practical use of Agile principles in product development. Finally, it studies the dynamics of cross-functional teams and collaboration and its benefits.

Next, we elaborate on the critical components of APM implementation for B2B SaaS startups.

2 The Use of Automation to Enhance the Operations

2.1 Centralization of Knowledge Management

Data centralization is essential for implementing knowledge management when decisions are based on the latest available information.

In early-stage startups, data enrichment often begins with manual processes, where team members individually enrich client data. For startups just beginning to master their operations and manage customer interactions, manual input in tools such as Kanban or Gantt charts on distinct platforms is often encountered. However, automation technologies advance, real-time situational adaptation becomes viable. The automation of data collection and analysis reduces the reliance on human intuition and enhances data-driven decision-making. As SaaS companies grow, fully automated data centralization is needed to handle larger volumes of data efficiently.

If manual centralization is a practical starting point, the goal is to transition incrementally to automated data management systems with a constant flow of qualified data. This will lead to faster, more informed decision-making. Large SaaS companies that have implemented robust integration tools demonstrate the potential of these systems to dominate niche markets and optimize knowledge management (Ekambaram et al., 2018). In the future, more SaaS companies will likely adopt fully automated systems to streamline operational tasks through real-time insights (Schrage, 2021).

Researchers like Crane and Self (2014) propose that big data could eventually complement or replace traditional knowledge management practices, but the transition must still be strategically managed. Consequently, organizations turn to extensive data-driven systems to scale, as they offer sophisticated algorithms to calculate real-time analysis.

The data come from different sources and centralized in one place. New data collected through customer service, marketing campaigns, or product usage, enriches the knowledge base. As the contact points are added, teams can find the client's personas and have a more detailed and accurate customer profile. This enables reviewing and adjusting to approach a persona with the right message. The meetings can be documented to improve the knowledge of future clients' needs continuously, and the expression of needs can be enriched. The information regarding its digital architecture is a precious base for the value proposition to be better communicated by the Sales team.

A primary business development goal is to use different channels to understand each prospect. Therefore, it is first necessary to identify if the prospect belongs to only one or more market verticals. Business developers use segmented data to craft personalized outreach campaigns, ensuring that each communication resonates with the challenges and goals of the target market. This approach enhances engagement and improves conversion rates, as prospective clients are more likely to respond to messages that correspond to their needs.

Lead segment types are defined based on criteria such as type of activities or regional presence. The providers of similar or complementary solutions already chosen by the potential client can also be considered. We can also explore the use of the actual platform, its frequency, and the most used features. In that way, the clients can be segmented from sporadic and casual users to frequent and power users. In both cases, the segments identified can be reached with crafted communications, explicitly detailing how the software or its advanced functionalities concretely answer an identified obstacle or room for optimization. Furthermore, customer relation management (CRM) systems facilitate the automation of these communication processes and automate follow-up tasks.

For the existing clients, the product's efficiency and the project's unfolding matter. The reactivity to client inquiries throughout the project can be derived from the onboarding process to the annual report of key performance indicators (KPIs). Client satisfaction is based on the ability to reach the goals set during the kickoff meeting and is found to be the amount of time and money saved, as well as progress control and justification (Schnitzer et al., 2020).

2.2 The Transition from Manual to Automated Data Entry

Automation across marketing, sales, and customer support teams saves time and reduces repetitive tasks. The optimization of workflows leads to:

- Quality improvement through data enrichment
- Sales increase via multi-channel engagement and tailored communication
- Customer support with timely response
- Client retention with continuous feedback

One goal of the automation toolset is to scale operations and increase the volume of tasks. If the workflows are well-defined, hundreds and thousands of prospective clients can receive personalized information in a streamlined manner, and business developers can quickly react to proof of interest. Resources are wisely managed in this way, and the scale of operations can grow efficiently without requiring proportional hires.

In their daily interactions with existing clients, customer support teams often spend more time than the duration agreed on in the existing contract. The vital need for customer satisfaction, which makes the company believe that a good reputation is necessary for growth, drives the team to spend more time on interactions. It is, however, possible to personalize and inflate customer engagement through personalized scenarios designed with structured processes to ensure that the support will have the maximum amount of knowledge when answering a client.

While useful, business development automation is a separate layer that assists mainly in scaling and maintaining customer engagement for client-facing teams. Agile frameworks also benefit from automation tools, which we will explore further in development.

3 Agile Method Applied to Product Development

3.1 Product Diversification

When using APM, software developers need time in two key areas: innovation and maintenance, or "run." The time dedicated to innovation includes developing advanced features or adapting the tool for niche markets. Maintenance of the existing architecture can optimize the workflow. This time allocation directly impacts on how the product will be positioned within the market by time.

In the SaaS industry, users' needs and technological capabilities to answer them constantly evolve (Denning, 2018). Since the team opts for a tailored and iterative product development approach, the company gains a competitive advantage and achieves a higher client retention. In practice, Scrum teams run sprints, which can last from 1 to 4 weeks, with a careful split of time on the run or innovation.

Figure 1 illustrates the cyclical flow from Sprint Planning, Development, Testing, Review, and Retrospective. Each sprint returns to the planning phase, supporting continuous improvement and iteration. The team knows the workload, and developers attend stand-up meetings throughout the week and reassess upcoming developments (Rigby et al., 2016). Team members are updated with automated notifications on the status of tasks.

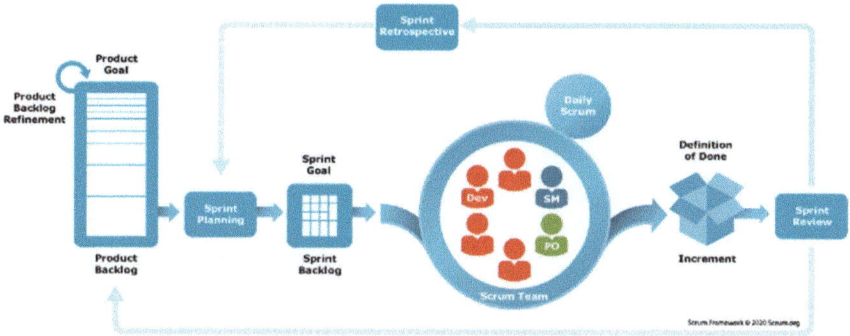

Fig. 1 Scrum framework (Schwaber & Sutherland, 2017)

Platforms like Jenkins or CircleCI facilitate product development since they automatically test and deploy new code and reduce the risk of errors. Teams can detect bugs earlier and fix them faster.

Jira, a widely adopted tool, is an integrated platform for sprint planning and task prioritization. By setting up workflows in Jira, the development teams can automate repetitive processes such as creating sprint backlogs, assigning tasks. Human error and the need for manual intervention can be minimized. Spotify uses Jira's automation capabilities to streamline sprint planning, enabling their development teams to handle multiple features simultaneously without losing track of high-priority tasks.

Successful Agile teams integrate product roadmaps that serve as living documents to match the platform's responsiveness in the development phase and the company's strategy. These roadmaps facilitate a detailed analysis of the product's trajectory. (Kapitsaki & Christou, 2015). Another tool, the sprint burndown chart, illustrated in Fig. 2, represents each task's completion level and a real-time view of the sprint progress.

In the case of software development for a niche market, creating different versions that incorporate terminology known and used daily by the target users will build a better product-market fit (Anderson & Narus, 2011). From the demo meeting and training, once teams operate the tool independently, the vocabulary adaptation will resonate with users in those sectors and increase the retention rate. For instance, a project management tool for a sports federation might display terms like "game" and "sponsorship." On the other hand, a version designed for cultural institutions would prioritize "exhibition" and "donor relation," aligning more closely with user expectations. SaaS follows small, frequent iterations and feature flagging, to allow specific deployment to users or regions for testing without affecting the entire user base. Innovation can be constantly applied in feature expansion, customization, and integration per vertical. At the same time, these updates are rolled out and tested in real-world conditions, lowering the chances of customer disruptions.

Customer success highly depends on discovering the features that have the highest impact on the perceived value of the software while reducing churn (He & Wong, 2004).

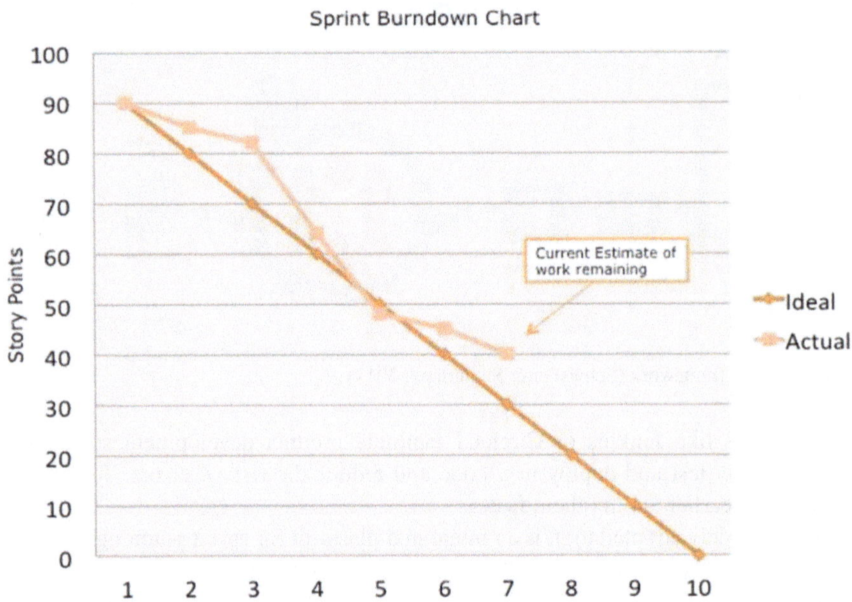

Fig. 2 Sprint Burndown Chart (Schwaber & Sutherland, 2017)

3.2 Product Improvement

Unlike the innovation phase, which focuses on new features and growth strategies, the run phase is dedicated to refining the existing product. Analyzing clients' past and daily data provides insights into their performance and identifies which strategies are working, and which need adjustment (Denning, 2016).

Agile frameworks allow collecting data whenever a new software element is developed. The collaboration between beta testers and the team is crucial as they need to understand that they will be the first to see a glimpse of a new feature, which will be developed with them and thanks to them (Chen & Nath, 2018). Conditions in niche markets can be unfavorable to this application as clients might find this role too abstract and time-consuming if based on an early-stage prototype. When suitable conditions are met, users can engage more in the development. New developments must comply with regulations, and the data security layer implies major reviews to be continuously integrated into the workflow.

Research shows that companies prioritizing feedback loops in their development process outperform competitors in terms of customer retention and satisfaction (He & Wong, 2004). The product team ought to analyse feedback to guide iterative improvements with changes ranging from minor usability improvements to substantial feature adjustments. The continuous improvement model, often associated with frameworks such as Kaizen or Lean, is central to Agile's run phase and reduces the risk of significant disruptions (Anderson & Narus, 2011).

Agile facilitates a value-driven lean approach, where teams focus on delivering the most valuable features first, so that the customer receives immediate benefits. This aligns well with the subscription-based revenue model of SaaS businesses, where continuous engagement and satisfaction are essential for retention.

3.3 Data Visualization Tools and Metrics to Follow

3.3.1 Product Development

While Scrum is familiar among SaaS, teams can also use the Kanban practice for aspects that need to visualize work progress and limit its amount. Managing tasks is dynamic, responding quickly to changing priorities, and visual perception prevents tasks from remaining in the same stage for too long. This visual breaks down tasks into the stages To Do, In Progress, and Done, preventing bottlenecks with a smooth transition between tasks (Fig. 3).

This method is advantageous for continuous product delivery where development, testing, and deployment cycles overlap (Masood & Farooq, 2017). Agile encourages regular retrospectives, which involve reviewing the incidents or vulnerabilities and implementing preventive measures in the future sprints.

3.3.2 Operations

Data visualization tools such as dashboards, heat maps, and Gantt charts help to monitor processes and find out the inefficiencies quickly. Teams can monitor KPIs such as lead conversion rates, customer retention, or sales activity without navigating through reports. This instantaneous access to insights provides flexibility and

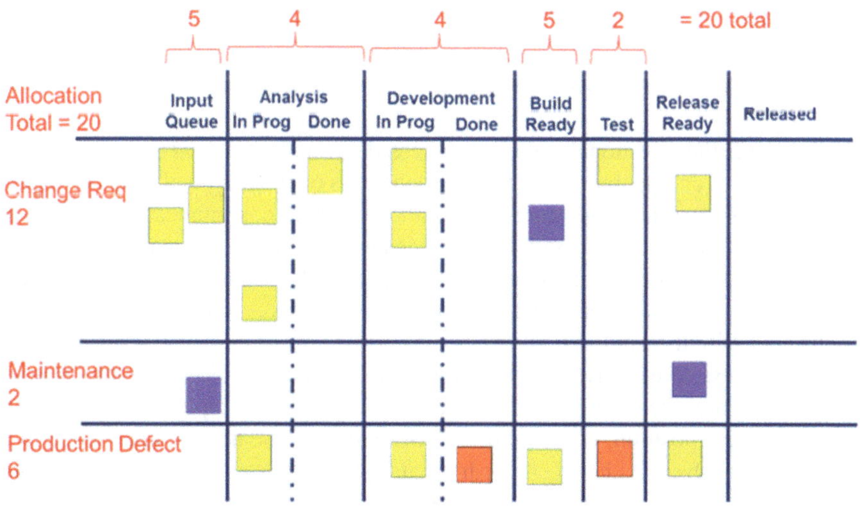

Fig. 3 Example of a Kanban board (Anderson & Narus, 2011)

allows for the adjustment of processes when blocks or opportunities are identified (Serrador & Pinto, 2015).

CRM systems provide sales and customer data using bar graphs or pie charts to track the meetings with prospects or monitor sales teams' performance over time. These reports give a granular view of sales pipelines, but also crucial metrics such as customer acquisition costs (CAC), churn rates, and customer lifetime value (CLV) to refine strategies and improve profitability (Hneif & Ow, 2009).

For customer success teams, visual dashboards track satisfaction indicators, and the number of support tickets resolved within a specific timeframe. When the customers at risk of churning are pinpointed, prompt proactive engagement strategies can be engaged (Masood & Farooq, 2017). For marketing teams, tracking campaign performance metrics such as email open rates, click-through rates (CTR), and lead source attribution through visual tools allows them to optimize their outreach efforts. For example, trend analysis helps to identify the emerging opportunities or detect potential threats, allowing the business to react effectively (Sinha, 2019).

Spending time on benchmarking to document growth trajectories and potential disruptions focuses efforts on maximum impact. Expertise comes with a heavy absorption of knowledge, called knowledge-as-data, representing data study in connection with knowledge management. We are used to perceiving how humans create logical meaning in what we think, say, and do; this is called knowledge-as-meaning. We are also familiar with learning through relatively rational, intuitive, impulsive, and creative activities, known as knowledge-as-practice. Practice and meaning are described as linear learning processes, where knowledge-as-data is lively. (Ekambaram et al., 2018) Apart from being present in the minds of knowers, the study of knowledge-as-data will reflect new organizational routines, processes, practices, and norms. Data visualization enables the speed and accuracy of decisions, making it a cornerstone for any organization practicing Agile development (Kapitsaki & Christou, 2015).

4 Cross-Functional Teams and Collaboration

Breaking up the traditional approach where development, marketing, sales, customer support, and operations managers each focus on their defined scope of supervision, agile practices opt for collaboration with a communicative approach. Communication platforms and Project Management tools let teams pool their expertise and let other members visualize progress. They can use a dedicated channel to discuss, analyze the progress, and align their tasks with the project goals. (Schwaber & Sutherland, 2017).

The success of effective collaboration relies on a clear role definition. Startup departments are often represented by one person who has multiple functions. When creating a new position, tasks are delegated, and so is the flow of knowledge to a certain point. Overlaps between departments can be the source of assistance from one team member to another and result in tackling challenges from multiple angles.

Even though cross-functional teams thrive on diversity of skills, defining roles in a flexible environment encourages a stronger sense of ownership and accountability.

Today, online communication platforms offer to collaborate across geographically dispersed offices, even asynchronously. While teams can work autonomously, the Project Management tool is enriched by sharing data. Quick decision-making is fostered by contributing all employees' expertise without necessary hierarchical approval. Agile teams often see leadership as decentralized, meaning that each employee must rely on trust and shared responsibility rather than hierarchical direction, thus reducing development cycle times as there are fewer department handoffs. Frequent face-to-face meetings are the most effective way to align team members, identify future issues early, and reduce the error risks due to the misunderstandings (Rigby et al., 2016).

The value of collaboration depends on everyone's contribution and ability to communicate openly, whether through writing a direct message or speaking in group video calls. It is beyond doubt that the company culture must be a culture of trust to foster empowerment (Denning, 2016). Valuing each team member can encourage them to share ideas and feedback. Agile leaders should act as facilitators, enabling teams to get involved in decision making. This involvement enhances performance and job satisfaction (Rigby et al., 2016). They need to manage conflicts because of the mismatching of the priorities, which differ from one team to another.

5 Conclusions

Adopting Agile methodologies in the B2B SaaS sector can present several challenges. One of the most common barriers to its adoption is resistance to change, especially within teams accustomed to traditional project management methods like Waterfall. Employees may need help to adjust to Agile's iterative nature (Masood & Farooq, 2017). Using hybrid approaches can also work to adapt more quickly and effectively.

Another significant challenge is scaling the agile team in large organizations. While small, cross-functional teams can effectively use Agile practices, scaling these principles across departments or multiple teams can create communication gaps and coordination issues (Sinha, 2019).

Encouraging executive buy-in is critical for adopting Agile as a development method and a company-wide managerial approach. Agile coaches and Scrum masters play a crucial role in facilitating the adoption process by helping teams understand why each method is applied to defined parts of the project.

This chapter has highlighted the critical role that Agile Project Management practices play in the SaaS industry. By centralizing data and continuously seeking areas for improvement, these companies can maintain a competitive edge in a fast-paced market. SaaS startups face unique challenges that are answered by combining Agile frameworks and automation. Teams will apply the iterative methodology to build a long-term vision while retaining the flexibility to adapt, ensuring that both short term objectives and business goals are met. By embracing Agile, startups improve their development cycles and foster a culture of collaboration and continuous learning, essential for long-term success in the B2B SaaS sector.

The recommendation for young startups aiming for Agile implementation is to start small and then scale with automation. First, introducing Agile practices in small teams allows for an adjustment period to the cycles and mindset. Once teams are familiar with the framework, they implement automation tools to handle repetitive tasks, such as sprint planning, testing, and deployment.

Second, they support adapting the framework to fit the specific challenges faced by the company always and emphasizing the collaboration. Then, implement tools that automate the collection and analysis of customer feedback and use this data to develop new features or propose design improvements. Third, new features can be deployed incrementally to selected customer groups before being broadly rolled out. This helps reduce risks and ensures that updates are tested in real-world conditions.

References

Anderson, J. C., & Narus, J. A. (2011). *Business market management: Understanding, creating, and delivering value*. Pearson.

Chen, L., & Nath, R. (2018). Automation of sales processes in SaaS businesses: Opportunities and challenges. *Journal of Business Research, 95*, 288–295.

Crane, L., & Self, R. J. (2014). Big data analytics: A threat or an opportunity for knowledge management. In L. Uden et al. (Eds.), *KMO 2014, LNBIP 185* (pp. 1–10). Springer International Publishing Switzerland.

Denning, S. (2016). Agile: It's time to put it to use. *Forbes*.

Denning, S. (2018). Succeeding in an increasingly agile world. *Strategy and Leadership, 46*(3), 3–9.

Ekambaram, A., Sørensen, A. Ø., Bull-Berg, H., & Olsson, N. O. (2018). The role of big data and knowledge management in improving projects and project-based organizations. *Procedia Computer Science, 138*, 851–858.

Fowler, M., & Highsmith, J. (2001). The agile manifesto. *Software Development Magazine*.

He, Z. L., & Wong, P. K. (2004). Exploration vs. exploitation: An empirical test of the ambidexterity hypothesis. *Organization Science, 15*(4), 481–494.

Hneif, M., & Ow, S. H. (2009). Review of agile methodologies in software development. *International Journal of Research and Review in Applied Sciences*.

Kapitsaki, G. M., & Christou, M. (2015). Learning from the current status of agile adoption. In *Springer, ENASE 2014 conference proceedings*.

Masood, Z. A., & Farooq, S. (2017). The benefits and key challenges of agile project management. *International Research Journal of Management Science*.

Rigby, D. K., Sutherland, J., & Takeuchi, H. (2016). Embracing agile: How to master the process that's transforming management. *Harvard Business Review*, 41–50.

Schnitzer, M., Kronberger, K., Bazzanella, F., & Wenger, S. (2020). Analyzing project management methods in organizing sports events. *SAGE Open, 10*(4).

Schrage, M. (2021, August 31). *How the big data explosion has changed decision making*. Harvard Business Review.

Schwaber, K., & Sutherland, J. (2017). *The scrum guide*.

Serrador, P., & Pinto, J. K. (2015). Does agile work? A quantitative analysis of agile project success. *International Journal of Project Management., 33*, 1040–1051.

Sinha, S. (2019). Exploratory study on the influence of agile on project management. *International Journal of Computer Science & Engineering*.

Software As A Service (SaaS) Market Size, Share, Growth Analysis, By Component (Software, Services), By Deployment Mode (Private Cloud, Hybrid Cloud), By Application (CRM, ERP), By Enterprise-Size (Small & Medium Enterprises, Large Enterprises), By Region–Industry Forecast 2024-2031, *Skyquest*. https://www.skyquestt.com/report/saas-market

Harmony of Discord: The Paradoxes of Artificial Intelligence and Innovative Teams

Seyda Zeki Deligonul

Abstract

This chapter delves into the paradoxes within innovative project teams, highlighting the interplay between technology and practice and the inherent tensions in AI implementations. We conceptualize these paradoxes as polar ends on a continuum, identifying critical tension nodes and their characteristics. We reveal the theoretical foundations and implications for technological adoption and integration. Looking ahead, we consolidate these paradoxes into distinct clusters to investigate the underlying patterns in the transformative digital landscape. These clusters offer a structured framework for understanding technological complexity. They identify core issues, anticipating future dilemmas that organizations must navigate.

1 Introduction

This chapter explores the nexus of tensions that emerge from the fusion and frictions of technological advances. Our focus remains on artificial intelligence (AI). The study instigates paradoxes in the context of innovative project teams. It reflects the interplay between technology and practice, embodying the tensions and conflicts inherent in AI implementations. We conceptualize these paradoxes as polar ends within a continuum. In that analysis, critical tension-nodes surface and characteristics of their polarity emerge. We reveal their theoretical underpinnings and implications for technological adoption and integration. Next, we look forward to the future. By consolidating these paradoxes into distinct clusters, we probe the underlying patterns of tension that trouble the transformative digital landscape.

S. Z. Deligonul (✉)
St. John Fisher University, Rochester, USA

Ö. Hazır, M. E. Bruni (eds.), *Tomorrow's Data Empowered Project Management*, Future of Business and Finance, https://doi.org/10.1007/978-3-031-84017-3_10

These clusters provide a structured framework for understanding technological complexity and uncovering the core issues by highlighting future tensions. Also, these are harbingers of the future dilemmas that organizations must navigate. With a nuanced perspective of this unique approach, we put a new lens on technology adoption in the digital age.

We explore the topic in the context of innovative project teams. To integrate competing task demands, project teams need to reconcile inconsistent perspectives. By adopting opposing mental templates, they recognize and embrace the simultaneous existence of contradictory ideas. The opposition in those, we argue, makes a team run rife with paradoxes. Below, we present specific reasons for this condition in collective interactions. Our list includes factors such as the team's temporary nature and the role of weak-ties by Granovetter (Granovetter, 1973; Granovetter, 1983). Also, we propose the relevance of the richness in role-sets, cognitive diversity, and exposure to competing demands (Miron-Spektor et al., 2022). Finally, the network features, we argue, contribute to the discussion owing to the structure of relational voids, bridges, and the process of facilitating brokerage across structural holes (Burt, 1976). All those we discuss below suggest that the fluid and dynamic nature of project teams and their structure create a unique environment conducive to fostering paradoxical viewpoints.

Life embodies a confluence of opposing complexities. In that, technology fundamentally alters the social fabric, transforms production mechanisms, and reshapes societal roles. Such entanglement, the task of the project teams, is about navigating impasses. As they do, they play a dual role. First, they actively contribute to creating paradoxes. They do so because they recognize the inherent value in embracing contradictory positions. Second, project teams not merely create paradoxes but also become their pivotal consumers of paradoxes. By embracing opposing ideas, they navigate the complexities of the technology landscape with deeper insight, agile strategies, compatible structures (Fraser et al., 2021), and more effective actions (Poole & van de Ven, 1989). Hence, this chapter focuses on the technology-induced tensions and paradoxes from the lens of reactionary instrumentalism and technological determinism.

As a transformative force, artificial intelligence draws us between two extreme perspectives: technological determinism and reactionary instrumentalism. Technological determinism portrays AI as a driver of societal change, autonomously steering society down a path with little room for human agency or interference. Conversely, instrumentalism regards AI as a neutral tool and downplays its transformative power. It highlights human agency and intentionality in shaping AI's role in advancing society. Given these two philosophical extremes, our view presents technology as a force that simultaneously constrains and enables creativity. Hence, innovative teams may find themselves in a Sisyphean cycle, where pursuing technological innovation becomes both a driver and a barrier to creativity. Technologies that were once enabling can become constraining, leading to tension between the human agency and the limitations imposed by existing technological frameworks. This view warns us of a potential loss of control, urging us to be mindful of the unintended consequences of technological advancement. Meanwhile, it encourages a proactive stance, advocating for technology's deliberate and ethical use to serve human values and goals.

2 Explicating the Concept of Paradox

A paradox is a group of conditions that lead to a contradiction or defy intuition. In their resolution, an apparent lack of consistency prompts unity, spurring the need for sense-making. Hence, engaging with a paradox catalyzes a process of reexamining and responding to the inconsistencies. Project teams more than often encounter paradoxical frameworks and need to find a cohesive approach to integrate practices that are logically discord with one another (Lampel et al., 2000). Their polarity reveals the coexistence of opposing yet interdependent demands, creating tensions. Such tensions manifest as impasses to be navigated for organizations and group activities such as in project teams.

The above is the definition we apply in our study. In some other studies, a paradox implies a two-sided statement that is not contestable separately but seems inconsistent when conjoined (Berti et al., 2022). Each part in it appears logical but defies compatibility with the other parts (Smith et al., 2017). In a strict sense, paradox differs from dilemmas, contradictions, and dualities (Lewis, 2000). Such concepts share similarities but differ in their nuances. For instance, a dilemma involves a choice between alternatives, often with unfavorable outcomes. On the other hand, a contradiction embodies logical inconsistencies without the innate harmony or potential for the resolution that a paradox suggests. Finally, a duality acknowledges the presence of two opposing forces. However, it often implies a mutual dependence instead of the tension inherent in paradoxes.

In our discussion, the breeding grounds for paradoxes are temporary work groups assembled for innovative endeavors. These groups act as open exchanges where conflicting ideas are debated with latitude to allow inconsistencies. It is through these inconsistencies that creative tensions arise and give rise to unconventional ideas and paradoxical perspectives. Examples of such teams abound in the literature. The production of theatre plays (Goodman and Goodman, 1976; Eikhof & Haunschild, 2007; Uzzi & Spiro, 2005), video games (Cohendet & Simon, 2007; Guérin et al., 2006; Cadin et al., 2006), music (Lorenzen & Frederiksen, 2005a), the entertainment industry (Lorenzen & Frederiksen, 2005b), advertising campaigns or software (Grabher, 2004) epitomize the prototypical varieties of temporary communities for innovative projects.

3 Why Innovative Project Teams Breed Paradoxical Frames

Numerous factors play a role in nurturing paradoxical viewpoints in the context of innovative teams. Those factors motivate individuals as the team embraces diverse and contradictory perspectives and achieves a more thorough, rich, and accurate understanding of complex issues. This process is mitigated by the team's structure, routines, and dynamics, extending to the broader organization and technology. Hence, teams embrace unique features, making the team a medium where paradoxes are not only tolerated but are seen as valuable for driving creativity, innovation, and problem-solving.

Firstly, the temporary nature of project teams is a critical factor in fostering an environment ripe for multiple but not necessarily consistent views. As Burt (2002) points out, the concept of embeddedness and its impact on the decay of networks underscores the transient relationships within project teams. This impermanence means that the ties between team members, while potent during the project's lifecycle, are prone to decay once the project concludes. This transient nature of relationships encourages individuals to express and explore unconventional ideas without fearing long-term interpersonal repercussions, thus sowing the seeds of paradoxical viewpoints.

Secondly, project teams are often at the frontline of competing task demands. This exposure necessitates the reconciliation of inconsistent perspectives, as team members must navigate the complexities of diverse project goals and constraints. Such an environment naturally tolerates and, indeed, thrives on clashing viewpoints, as the management of these varied perspectives can lead to innovative solutions not evident from a single viewpoint.

Thirdly, the concept of "role-sets" within the broader organizational ecosystem highlights the diversity of perspectives that team members bring to the project. Each member's unique set of roles and responsibilities within the organization contributes to a rich tapestry of viewpoints. Their cognitive diversity is a fertile ground for contesting conventional ideas and nurturing opposing perspectives as team members challenge and refine each other's thoughts in pursuit of project objectives.

Fourthly, the applicability of Granovetter's theory of weak ties to project teams is particularly illuminating. Granovetter (1973) demonstrated that weak ties, or acquaintances, are more likely to provide new information than strong ties or close friends. In project teams, members often form weak ties, coming together from different parts of the organization or even with outside its boundaries. These ties are less about social involvement and more about task-oriented collaboration, making them powerful conduits for the flow of unconventional ideas and information that would not circulate within a network of strong ties.

Fifth, teams act as platforms where bridges are built from the members' strong networks. In doing so, they fill structural holes, as Burt (1976) described, where brokerage across these holes provides unforeseen options and opportunities. The team structure, therefore, becomes a network in which individuals can access and share diverse, often contradictory, information and viewpoints. This structural aspect of teams not only promotes the acknowledgment of diverse mental templates but also the embracing of seemingly contradictory frames, facilitating innovation.

Sixth, the essence of innovative projects is carved in uncertainty. The embrace of uncertainty is not just about acknowledging what we don't know; it is about leveraging the unknown as a tool for idea generation and more about switching from reactivity to creativity. To this end, it takes a counterintuitive mindset that accepts breakthrough ideas that defy conventional wisdom. Such a mindset presents a paradox in itself. In that, acknowledging limitations becomes the very source of strength, enabling the team to transcend traditional boundaries. The higher the uncertainty, the more the divergence. The more the divergence from conventions, the greater the variation of ideas. Accepting such plurality as indispensable rather than an obstacle, cultivates a culture where paradoxical thinking is not a threat but an opportunity for the team.

4 Why Artificial Intelligence Breed Paradoxical Frames

The artificial intelligence community is a quintessential example for our discussion. Such a role is characterized by a dynamic interplay of divergent perspectives and lengthy debates over its future and potential risks. Also, it is heralded as a transformative force with its unique paradigm. For one, it is distinct by its capacity for being generative; the models in this industry generate and inspire the creation of subsequent innovations. In AI, each product catalyzes new applications and collective experimentation. The modern wave for harnessing collective creativity is not merely reminiscent of past revolutions; it actively redefines them, exerting a profound influence across all facets of life (i.e., von Hippel, 2005). Hence, we select AI as our case for its transformative impact, highlighting its role as a perpetual engine of innovation and a testament to the power of collaborative creativity.

In AI the perforation of the boundary between producer and user blurs the roles (Jeppesen & Molin, 2003). Users become developers. Products remain 'permanently beta in use (Neff & Stark, 2010)', and innovation persists. When innovation has no end, the innovation cycle is never fully completed; each new product triggers ideas for new uses and leads to collective tinkering for the next steps. Taking off from pioneering times, these novel ways of leveraging collective creativity are akin to the revolutions that have gone under labels such as 'open innovation' (Christensen et al., 2005), touching every realm of our lives (von Hippel, 2006; Kumar et al., 2023). Given the interdependence between society and technology is cyclical, technology plays a crucial role in shaping our lives and societal norms. First, it heralds significant transformations for society at large. Second, it holds a promise of democratizing information. Third, it is poised to redefine the notions of authority, control, trust, and governance. Finally, in time, it will likely encourage a shift towards consolidation in power, eroding doubt and promoting passive acceptance of values. Hence, its deployment reflects interlinked benefits and risks.

Artificial intelligence is one of the most disruptive technologies of our time. Freeing us from the tedium of recurrent routines and monotonous tasks, it can improve efficiency and productivity across finance, healthcare (World Health Organization, 2021), education, manufacturing (Elahi et al., 2023), and beyond. The delegation of tasks to AI systems symbolizes a form of liberation (Hou, 2021). Such liberation is not merely an operational issue for a group but inclusive of cognitive processes for the individual. So, we can engage in higher creative endeavors by offloading arduous tasks to AI (de Miranda, 2020).

However, with AI, we encounter a dual-edged phenomenon. Such technologies reconstruct the idea of liberation and dependency. They reshape our conceptualization of control and the involvement of human agency in decision processes. As AI takes over, our hunger for efficiency and productivity engenders more reliance on these systems. The more reliant we become, the more we tend to delegate tasks to AI. As a result, there will be more dependency on the human-technology interface. This will accelerate, and the growing use of AI systems will gradually erode the human touch in critical decision processes. Ethics, altruism, empathy, or similar human processes will be replaced by self-ruling mechanisms.

The above discussion highlights the balance between creativity and the unforeseen repercussions of technological advancement. This dual-edged nature of AI is a source of significant tension within both organizational and societal contexts. On the one hand, AI offers unparalleled opportunities for enhancing welfare. It heralds an unprecedented level of innovation and automation. On the other hand, this progress does not come without its challenges and potential pitfalls. The development and deployment of AI systems often lead to unintended consequences that can exacerbate issues, new and old. These tensions foster cycles of effect and repercussion, making AI a breeding ground for diverse ideas diagonally opposite logics.

Artificial Intelligence (AI) is a context for counterintuitive frames for another reason. Moravec observes that machines find complex reasoning tasks easier than perceiving and understanding the world like humans do (Agrawal, 2010). The idea is that machines excel at analyzing vast data sets and winning complex games like Go, yet struggle with the intuitive logic in seemingly simple tasks. AI models lack intuitiveness but can combine multiple logical ideas to create broader logical constructs. They can effectively bootstrap instead of using an instinctual approach. Their reasoning does not necessitate a high-level analytical model. Instead, they feed a preconception back into the inference, bootstrapping the process without a pre-established logical framework. Replacing intuition with the capability to explore a broader range of possibilities, unhindered by the constraints of human experience or biases, potentially leads to novel and unexpected diversions in ideas.

5 An Array of Paradoxes

As we venture further into the AI era, we must foster AI models that improve our capabilities without undermining societal frameworks and values. This condition requires a broad view. It calls for a reassessment of autonomy, self-determination, and ethical accountability. Blind reliance on AI may distort the conventional idea of autonomy and human agency. It may miss the balance and sophisticated relationship between human and machine interaction. This concern necessitates attention to ethical guidelines and control models to ensure that AI operations align with our social values and norms.

The fertility of AI to generate paradoxes lies in its impact on foundational societal constructs: identity, governance, economy, and ethics. These constructs, once redefined, force us to confront the duality of empowerment and control, autonomy and dependency, transparency and privacy. Simply, they challenge us to reimagine societal norms and values. In that sense, the emergence of AI technologies serves as a mirror, reflecting complexities and contradictions. They compel us to question the nature of truth, the essence of human autonomy, and the structures of power and governance that underpin society. In doing so, they generate paradoxes and invite us to engage with them, encouraging profound understanding and innovative solutions that reconcile these tensions.

5.1 Ethical Issues and Bias Paradox

AI systems can provoke ethical dilemmas and biases. With the progression of generative AI, ethical concerns and risks in areas like data privacy, security, and adherence to regulations can become more pronounced. The spectrum of risks expands. It upsurges from the new forms of plagiarism, spreading misinformation, copyright violations, and distributing harmful content. Furthermore, overreliance on autonomous algorithms limits our autonomy and agency. With them, we hamper our ability to make decisions aligned with our values and ethical judgments. Such constraints are likely to introduce prejudices where algorithmic determinations, devoid of empathy and ethical nuance, dictate human actions and interactions. Also, AI algorithms may perpetuate the biases from their training phase, distorting their service with social injustice or discrimination. Such impairments present a paradox: a tool intended to improve objectivity and efficiency serves its purpose without a hitch. At the same time, it may embed and magnify biases, challenging the ethical foundations of project management practices.

5.2 Over-Reliance Paradox

As AI technologies become more integrated into project management tools, a paradox emerges where the reliance on AI for decision-making can both enhance and undermine project outcomes. On one hand, AI can process vast amounts of data to develop insights and predictions that far exceed human capabilities, potentially increasing efficiency and accuracy. On the other hand, over-reliance on AI can lead to a loss of critical human judgment and intuition, which are essential in navigating uncertainties and complex stakeholder dynamics that AI may not fully grasp. Under these conditions, with blind dependence on AI, we lose richness in human experience, exacerbate societal burdens and perpetuate biases, thus reinforcing existing social injustices rather than alleviating them (Tai, 2020). The concerns extend to economic uncertainties, employment dislocations, the creation of societal divisions, and even a shift toward a surveillance society (Werthner et al., 2024). Moreover, having a false sense of its infallibility, we may mask limitations and potential errors between humans and technology interfaces (Kostick-Quenet & Gerke, 2022). For example, legal and procedural access to justice can be compromised when AI systems make decisions. Without transparent processes, individuals face inadequate means to challenge or seek redress for those decisions.

5.3 Innovation vs. Control Paradox

Introducing AI into project management processes challenges the traditional balance between innovation and control. AI can drive innovation by identifying new opportunities, enhancing creativity, and pushing the borders of habitual routines. However, this vitality can sometimes conflict with the need for control and predictability in project outcomes. Indeed, the paradox of AI's potential to both enhance and diminish our capabilities may have profound implications for human agency, decision-making, and societal evolution. On the positive side, AI's ability to analyze large datasets can uncover patterns and insights beyond human reach, leading to breakthroughs in medicine, environmental protection, and many other fields. This technological leverage can enhance efficiency, accuracy, and creativity by providing tools that augment our natural abilities. However, the over-reliance on AI introduces significant risks and challenges. Firstly, the blind use of AI can erode critical human skills and judgment. As AI systems make more decisions, lacking empathy and moral judgment, they may perpetuate biases in the training process (Kreps et al., 2023).

5.4 Skillset Transformation Paradox

The integration of AI in project management necessitates a transformation in the skillsets required for project managers. While AI can automate routine tasks, it simultaneously elevates the importance of soft skills such as emotional intelligence, critical thinking, and stakeholder management. This creates a paradox where the technology that makes specific skills obsolete simultaneously makes other, more traditionally human-centric skills more crucial than ever. This duality is related to the automation vs. augmentation dilemma, highlighting fundamental tension within the workforce and broader society. Automation refers to machines taking over tasks previously performed by humans, aiming for efficiency and reducing the need for human labor. Conversely, augmentation signifies a collaborative approach where humans work closely with machines, enhancing human capabilities rather than replacing them. The tension arises because, while automation seeks to reduce human involvement, augmentation aims to empower humans, creating a scenario where the two concepts seem at odds.

5.5 AI for Smarter Ecosystems of Projects

Fusing AI with smart contacts promises more efficient ecosystems for managing projects. Smart contracts, self-executing with the terms of the agreement being directly in the code, promise to automate and streamline complex processes, ensuring transparency and trust. However, the marriage of these cutting-edge technologies also brings several complex challenges and questions to the fore. Trust and decision-making authority become pivotal concerns as stakeholders must navigate the intricacies of relying on AI-driven decisions. Consequently, the potential for unforeseen vulnerabilities or biases within AI algorithms poses significant risks. These biases could inadvertently be codified into smart contracts, leading to unfair outcomes or systemic inefficiencies. As such, while the fusion of AI and blockchain offers transformative potential for project management ecosystems, it also demands a careful and considered approach to mitigate risks and ensure equitable, practical outcomes.

5.6 Scalability of AI

Incorporating AI with technologies such as blockchain stands at the frontier of innovation, promising to revolutionize how large-scale and complex projects will be managed. However, a paradox emerges as the scalability challenges inherent in this fusion pose significant barriers to realizing the intended potential. AI, with its capacity for continuous learning and adaptation, requires substantial computational resources, especially as the complexity of tasks increases. Concurrently, adjoint technologies such as blockchain also rely on increasingly more resources. The juxtaposition of each technology's strengths with the scalability limitations presents a common sense-defying issue, where the very features that make AI so promising become constrained when applied together in extensive, intricate project scenarios. Addressing these scalability challenges is, therefore, not just a technical necessity but a crucial step toward unlocking the synergistic potential of AI and adjoint technology integration. The immense benefits versus scalability limitations, affecting their practical application in complex project management scenarios, present another technology paradox.

5.7 Algorithmic Management and Work

There is a fear that integrating AI into the workplace introduces issues such as technological unemployment, algorithmic management, and the transformation of platform work. Indeed, AI in the workplace can precipitate a profound transformation, not only in how tasks are performed but also in the fundamental dynamics of employment and management. Such developments introduce a myriad of challenges, chief among them being technological unemployment, where machines and algorithms replace human roles, leading to job displacement and a reevaluation of skills in the labor market. Additionally, the rise of algorithmic management—where decisions about work allocation, performance evaluation, and even disciplinary actions are made by algorithms—heralds a new era of highly efficient and profoundly impersonal oversight. Also, work that is mediated by AI-driven platforms further complicates traditional employment relationships. It blurs, for instance, the lines between employees and contractors. While maximizing productivity, this style of managing strips away the nuances of human judgment and interaction, potentially leading to unfair or opaque processes. These developments collectively challenge established notions of job security, managerial oversight, and the very nature of work, prompting a reconfiguration of workplace norms and the relationship between technology and labor.

5.8 Institutional Challenges of AI and Smart Contracts

The concurrent evolution of AI, along with a suite of groundbreaking technologies—including the Internet of Things (IoT), 5G networks, quantum computing, augmented reality, and robotics—marks a pivotal moment in technological advancement. While amplifying capabilities through enhanced connectivity, faster processing speeds, and more immersive experiences, these technologies intersect with emerging concepts like smart contracts, edge computing, and blockchain, raising complex cybersecurity challenges. Such an amalgamation of progress drives a structural transformation to disrupt existing societal and institutional frameworks. For example, the rapid pace of these advancements outweighs the ability of current legal systems to adapt. It creates a pressing need to address novel challenges related to smart contracts, liability, intellectual property rights, and data privacy. As the pace of technological advances dismantles established institutional systems, they necessitate reevaluating our regulatory systems to ensure the creation of new paradigms. This tension between fast-paced innovation and slower institutional adaptation highlights a critical tension. It develops a paradox between the lure of the benefits of autonomous technology and the burdens of the slower genesis of adaptive frameworks.

5.9 Performance Resilience and Technology

Increased embeddedness of AI tools in upstream and downstream operations promises to improve performance. Additionally, it enhances resilience against a backdrop of global volatility and uncertainty. Using AI, managers can predict disturbances, optimize logistics, and manage inventory. They can achieve unprecedented precision, improving performance stability and risk mitigation. However, this transformative dependency on autonomous technology launches new vulnerabilities. Cybersecurity threats emerge as critical concerns through the linkages offering multiple entry points for potential breaches, jeopardizing sensitive data and operational continuity. Additionally, relying on algorithms for critical decisions introduces the risk of systemic errors or ingrained biases, which could lead to flawed decision-making and exacerbate risks instead of mitigating them. This paradox underscores the need for robust safeguards, ethical AI practices, and ongoing scrutiny to ensure the drive toward technological empowerment does not inadvertently amplify the risks it seeks to diminish.

5.10 Semantic Analysis Paradox

This concept refers to the ability of AI systems to acquire and understand complex meanings and contexts without human intervention. From one perspective, AI enables machines to interpret and interact with the world in ways that imitate human cognitive processes. However, the more capable and autonomous AI becomes in generating semantics, the more difficult it is for humans to predict or even comprehend the basis of AI's decisions and behaviors. The more significant the gap between AI and human sense-making, the greater the ethical, safety, and reliability concerns. As AI systems drive more actions, their semantically valid interpretations within their learned framework may diverge significantly from human values or intentions. Thus, autonomous semantic development in AI is a two-sided issue. While it offers immense potential for benefits, at the same time, it exacerbates the complexity of AI's alignment with human oversight and ethical standards.

5.11 Transparency vs. Privacy Paradox

Integrating autonomous machines into business brings a critical duality between openness and privacy to the forefront. For one thing, transparency is essential for building trust in autonomous systems, requiring that the algorithms and data guiding their decisions be open to scrutiny. This control is crucial not only for ensuring their reliability and safety but also for allowing users and regulators to understand and predict their actions. This push for transparency often clashes with the imperative for privacy, as these machines collect, process, and act upon vast amounts of personal data to function effectively. The more these systems know about us, the better they can serve our needs; however, this same knowledge poses significant privacy risks if misused or inadequately protected. Thus, as autonomous machines become more embedded in operations, there will be polarity between reconciling the need for transparent operations and the equally vital need to protect.

5.12 Contradictory Nature of Sustainable Project Objectives

Sustainability projects face the challenge of achieving conflicting goals. First, a responsible green project requires analytical methods and, usually, a gradual approach. This means carefully choosing materials, processes, and technologies that reduce carbon footprints and conserve resources. Also, this approach may be demanding as it requires extensive planning, innovative methods, and sometimes the development of entirely new technologies, all of which can extend timelines and increase costs. In contrast, contemporary businesses require agile development, resource reduction, and fast deployment to remain competitive. For that reason, AI must balance time, cost, and quality within tight constraints to compete. When AI runs into conflicting objectives, as in this case, between ecological responsibility and business requisites, it comes to a paradoxical impasse.

5.13 Coopetitive Tensions and Stakeholders Paradox

The coopetition tension paradox emerges from the clashing interests of stakeholders. On the one hand, a project team attempts to achieve unified objectives that promote collective benefits; on the other hand, it encounters conflicting ambitions to compete for dominance, resources, or leadership roles. This duality creates a paradox in which overlapping pressures spark tensions to severe internal organizational ties. Against this ferment, neither explicit competitive action nor collaborative response resolves the issues. Instead, those in a coopetitive environment must follow a path that involves sharing insights, resources, and platforms while guarding their interests. In this scenario, participants take on roles neither as allies nor adversaries but rethink and often overhaul their positions.

6 Clustering Paradoxes into Tension Nodes

Organizing the paradoxes into clusters allows for a nuanced understanding of the logic in emerging technologies and organizational dynamics. The first group focuses on how these technologies affect decision-making and the necessary skills for management. The second group explores the tension between fostering innovation and maintaining control alongside the adaptability of contracts and processes. The third group highlights the ethical and legal concerns of adopting these technologies, underscoring the need for careful consideration of their broader implications.

6.1 Regulatory (Institutional, Ethical, Legal Land Privacy) Considerations

Grouping these paradoxes together highlights the ethical and legal challenges arising from the deployment of AI. The upshot is that we express concerns about bias, privacy, and the evolving legal landscape. We believe that future work teams will have significant challenges related to regulatory institutions, ethics, morality, and privacy, promising a landscape where work is not only about innovation but also about responsibility. As professionals navigate these paradoxes, integrating technology into projects will become increasingly sophisticated, guided by strict principles, legal understanding, and a commitment to protecting stakeholder rights. These developments suggest a future where teamwork will not only be judged by its commercial success but also by its adherence to norms, standards, and respect for societal values.

We predict that innovative teams will organize and adopt ethical institutional structures that guide the development and deployment of AI in processes. These frameworks will aim to mitigate biases and ensure that creative outputs uphold ethical standards, respecting diversity and inclusivity. Second, as legal challenges concerning AI and smart contracts will become more pronounced, teams will be more legally literate, understanding the implications of their work within current and emerging legal frameworks. This knowledge will be crucial in navigating copyright issues, intellectual property (IP) rights, and the use of AI-generated content.

In a surprising turn, we expect that AI systems themselves will be developed to serve as ethical auditors within innovative processes. These AI auditors would analyze creative content for biases, ethical violations, and privacy concerns, providing real-time feedback to innovative teams. This role reversal, where AI shifts from being the subject of ethical scrutiny to an active participant in ethical governance, would mark a significant evolution in the use of technology within creative fields. Third, blockchain technology may evolve into a distributed network of ombudsmanship. Then it can arbitrate and mediate to resolve disputes related to copyright claims, ethical concerns, and privacy violations. These platforms might operate through community consensus mechanisms, offering an alternative to traditional legal systems that struggle to keep pace with the technology evolution (Verschure, 2016).

As part of the future developments as the transparency vs. privacy challenge intensifies, a new trend in the development of tools that inherently respect privacy could emerge. These tools would enable innovative collaboration without compromising the privacy of individuals' data, using techniques like differential privacy and secure multi-party computation to protect sensitive information. Second, organizations will begin to seek certifications for their innovative processes and outputs, similar to sustainability certifications in other industries. These certifications would attest to the ethical creation of content, adherence to privacy standards, and bias mitigation, becoming a competitive advantage in the marketplace.

Third, to address both transparency and privacy concerns, innovative teams will implement AI systems that maintain detailed logs of their decision-making processes, including the data used and the rationale behind creative suggestions. These logs would be accessible for audit purposes but designed to protect sensitive information, ensuring accountability without compromising privacy. Finally, organizations will establish advisory panels composed of ethicists, legal experts, technologists, and representatives from affected communities to oversee the ethical implications of their work. These panels would provide guidance on complex issues, ensuring that innovative outputs reflect a broad spectrum of perspectives and uphold societal values.

6.2 Technological Synergy and Conflict

In the context of group work, we turn to the future evolution of technological synergy and conflict. We anticipate that teams, in the future, will be poised on the edge of paradoxes that challenge our conventional understanding of creativity, collaboration, and the role of technology. Surprising trends will evolve. For instance, there might be waves of going back to analog methods, very much like what happened in the music industry. Also, AI might offer opportunities to become co-creators, institute decentralized innovative platforms, and self-regulating systems. These developments point to a future where the boundary of innovation is continually redefined. As these trends unfold, teams will need to navigate the complex interplay between leveraging AI's potential and preserving the irreplaceable value of human creativity.

First, we predict that the over-reliance paradox will lead to lead to a resurgence of "analog" methods, where traditional techniques become valued for their inherent "imperfections" and human touch, creating a new appreciation for crafts and skills that AI cannot replicate perfectly. Second, the tension between human agency and AI automation presents a dual-edged sword. The future will see teamwork leveraging AI to undertake mundane or repetitive tasks, freeing humans to focus on high-level conceptual work. However, the real surprise could come from AI systems that not only suggest ideas but also critique and refine human-generated concepts, effectively becoming co-creators. This could challenge the notion of authorship and creativity, leading to debates about the value and ownership of AI-assisted creations.

Third, scalability in AI technology, particularly in innovative domains, poses a significant challenge. As AI systems become more advanced, their resource demands escalate, potentially limiting their ownership to well-funded organizations. This could initially widen the gap between teams from different organizations (Norton, 2017). However, it is also likely that a counterintuitive trend might emerge, where decentralized AI platforms powered by blockchain technology democratize access to powerful creative tools, enabling small groups to compete on equal footing with industry giants.

Fourth, the duality of innovation versus control in the context of AI is particularly poignant. Regulatory frameworks designed to control the ethical use of AI could inadvertently stifle innovation, particularly in innovative fields. However, a surprising future trend might be the development of AI systems capable of self-regulating their outputs to adhere to norms, effectively balancing innovation with societal expectations. This could lead to a new era of "responsible creativity," where AI systems are programmed to avoid creating content that could be harmful or divisive.

6.3 The Interplay of Innovation, Control, and Adaptation

Considering the paradoxes of innovation vs. control and skillset transformation, alongside the ambiguity and evolving nature of smart contracts, sets a complex stage for the evolution of group work. These dynamics introduce significant challenges but also open doors to surprising and counterintuitive future trends that defy traditional expectations. Below is a speculative exploration into how these dimensions may shape the future of creative collaboration, highlighting unexpected predictions and intriguing future trends.

In innovative group work, the tension between fostering innovation and maintaining control is paramount. This paradox will lead to the development of dynamic governance models that are both flexible and structured, allowing for creative freedom while ensuring alignment with organizational goals. A surprising prediction here might be the rise of AI-driven decision-making platforms that can assess the potential impact of innovative projects in real-time, offering a balance between risk and reward. These platforms could enable innovative teams to pursue bold ideas with an understanding of their potential implications, effectively navigating the innovation-control dichotomy.

Second, as technology evolves, so must the skillsets within project teams. The paradox lies in the need to rapidly adapt to new technologies while also maintaining a deep mastery of existing skills. A counterintuitive trend might emerge, where instead of solely focusing on technical skill acquisition, there's a renewed emphasis on soft skills like critical thinking, adaptability, and emotional intelligence. These skills could become the cornerstone of creative work, as they enable individuals to navigate the complexities of technological change more effectively. Moreover, we might see the rise of "hybrid" roles that blend artistic creativity with technical proficiency, challenging the traditional separation between innovative and technical teams.

Third, smart contracts, with their promise of decentralization and automation, introduce a new layer of complexity to innovative work. As these contracts become more prevalent, we might witness a surprising shift towards more decentralized configuration of processes. For instance, blockchain technology could enable a new model of creative collaboration where contributors from around the world work together seamlessly, with smart contracts automatically managing rights, royalties, and project governance. This could challenge the traditional hierarchy within innovative organizations, leading to a more egalitarian and collaborative work environment.

We expect that beyond just facilitating collaboration, novel work platforms could leverage blockchain to ensure transparency and fairness in innovative endeavors, disrupting how creative work is commissioned, produced, and compensated. Second, while AI's role as an assisting teamwork is already recognized, a future trend might see AI not just supporting but actively participating in the innovative process, using its capabilities to generate ideas that humans might not conceive, effectively becoming a co-creator.

Third, in response to the global push for sustainability, a surprising trend could be the prioritization of eco-friendly technologies and practices in innovative work. This might include the use of green data centers for digital work or sustainable materials in physical creations, merging environmental consciousness with innovation. Fourth, given the potential for technology to have unintended negative impacts, a future trend might focus on ethics-first design principles. Innovative teams might adopt frameworks that prioritize ethical considerations from the outset, ensuring that innovation serves the greater good.

7 Conclusions

Within project teams, paradoxes should not be construed as problems necessitating resolution but rather as tensions to be navigated. This perspective advocates for a reflective and iterative approach. Neglecting to engage with such a process suppresses creativity. It impedes the development of critical insights and narrows the decision down to a series of simple choices. For example, consider the act of managing the imperatives of adhering to strict deadlines versus the necessity of flexibility so that you tolerate unexpected disruptions. In response, traditional practice devises the answer from a simple trade-off. Instead, our answer transcends this convenient path. Instead, our perspective demands a continuous learning process that involves agility, resilience, and responsiveness.

The distinction between instrumental and humanist perspectives of creativity reflects a duality. Teams may strive for innovation (an instrumental aim) while also seeking to fulfill more humanist objectives, such as self-expression or societal impact. This dual pursuit can create tension, as the instrumental use of technology for efficiency or productivity may clash with the desire for creativity that transcends utilitarian purposes.

Managing these challenges requires a conscious effort to balance the deterministic influences of technology with the instrumental control teams have over their innovative tools. It involves recognizing the potential of technology to inspire and restrict creativity and navigating these dualities to foster innovation while maintaining the humanistic values of the creative drive. The challenge lies in navigating this tension, striving for a balance that harnesses the benefits of technology while remaining vigilant against its potential to shape society in ways that may not align with human welfare and ethical standards.

References

Agrawal, K. (2010). To study the phenomenon of the Moravec's Paradox. In *Arxiv*, pp. 1–8. Available online at http://arxiv.org/pdf/1012.3148.pdf

Berti, M., Clegg, S., Gaim, M., & Cunha, M. P. (2022). *Organizational paradox*. Cambridge University Press. (Elements in Organization Theory). Available online at https://www.cambridge.org/core/product/12CF7333392DE655D9D9AE38015FAE55

Burt, R. S. (1976). Positions in networks. *Social Forces, 55*(1), 93–122.

Burt, R. S. (2002). Bridge decay. *Social Networks, 24*(4), 333–363.

Cadin, L., Guérin, F., & DeFillippi, R. (2006). HRM practices in the video game industry: Industry or country contingent? *European Management Journal, 24*, 288–298.

Christensen, J. F., Olesen, M. H., & Kjær, J. S. (2005). The industrial dynamics of open innovation. Evidence from the transformation of consumer electronics. *Research Policy, 34*(10), 1533–1549.

Cohendet, P., & Simon, L. (2007). Playing across the playground: Paradoxes of knowledge creation in the videogame firm. *Journal of Organizational Behavior, 28*(5), 587–605.

Eikhof, D. R., & Haunschild, A. (2007). For art's sake! Artistic and economic logics in creative production. *Journal of Organizational Behavior, 28*(5), 523–538.

Elahi, M., Afolaranmi, S. O., Lastra, M., Luis, J., Garcia, P., & Antonio, J. (2023). A comprehensive literature review of the applications of AI techniques through the lifecycle of industrial equipment. *Discover Artificial Intelligence, 3*(1), 43. https://doi.org/10.1007/s44163-023-00089-x

Fraser, J., Ansari, S., Schultz, M. (2021). Navigating paradoxical tensions through the interplay of temporal structures. Available online at https://journals.aom.org/doi/abs/10.5465/AMBPP.2021.15400abstract

Goodman, R. A., & Goodman, L. P. (1976). Some management issues in temporary systems: A study of professional development and manpower-the theater case. *Administrative Science Quarterly, 21*, 494–501.

Grabher, G. (2004). Temporary architectures of learning: Knowledge governance in project ecologies. *Organization Studies, 25*(9), 1491–1514.

Granovetter, M. (1983). The strength of weak ties: A network theory revisited. *Sociological Theory, 1*, 201–233.

Granovetter, M. S. (1973). The strength of weak ties. *American Journal of Sociology, 78*(6), 1360–1380.

Guérin, F., Cadin, L., & DeFillippi, R. (2006). *HRM practices in the video game industry*.

von Hippel, E. (2005). Democratizing innovation: The evolving phenomenon of user innovation. *Journal für Betriebswirtschaft, 55*(1), 63–78. https://doi.org/10.1007/s11301-004-0002-8

von Hippel, E. (2006). *Democratizing innovation*. MIT Press.

Hou, H. (2021). On the three constraints of the development of artificial intelligence: Value, liberation and responsibility. *Cultures of Science, 4*(3), 159–168. https://doi.org/10.1177/20966083211052637

Jeppesen, L. B., & Molin, M. J. (2003). Consumers as co-developers: Learning and innovation outside the firm. *Technology Analysis & Strategic Management, 15*(3), 363–383.

Kostick-Quenet, K. M., & Gerke, S. (2022). AI in the hands of imperfect users. *NPJ Digital Medicine, 5*(1), 197. https://doi.org/10.1038/s41746-022-00737-z

Kreps, S., George, J., Lushenko, P., & Rao, A. (2023). Exploring the artificial intelligence Trust paradox. Evidence from a survey experiment in the United States. *PloS One, 18*(7), e0288109. https://doi.org/10.1371/journal.pone.0288109

Kumar, S., Lim, W. M., Sivarajah, U., & Kaur, J. (2023). Artificial intelligence and blockchain integration in business: Trends from a bibliometric-content analysis. *Information Systems Frontiers, 25*(2), 871–896.

Lampel, J., Lant, T., & Shamsie, J. (2000). Balancing act: Learning from organizing practices in cultural industries. *Organization Science, 11*(3), 263–269.

Lewis, M. W. (2000). Exploring paradox: Toward a more comprehensive guide. *Academy of Management Review, 25*(4), 760–776.

Lorenzen, M., & Frederiksen, L. (2005a). The management of projects and product experimentation: Examples from the music industry. *European Management Review, 2*(3), 198–211.

Lorenzen, M., & Frederiksen, L. (2005b). The management of projects and product experimentation: Lessons from the entertainment industries. *European Management Review, 2*(3), 198–211.

de Miranda, L. (2020). Artificial intelligence and philosophical creativity: From analytics to cre alectics. *Human Affairs, 30*(4), 597–607. https://doi.org/10.1515/humaff-2020-0053

Miron-Spektor, E., Emich, K. J., Argote, L., & Smith, W. K. (2022). Conceiving opposites together: Cultivating paradoxical frames and epistemic motivation fosters team creativity. *Organizational Behavior and Human Decision Processes, 171*, 104153.

Neff, G., & Stark, D. C. (2010). Permanently beta: Responsive organization in the internet era. In *Columbia University Academic Commons*. Institute for Social and Economic Research and Policy (ISERP Working Papers, 02–05). https://doi.org/10.7916/D8G44X47

Norton, A. (2017). *Automation and inequality. The changing world of work in the global South.*

Poole, M. S., & van de Ven, A. H. (1989). Using paradox to build management and organization theories. *Academy of Management Review, 14*(4), 562–578.

Smith, W. K., Erez, M., Jarvenpaa, S., Lewis, M. W., & Tracey, P. (2017). Adding complexity to theories of paradox, tensions, and dualities of innovation and change. introduction to organization studies special issue on paradox, tensions, and dualities of innovation and change. *Organization Studies, 38*(3–4), 303–317. https://doi.org/10.1177/0170840617693560

Tai, M. C.-T. (2020). The impact of artificial intelligence on human society and bioethics. *Tzu Chi Medical Journal, 32*(4), 339–343. https://doi.org/10.4103/tcmj.tcmj_71_20

Uzzi, B., & Spiro, J. (2005). Collaboration and creativity: The small world problem. *American Journal of Sociology, 111*(2), 447–504.

Verschure, P. F. M. J. (2016). Synthetic consciousness: the distributed adaptive control perspective. *Philosophical Transactions of the Royal Society of London. Series B, Biological sciences, 371*(1701). https://doi.org/10.1098/rstb.2015.0448

Werthner, H., Ghezzi, C., Kramer, J., Nida-Rümelin, J., Nuseibeh, B., Prem, E., & Stanger, A. (Eds.). (2024). *Introduction to digital humanism: A textbook*. Springer Nature Switzerland.

World Health Organization. (2021). Ethical challenges to use of artificial intelligence for health care. In *Ethics and governance of artificial intelligence for health* (pp. 31–64) Available online at Http://Www.Jstor.Org/Stable/Resrep40716.12.

Biases in Modern Project Management. Opportunities Connected to Artificial Intelligence (AI)

Roberto Linzalone, Antonio Bassi,
Alberto Michele Felicetti, and Salvatore Ammirato

Abstract

Project environments are increasingly characterized by uncertainty and, for this reason, require project managers to make frequent, quick decisions with poor and short-term information. In this context, project managers must shift from a rational and structured decision-making process to a simplified and less structured one leveraging heuristics. Heuristics are beliefs, experiences, mental models, frames, and other cognitive shortcuts for replacing parts of the rational and analytical process underpinning decisions. They are adequate support and very useful in many cases; nonetheless, they induce distortions in evaluations and estimates, with significant impacts, particularly in the context of projects. Heuristics are not free of the project manager's influence ("bias"). The challenge for project managers in today's uncertain project environments is to boost the use of heuristics while managing and controlling bias. Addressing and mitigating biases becomes crucial to improve decision-making effectiveness and outcomes. Artificial intelligence (AI) emerges, in such a context, as a potential support harbinger of tangible benefits for the project managers' decisions.

R. Linzalone (✉) · A. M. Felicetti · S. Ammirato
Department of Mechanical, Energy and Management Engineering, University of Calabria, Rende, Italy
e-mail: roberto.linzalone@unical.it; alberto.felicetti@unical.it; salvatore.ammirato@unical.it

A. Bassi
Department of Innovative Technologies, Scuola Universitaria Professionale della Svizzera Italiana, Polo universitario Lugano, Lugano, Switzerland
e-mail: antonio.bassi@supsi.ch

Ö. Hazır, M. E. Bruni (eds.), *Tomorrow's Data Empowered Project Management*, Future of Business and Finance, https://doi.org/10.1007/978-3-031-84017-3_11

1 Introduction

Project managers in modern projects must quickly make decisions that can significantly impact the outcome of their projects. In this situation, biases are consistent deviations from organized judgments or logical decisions that affect decision-making and impact project activities' planning, monitoring, and control. Cognitive biases are deviations from the norm or rationality in judgment processes. While rational and structured project management activities take time and require data, cognitive biases simplify decision-making; nonetheless, they can lead to incorrect evaluations, ineffective decisions, and suboptimal project outcomes. In any case, they significantly affect the performance of the project management process and, consequently, the effectiveness of project managers. Recognizing and mitigating the impact of these biases is essential for project success, and it is necessary to develop a strategy that is both aware and strategic, including promoting diversity of thought within teams, adopting data-driven decision-making methodologies, and encouraging a culture of critical review and continuous learning. AI is then an opportunity to mitigate project managers' bias and improve the quality of decisions, creating a more inclusive, resilient, and adaptable work environment, which is essential characteristics in a business context increasingly subject to rapid changes and growing uncertainty.

The mind of the project manager, due to the concurrent intertwining of rational and not rational, objective and subjective elements that enable decision-making, is particularly susceptible to distortions in perception and evaluation. While these elements can reveal themselves crucial in overcoming rigid and rational planning and overcoming limitations and constraints that would otherwise stay insurmountable, exploring the opportunities that Artificial Intelligence (AI) can open in this regard becomes necessary. By replicating analysis and decision-making processes typical of the human mind.

Through various techniques like Machine Learning (ML), Deep Learning (DL), Neural Networks (NN), Fuzzy Logic (FL), AI can process data and create a fast and bias-free decision. Alternatively, AI can countercheck and control project managers' bias. For example, ML algorithms can be used to analyze large volumes of data and identify patterns that suggest the presence of biases, enabling project managers to intervene promptly.

The adoption of AI in Project Management is already underway in various companies. Many scholars argue that AI can successfully improve project management, resulting in positive outcomes in accuracy, efficiency, and decision support. To effectively integrate AI into project management processes, it is important to follow some best practices, such as training staff on AI use, adopting appropriate tools, and measuring/managing the performance of the project management process to strategically drive the use of AI without being overwhelmed.

This chapter explores cognitive biases inherent to project managers that affect decision-making and management, often in subtle and unconscious ways. This can lead to distortions in Judgment that steer projects in unforeseen directions. The chapter examines how these biases can manifest through a detailed analysis, influencing decisions and management.

A cognitive analysis is proposed to highlight those Project Management (PM's) activities that can be replaced, supported, and mitigated with AI. A careful integration of AI with project managers' knowledge (that we may name 'human intelligence' to counterpoint and complement with 'artificial intelligence') to envision a project intelligence made up of a harmonic ecosystem of humans and software. The knowledge-based analysis of the project management process can show *where* and *how* to successfully integrate human intelligence with artificial one, thus showing effective and sustainable opportunities for application.

2 Project Manager's Decisions in Modern Projects. The Assumption of Uncertainty

Decision is even more critical for project managers in today's uncertain project environments. A first and general definition decision is choosing between two or more alternative options, representing solutions to a problem.

Decision is a process made up of steps according to the classical or Griffin's decision-making model: (1) identify the problem, (2) gather the information needed to make a rational decision, (3) generate all possible solutions without filtering any remote alternative, (4) generate objective criteria and measurements to assess the alternative solutions, and also define criteria for measuring the success or failure of the decision, (5) select the best option in the set of the best possible solutions, (6) put into practice the selected solution, (7) monitor and evaluate the outcome of the selected solution and the results that ensue. It may require some time for long-term results to become evident. However, after some time, evaluating the decision process according to its real outcomes' effectiveness is possible and comparing it with the outcomes that other solutions may have brought (Fig. 1).

More specifically, in the context of the project environment, the first phase of the decision involves defining the problem or needs to be satisfied and analyzing the project objectives and the expectations of the stakeholders (Meredith & Mantel, 2014). The second phase, information gathering, leads the project manager to consult the stakeholders, find sources and technical data, and collect historical data (Project Management Institute, 2021; Kerzner, 2017). The third phase involves the identification of possible and available alternatives, and the subsequent evaluation takes place based on objective criteria, such as costs, times, and associated risks (Lock, 2020). The selection of the optimal alternative is the one that offers the best balance between benefits and risks. The most common decision-making analysis tools include decision matrix, T-Chart, Decision tree, Multi-voting, Pareto analysis, Cost-benefit analysis, Conjoint analysis, SWOT analysis, PEST analysis. Combining these techniques can also be used to arrive at the final decisions.

Once the decision has been made, the project manager develops a plan for implementing the chosen solution, allocating resources, and defining the timing (PMI, 2021). Then, the project manager checks the progress of the activities, comparing

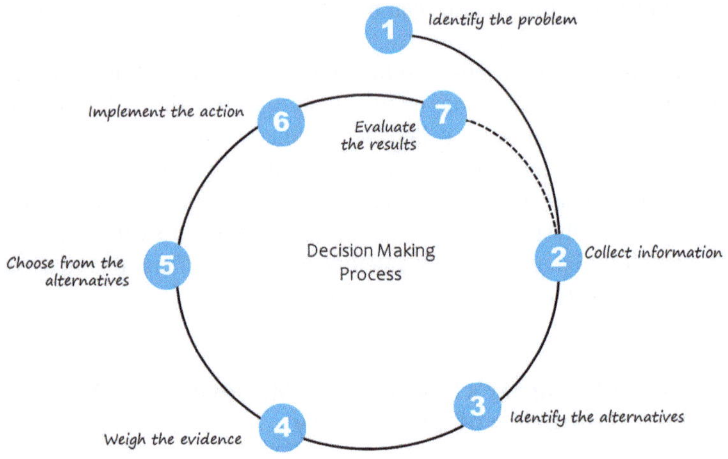

Fig. 1 Griffin's process for decision-making (Elmansy, 2015)

the actual results with those expected and taking corrective measures if necessary (Kerzner, 2017). After the project, the project manager evaluates the effects of the decisions and collects the lessons learned for future projects (Lock, 2020).

The final decisions can be made through either an intuitive or reasoned process or a combination of the two, depending on the nature of the decision. The reasoning is based on facts and information, disregarding emotions and other factors that could impact the decision-making process. However, intuition comprises previous encounters and individual beliefs. Considering intuition is important as it showcases life experiences. However, it could cloud Judgment as it is based on personal perspectives.

Not all the decisions are the same. There are different types of decisions that project managers face: programmed and non-programmed, routine and strategic, tactical (political) and operational, organizational and personal, major and minor, and individual and group (Chand, 2024). The project managers' decision process model, however, may change considerably according to the contextual conditions of the project environment. Key environmental factors affecting the decision process are uncertainty and complexity, stakeholder influence, resource availability, time constraints, regulatory/legal context, inadequate information, information overload, multistakeholder, vested interests, resistance to change, and lack of attachment (Pinto & Slevin, Critical success factors in effective project implementation, 1987; Floricel & Miller, 2001). Highly complex or uncertain projects require adaptive, flexible decision-making, as initial plans may need continuous adjustment (Pich et al., 2002). Project environments with diverse or conflicting stakeholder interests may prompt project managers to adopt a more consultative or collaborative approach (Aaltonen & Kujala, 2010). The scarcity of resources (e.g., budget, personnel) forces project managers to prioritize certain decisions and evaluate trade-offs more carefully (Pinto & Slevin, 1987). Projects with tight deadlines impose quick, often heuristic-based decisions that may risk cognitive bias (Kahneman, 2011). In regulated environments, project managers must integrate compliance considerations into decision-making (Hodgson & Cicmil, 2006).

Inadequate information refers to decisions made without sufficient data, often due to time or budget constraints (Pich et al., 2002). Information overload is a situation in which too much information hinders decision-making (Kerzner, 2017). In multistakeholder settings, divergent interests can complicate group decisions (Aaltonen & Kujala, 2010) due to heterogeneous views, values, and interests. Vested interests may bias the process (Flyvbjerg, 2009), and a fair decision-making process could be compromised, while resistance to change stems from attachment to established methods (Loch et al., 2008). Finally, a lack of attachment by the project manager to any of the alternative and possible solutions makes the decision process slow, stagnating, and unsettled.

When these factors characterize the project environment, the project manager adapts and adjusts the decision process, diverging from the Griffin's reference model. Namely, project managers deviate from a theoretical and rational decision process if uncertainty affects and characterizes the project environment. Actually, in highly uncertain projects like new product development (Loch et al., 2008), large infrastructure projects (Floricel & Miller, 2001), IT systems implementation (Pich et al., 2002), information is characterized by incompleteness, ambiguity, loss of timeliness and relevance, unreliability.

Information is often partial, forcing managers to make decisions without a full picture (Pich et al., 2002). Information is ambiguous, which can be open to multiple interpretations, complicating decision-making, primarily when no previous experience in that decision exists (Loch et al., 2008). In volatile settings, timeliness and relevance of information is critical for the effectiveness of the decision process; uncertain project environments involve the continuous change of the variables in play; that is, they lose relevance and timeliness, thus making the decision process ineffective and hard to make it work (Pinto & Slevin, 1987). Information sources may be unreliable or conflicting, and project managers must assess credibility to reduce decision risks (Floricel & Miller, 2001) (Fig. 2).

In conditions of certainty, the decision-maker can easily access good-quality information, thus providing adequate support to the decision process. Under risk conditions, information is of good quality. However, the potential payoffs and costs of the decisional alternatives are all associated with risks. In uncertainty, due to poor and ever-changing information, the project manager can only identify all the alternatives, risks, or consequences associated with each (Chand, 2024).

Thus, moving from 'certain' to 'uncertain' project environments, the level of ambiguity rises, and using heuristics becomes a useful shortcut to bypass the lack of information and improve the decision process's time and cost performance. Project manager switches from a structured decision-making process to a less structured one, where heuristics replace structured and formal process steps. Under 'uncertainty', the project manager's decision process turns towards empirical and practical solutions to arrive quickly and intuitively without necessarily guaranteeing the optimal solution.

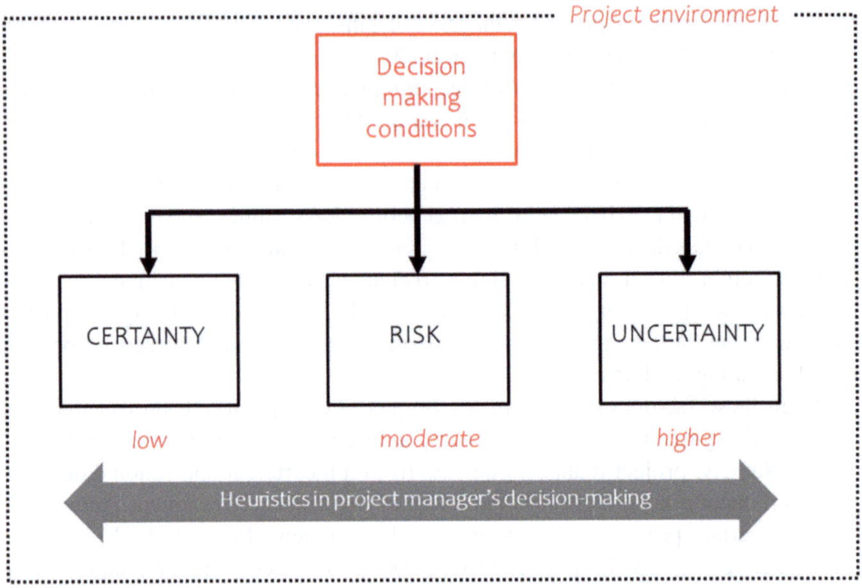

Fig. 2 The switch from a systematic to a heuristic and biased decision process, adapted from (Griffin, 2012)

3 Heuristics, Strategic Shortcuts to Catch up with Performance and Limited Information

Decision is a key activity in project management both strategically and operationally. Strategically, decisions define and inform project goals, allocating resources, and managing risks, with a long-term impact on companies' success. Operationally, decision-making concerns task assignments, performance tracking, and troubleshooting. Studies suggest that about **80%** of a project manager's time is spent on decision-related tasks, integrating strategic and operational components (Kerzner, 2017). This indicates the importance of effective and efficient decision-making for project managers and project success. In particular, the performance of the decision-making process is of the highest importance for the project manager. Key performances are effectiveness, efficiency, timeliness, risk, and adaptability. Effectiveness is the degree to which decisions align with project objectives and stakeholder needs (Pinto & Slevin, 1987). Efficiency is attaining the desired outcomes while minimizing resource usage (Kerzner, 2017). Timeliness is the speed of decision-making, particularly under time constraints (Atkinson, 1999). Risk management anticipates and mitigates risks in uncertain environments (Floricel & Miller, 2001). Finally, adaptability is the efficacy if adjustments as project variables change (Pich et al., 2002).

Project managers recur to heuristics in decision-making to overcome poor information and catch up with performance. Heuristics are cognitive shortcuts or simplified approaches to decision-making that individuals utilize to efficiently make judgments and decisions, particularly in complex or uncertain environments. In project management, heuristics assist project managers in making quick decisions without processing all available information or just using the piece of information available. Although heuristics can be beneficial, they can also result in cognitive biases that could harm project results if not managed properly. Heuristics are informal, intuitive problem-solving strategies that involve quick Judgment instead of thorough analysis. They are utilized when fast decisions are needed or when all information is unavailable. Heuristics frequently generate acceptable outcomes but are susceptible to mistakes because they are oversimplified (Tversky & Kahneman, 1974). Project managers often work in fast-paced settings with high uncertainty, limited information, and strict deadlines. Heuristics assist in handling these obstacles by offering a structure to make fast decisions under time and information constraints. Nonetheless, recurring heuristics in decision-making could lead to cognitive biases that impact the outcome of a project.

Heuristics operate in various ways and of various types. Project managers usually employ availability heuristics, anchoring and adjustment heuristics, and presentiveness heuristics. Project managers use the availability heuristic to assess the likelihood of events by considering how readily instances come to memory. For example, suppose a past project experienced a significant delay because of a supplier problem. In that case, the project manager might overestimate the chance of a similar delay occurring in upcoming projects, even if the probability is low (Kahneman & Tversky, 1973). The anchoring and adjustment heuristic pertains to the inclination to rely mainly on the initial information (the anchor) when making decisions. An initial budget estimate in project management can act as a reference point and impact future changes, regardless of accuracy (Tversky & Kahneman, 1974). Representativeness is when project managers ground their decisions on the similarity between a current situation and an experience without thoroughly examining the distinctions. Suppose a manager sees a similar project succeed with a particular approach. In that case, they may believe that using the same approach will be successful again without considering potential risks (Kahneman & Tversky, 1982).

Key elements of heuristics are simplification, experience, and time-saving. Heuristics streamline complex decisions by concentrating on a restricted number of factors or experiences. This decreases the mental burden while also taking the chance of missing important data. Project managers develop rules of thumb based on their previous experiences. This hands-on experience is useful but may also lead to biased decisions if the previous background doesn't directly apply to the current project. In addition, heuristics enables fast decision-making, which is beneficial in situations with tight deadlines.

Nevertheless, the trade-off is that quick decisions can be uninformed or biased systematically. Uncertainty is defined by changing goals, changing environments, and a lack of reliability and stability of the information in the long term. Such a project context highlights the importance of heuristics for the success of project managers.

Heuristics impact on Project Managers' activity both positively and negatively. Heuristics benefit project managers as they enable quick and efficient decision-making when time or information is limited. They help prioritize tasks, manage resources, and respond promptly to new challenges. In turn, they may result in cognitive biases, such as overconfidence, anchoring, or confirmation bias, which can negatively impact decision-making. For instance, depending too much on previous experiences or underestimating risks could result in delays, budget overruns, and stakeholder miscommunication (Pinto, 2013).

Heuristics are essential decision-making tools in project management; however, the inherent risk is that these mental shortcuts may bring to cognitive biases that affect project outcomes. Understanding the role of heuristics and managing their influence can help project managers improve decision quality and project performance.

4 Bias on Project Manager's Decisions

Decisions combine objective and subjective information. Objective information is data or facts that are unbiased, measurable, and verifiable. It is reliable for decision-making in project management. Examples of objective information are statistical data, budget figures, and schedules not influenced by personal Judgment. Objective data, like performance analysis, resource allocation, and risk assessment, is crucial for project managers' activities, as it offers a factual basis that minimizes uncertainty. Instead, subjective information is created by humans according to their personal viewpoints, beliefs, or feelings. It can vary between individuals, according to their unique combination of experiences, biases, prejudices, and intuition. Project managers' subjective insights come into play when they analyze team interactions, evaluate stakeholder satisfaction, and forecast project outcomes based on experience. Although subjective information may create bias, it also offers important context that objective data alone cannot provide, especially in complex decision-making situations involving human factors (Kerzner, 2017; Project Management Institute, 2021).

Objective information is consistent and replicable, useful for quantifiable aspects of decision-making. Subjective information offers flexibility and nuance, which is crucial when decisions depend on qualitative judgments or stakeholder relations (Kerzner, 2017). Effective project management requires both since objective data provides a solid foundation, while subjective insights allow for adaptation to unique project circumstances. Despite being less consistent, subjective information often drives the decision, thus pondering much more than objective elements. Subjective information is very important in project management, where managers make estimates, assign responsibilities, and decide on risk strategies and investments. Thus, their decision affects the success of projects, resulting in wise or bad decisions.

According to the environment's uncertainty level, the decision process can require the project manager to have a consistent share of subjective bias to come to the decisions. Various biases, from personal, social, and emotional dimensions like beliefs, experiences, mental models, convincement, and emotional state, are unavoidable and necessary at the same time to process decisions (Kahneman, 2011;

Flyvbjerg, 2021). The more the uncertainty in the project environment, the more the project manager's bias on the decisions.

Further, the more the deadlines and budgets are tight, the more the project managers use heuristics to shortcut the decision process. It follows that the level of biases rises, thus making it crucial to prevent bad decisions. Bias in decision-making by project managers is generally unintentional. It results from cognitive limitations and psychological factors rather than deliberate choice. Thus, while project managers do not intend to bias decisions, various unconscious cognitive, emotional, and social factors intervene in the decision-making process.

Coming to a more rigorous definition, bias is "a strong feeling in favor of or against one group of people, or one side in an argument, often not based on fair judgment" (Oxford University Press, 2024). So, a bias is a disproportionate weight in favor of or against an idea or thing, usually in a way that is inaccurate, closed-minded, prejudicial, or unfair. In science and engineering, bias is a systematic error that influences the ability to make a specific decision based on facts and evidence (Busenitz, 1997; Schwenk, 1986).

In literature, a distinction is made between cognitive bias and behavioral bias. Cognitive biases are systematic errors in thinking and interpreting information. They originate from the brain's tendency to use shortcuts (heuristics) to simplify decisions in complexity or uncertainty. These biases are essentially cognitive distortions or errors in reasoning. They occur unconsciously and affect how we interpret information, form judgments, and make decisions. Cognitive biases stem from cognitive limitations and the brain's need to process large amounts of information quickly.

On the contrary, behavioral biases are systematic behavior deviations from emotional or social factors. They influence how project managers act rather than how they think. These biases are behavioral patterns influenced by emotions, social pressure, or habits. Behavioral biases impact how people react, respond, and behave, often by deviating from rationality. A typical example is loss aversion, which is the tendency to prefer avoiding losses rather than acquiring equivalent gains, often leading to risk-averse Behavior (Tversky & Kahneman, 1974). Another example is herd behavior, which is the tendency to follow the actions or decisions of a larger group, overlooking personal beliefs. This can lead to irrational decision-making (Banerjee, 1992).

All in all, cognitive biases influence how people think, distorting reasoning and Judgment. They are often mental shortcuts that lead to flawed conclusions. Behavioral biases affect how people act, leading to irrational behaviors driven by emotions, habits, or social pressures.

In these situations, project managers use personal judgment, experiences, perceptions, mental models, emotional states, and many other psychological and mental supports that can lead to incorrect judgment and, as a result, a miscalculation of the situation or project at hand. These errors are often systematic and not random; therefore, they are called *Systematic biases* (Kahneman & Tversky, 1979). Systematic biases are frequent distortions in the human mind, often contrary to rational thought.

Cognitive biases are systematic patterns of deviation from rationality in Judgment, where individuals make decisions based on subjective criteria rather than objective evidence. Examples include confirmation bias (favoring information that confirms preconceptions) and availability bias (relying on immediate examples that come to mind). Bias can be harmful, especially when it leads to unfair treatment or incorrect decisions. Recognizing and addressing bias is crucial in various fields. It is fundamental in Project management, where neutrality and objectivity concerning plans, evaluations, and decisions are fundamental to ensure fair and accurate management.

Cognitive biases help when a quick response is more valuable than an exact fitting solution. In certain circumstances, it is essential to make timely decisions, such as in life-threatening emergencies. In their professional lives, project managers typically do not encounter such scenarios. They prioritize accuracy over quick responses, so biases are generally viewed as drawbacks in project management. It is, however, important to recognize that the increasing urgency of decisions and the pace of planning in projects pressure toward quick responses.

5 Bias in the Decision-Making Process. Nature and Typologies

Project managers are constantly exposed to biases due to the continuous decisions involved by the role. Because of biases they deviate the project from its optimal path. The biases that rise in the decision-making process can be of various nature and typology. Optimism bias, confirmation bias, anchoring bias, groupthink, overconfidence bias, availability bias, are just a few of about 200 types of biases acknowledged by managerial literature (Flyvbjerg, 2021). They have three different natures: cognitive, emotional, and social-organizational (Table 1).

6 Improving Project Management by Managing Biases

Awareness of cognitive biases offers the opportunity to improve the quality of decisions significantly. Using data-driven methodologies and promoting diversity of thought helps make more informed decisions, reducing the influence of subjective intuitions and prejudices. Understanding cognitive biases and adopting strategies to mitigate them reduces the likelihood of errors and promotes more precise and reliable decisions. To significantly improve the quality of decisions, it can be useful to leverage the understanding of cognitive biases. In this context, using data-driven methodologies and promoting diversity of thought helps make more informed decisions and reduce the influence of subjective intuitions and prejudices. Awareness of cognitive biases and adopting strategies to mitigate them reduces the likelihood of errors, fostering more precise and reliable decisions.

Adopting data-driven methodologies and promoting diversity of thought can play a relatively important role in ensuring that decisions are based on a broad range

Table 1 Main biases and their origins

Origin	Rationale	Bias
Cognitive	Project managers rely on cognitive shortcuts (heuristics) that simplify decision-making but can lead to systematic errors.	**Optimism bias.** Project managers overestimate positive outcomes and underestimate risks, leading to unrealistic timelines or budgets. This is often due to a desire to successfully deliver projects and gain stakeholders' approval (Flyvbjerg, 2006).
		Confirmation bias: It is the inclination to search for or interpret information in a manner that validates one's preexisting beliefs. In project management, this may result in focusing only on data that backs up a chosen plan while disregarding contradicting evidence. This bias can hinder project reviews and risk assessments by impeding the detection of possible problems (Kahneman & Tversky, 1979). Examine the effect of confirmation bias on decision-making in uncertain situations, as often happens in project management.
		Anchoring bias: The project manager's decisions tend to stay close to initial estimates or assumptions (such as cost estimates), the 'anchor' even when additional information during project development indicates otherwise (Kahneman, 2011). (Lovallo & Kahneman, 2003) supported that anchoring bias can result in suboptimal strategic choices in business and project settings.
		Survivorship bias consists of grounding on past successful projects or outcomes, thus influencing the assessment of future project success probabilities. In project management, this happens with an over-reliance on positive lessons learned and poor focus on the negative lessons coming from failed projects. (Nelson, 2005) discusses this bias within the framework of project outcomes, stressing the significance of drawing lessons from both successful and unsuccessful projects.
		Overconfidence bias is the tendency to overestimate one's knowledge, abilities, or the accuracy of one's predictions. In project management, this could result in underestimating risks, disregarding possible pitfalls, and making overly ambitious commitments. (McGraw et al., 2002) explore the impact of overconfidence bias on decision-making in uncertain conditions, a prevalent obstacle in overseeing intricate projects.
		Status quo bias is the tendency to stick with the current state, leading project managers to resist or slow changes even when supported by evidence. This prejudice can impede innovation and block the implementation of more effective technologies or methodologies.
		Availability bias causes managers to rely on easily accessible or recent information when making decisions, instead of considering all relevant data. This could result in an inaccurate evaluation of potential risks and benefits.

(continued)

Table 1 (continued)

Origin	Rationale	Bias
Emotional and motivational	Project managers may attach emotionally to previous decisions, thus affecting rational thinking.	**Escalation of commitment**: Project managers might persist in investing resources in unsuccessful projects to justify previous investments. This Behavior is linked to the sunk cost fallacy (Arkes & Blumer, 1985). This is often due to pressure to show persistence or avoid admitting failure (Drummond, 1996).
		Emotional Decision-Making. Decisions influenced by emotions can cloud Judgment, causing project managers to act impulsively rather than logically, impacting project outcomes negatively (Loewenstein et al., 2001).
		Regret Aversion: This bias causes individuals to avoid decisions that might lead to regret, hindering innovative approaches and maintaining the status quo in project management (Loomes & Sugden, 1982).
Social and organizational pressures	Social and organizational influences induce project managers to shape decisions accordingly.	**Groupthink**: In teams, the desire for consensus can override critical thinking, leading to suboptimal decisions because alternative viewpoints are not fully considered (janis, 1972). This bias is particularly strong in hierarchical or highly cohesive teams.
		Conformity Bias: Project managers may align their opinions with group norms or pressures, even against their better Judgment, resulting in suboptimal choices in project management (Asch, 1951).
		Social Loafing: The phenomenon where individuals exert less effort in a group setting impacts overall productivity and decision-making effectiveness in projects (Karau & Williams, 1993).

of information and perspectives. Objective data provides a more precise and accurate view of the current situation and reduces dependence on intuition and subjective impressions. For example, a team composed of members with diverse skills can better identify hidden risks and opportunities, improving the overall quality of decisions. Awareness of cognitive biases and implementing strategies to mitigate them can reduce the likelihood of errors stemming from unconscious prejudices. Specific training on cognitive biases helps team members recognize and address their biases and improves their ability to make impartial decisions.

Furthermore, debiasing techniques, such as pre-mortem analysis and decision checklists, can prevent common errors. Pre-mortem analysis, for instance, involves team members imagining a scenario in which a decision fails before it is implemented, allowing them to identify potential problems and develop mitigation plans. Decision checklists help ensure that all relevant aspects are considered and reduce the impact of cognitive biases in the decision-making process. By implementing these strategies, organizations can significantly reduce errors caused by cognitive biases, improving the accuracy and reliability of decisions made.

Recent studies have pointed out the challenges of managing project managers' cognitive biases in project management. Challenges mainly regard recognizing and identifying biases in high-pressure situations, as these can affect risk assessment, resource allocation, and stakeholder management. Project managers often fall into overconfidence, anchoring, or confirmation biases, with impacts on decision accuracy (Flyvbjerg, 2009). For scholars, instead, the challenges lie in developing reliable frameworks to measure biases and defining training programs to enhance project managers' awareness and the definition of mitigation strategies (Shepperd et al., 2018). However, more recent literature is highlighting and focusing on the role of digital technologies as tools to mitigate biases by providing data-driven insights and decision support. Artificial Intelligence, Predictive Analytics, and Decision Support Systems, to name a few, offer opportunities to disrupt project managers' decisions. AI can collect and analyze large amounts of project data to discover patterns, inconsistencies, and risks that human managers might overlook, while reducing biases such as confirmation bias (Mahmood, 2021). Predictive analytics offer forecasts based on historical data, improving project managers objectivity in decisions by highlighting potential pitfalls (Sharma & Verma, n.d.; Taylor & Tomaschek, 2020). Decision Support Systems provide structured frameworks for evaluating options, minimizing the influence of cognitive shortcuts (Turban et al., 2011).

7 'Human Intelligence' and Artificial Intelligence in Modern Project Management

Despite the enormous opportunities looming on the horizon of modern project management, very few studies have to date investigated *where* and *how*, in the project management process, AI can suitably support project managers' decisions and boost performance.

Taboada et al., 2023, explored the application of AI in modern project management by crossing AI techniques with PMBOK 7 Performance dimensions (PDs). They find among practitioners the use of machine learning, fuzzy approach, heuristics, NLP, deep learning, neural networks, expert systems, computer vision. Also, they suggest the activities the project managers support with AI: forecasting, decision-making, optimization, automation, estimation, and learning. It comes out from their study that project managers adopt AI to face planning, measurement, uncertainty, generic activities, delivery, work, stakeholder, team.

However, to address the mentioned question, the deepening of the concept of *intelligence* seems useful. Assuming that today's project manager's intelligence is a wider concept including both the *human intelligence* (based in the mind of the person) and the *artificial intelligence (*based in AI tools*)*, we can see the opportunities of AI for the modern project manager by exploring AI contributions project manager's human-intelligence. Intelligence is using *knowledge* to solve problems and adapt to new situations. In Organization and Management sciences, intelligence is a multi-faceted concept encompassing cognitive, emotional, and social dimensions (Gardner, 1986). Cognitive intelligence pertains to problem-solving and decision-making (Mumford et al., 2000). It concerns the ability to process information, solve problems, and understand complex concepts, traditionally measured through intelligence quotient (IQ). Emotional intelligence (EI) underpins the ability to manage one's emotions and understand others' emotions (Goleman, 1995), facilitating effective interpersonal relationships and balanced decisions crucial for effective leadership and team dynamics. Social intelligence, theorized by (Thorndike, 1920) and further developed by (Salovey & Mayer, 1990), focuses on interpersonal skills and adaptability in social contexts. It is the ability to navigate and interact in social dynamics, understand and influence relationships and social norms, promoting cooperation and effective leadership (Gardner, 1983). Intelligence is, therefore, the ability to learn and apply cognitive, emotional, and social knowledge ineffective and adaptive ways. These three basic intelligences interact in one holistic model of intelligence, where the interplay of cognitive, emotional, and social are crucial for the effectiveness of managers' role (Robinson, 2018; Judge et al., 2004). Intelligence in management rises as a complex and strategic issue, particularly for dynamic and changing environments, like projects.

It is the case to remark that knowledge and intelligence are distinct but interconnected concepts. Knowledge is the information and skills the manager acquires through experience or learning. Knowledge can be tacit or explicit (Polanyi, 1966; Nonaka & Takeuchi, 1995). Tacit knowledge is based on personal experiences and intuitions (i.e. *learning by doing* It is transferrable through social interactions perhaps by co-participation in activities, that becomes authentic 'shared experiences'. Hence, they are developed or acquired through practice and interaction. Explicit knowledge is instead formalized, codified, and organized. Therefore, do Hence, they are developed or acquired through practice and interaction. Explicit knowledge is instead formalized, codified, and organized. Hence, they are developed or acquired through practice and interaction. Explicit knowledge is instead formalized, codified, and organized. Hence, they are developed or acquired through practice and interaction. Explicit knowledge is instead formalized, codified, and organized. Therefore, it is documented in written or digital forms. It is easy to share through manuals, reports, and other codified resources (Nonaka & Takeuchi, 1995). Explicit knowledge is usually distributed among organizations and is not exclusive, distinctive, or appropriable by competitors. According to the Knowledge-based View of organizations, it is not strategic and destined to belong to all competitors unless protected.

Competence is applying knowledge and skills in specific contexts to obtain the desired results (Spencer & Spencer, 1993). It consists of the ability to integrate knowledge, experience and know-how. On the other hand, an informed decision is the choice of the best option, based on an accurate evaluation of the available information (Tversky & Kahneman, 1974). It is characterized by the critical analysis of data and reflection on the possible consequences. Informed decision-making requires a long and demanding decision-making process. The most widely accepted model of 'informed decision making' is that of *Prospect theory* (Kahneman & Tversky, 1979); the decision maker grounds the decisions on the perception of the prospective gain and/or loss, compared to the absolute value. The perception actually helps the decision maker replace complex evaluations and lengthy decisions. However, this way, managers' decisions are influenced by cognitive biases and subjective evaluations rather than by complete rational analyses (Kahneman & Tversky, 1979). All in all, decisions are contingent trade-offs between quality and cost. What comes up from the above review is that knowledge is at the bottom of a hypothetical pyramid, where a step up there is intelligence.

8 What Opportunities Do Artificial Intelligence Offer to Project Managers' Decisions?

Adopting data-driven methodologies enhances decision-making effectiveness by reducing the influence of biases and intuitions. AI tools and adequate training can empower the decision-making process, ensuring continuous monitoring to align strategies with objectives and maximize their effectiveness. Namely, analyzing large amounts of data impartially using AI tools is essential to provide recommendations based on solid evidence. AI tools can process huge volumes of data in real-time to identify patterns and trends that may not be visible to human analysis. AI helps predict future outcomes and allows companies to plan more accurately and mitigate risks. For example, machine learning algorithms can analyze historical data to forecast product demand, optimize supply chains, and improve inventory management. This approach increases operational efficiency and reduces costs associated with errors and inefficiencies.

An analysis of the whole project management process is essential to understand the challenges of the modern project manager and the opportunities that AI offers in a sustainability framework of healthy and balanced 'coexistence' between humans and machines. However, it is a crucial requirement to adopt a suitable and effective analysis perspective. An 'intelligence-based analysis' of a process refers to detecting, mapping, and analyzing various forms of intelligence—cognitive, emotional, and social—to assess and enhance process efficiency and efficacy (Gardner, 1986; Mumford et al., 2000). This analysis is coherent with an *intelligence-based* perspective of investigation.

Thus, we push forward an analysis of the project management process according to Gardner's model to highlight intelligence-based activities, tools, and criticalities project managers encounter; following, we analyze and discuss opportunities to support human intelligence with AI. The intelligence-based perspective enables mapping the project management process and creating a standard model for concurrent analysis of both bits of intelligence, consistent and suitable to identify and evaluate *where* and *how* to support project managers with AI, particularly regarding biases. With this regard, the term *opportunity* coincides also with the concept of what is appropriate and useful to delegate to AI, for a sustainable and ethical improvement of project management performance.

Project management ethics requires the management of projects by moral principles and ethical standards, ensuring transparency, fairness, and responsibility, essential elements of today's projects to maintain stakeholder trust and prevent unfair practices (Pinto, 2013). Further, it is crucial to delve into the merits of the intelligent activities of project management and make them explicit, perhaps via practical synthesis and graphical tools, in order to ground an open and plural cultural and scientific discussion, as long as it is based on a clear and shared vision of the project management process.

By crossing the project management process (Project Management Institute, 2021) with Gardner's model (Gardner, 1986), we are able to achieve an intelligence-based characterization (Goleman, 1998) of the process. A critical review of the PMI's processes, in light of the mentioned characterization allows to advance the following opportunities for the application of AI in project management (Table 2).

As emerges from the above findings AI is a harbinger of opportunities to mitigate and control biases in Project Management Decisions. We are probably still not fully aware of all possible opportunities, nonetheless we have insights and evidence that allow to make a point on it so far. The integration of AI into project management processes represents a transformative opportunity to control and mitigate the biases that accompany project managers' decisions and tacitly drive project management outcomes and performances. Each phase from initiation to closing, are not free of cognitive, emotional, and social biases.

During project initiation, Natural Language Processing (NLP) can analyze stakeholder communications across various channels, regardless of their volume and help to uncover latent interests and concerns that may not be immediately apparent, or not clear in priority. This data-driven approach can improve stakeholder analysis in quantity and quality, allowing project managers to make more informed, unbiased decisions thanks to quantitative, pervasive, consistent information sources.

During the planning phase, cognitive and emotional biases can lead to optimistic overestimations or underestimation of potential risks. Predictive analytics can analyze historical data to identify and forecast risks more accurately, reducing the impact of biases in risk assessment. Additionally, AI-driven optimization algorithms

Table 2 Comprehensive overview of intelligence-based project management processes, and AI opportunities

P.M. processes	Project management intelligence-based tasks			AI Opportunities	
	Cognitive	*Emotional*	*Social*	Project management task/ AI Technique	*AI support*
1. Initiation	Cognitive intelligence is used by Project Managers (PMs) to define the project's scope, objectives, and feasibility. They analyze business needs, and conduct feasibility studies (Project Management Institute, 2021). Cognitive skills help in creating the Business case and the Project charter that align with organizational goals (Kerzner, 2017)	Emotional intelligence is needed to engage stakeholders and manage their expectations from the outset. High emotional intelligence is strategic to understand stakeholders' needs and establish trust (Goleman, 1995)	Social intelligence enables project managers to identify key or critical stakeholders, navigate organizational politics and gain support (Salovey & Mayer, 1990). This type of intelligence allows effective stakeholder analysis and relationship-building	Stakeholder analysis/natural language processing (NLP)	AI can analyze stakeholder communications (via many channels, e.g. whatsapp, emails, etc.) and social media, to identify and map their interests and influence (Cambria et al., 2013).
2. Planning	PMs carry out detailed planning and resource allocation. Cognitive skills are essential for developing project plans, schedules, and budgets, and for using tools such as Gantt charts and risk management frameworks (Project Management Institute, 2021). Further, analytical abilities are put in place to obtain clear, measurable objectives and KPIs (Kerzner, 2017)	Emotional intelligence is used by the FM to form the team (team formation), to facilitate team collaboration and communication. Also, according to Tuckman's scale (Project Management Institute, 2021) to manage 'storming' that is conflicts, to ensure team engagement, and address concerns proactively (Goleman, 1995)	Building relationships with stakeholders and ensuring their buy-in are strategic for the PM's performance. Social intelligence is needed to an effective negotiation and management of stakeholder expectations (Salovey & Mayer, 1990)	Risk management/ predictive analytics.	Machine learning algorithms can be used to predict potential risks based on historical project data and simulations (Chong et al., 2017)
				Schedule optimization/ optimization algorithms	Automatic adjustment of project schedules and resource allocations to optimize timelines and resources (Jouzdani et al., 2016)

(continued)

Table 2 (continued)

P.M. processes	Project management intelligence-based tasks			AI Opportunities	
	Cognitive	*Emotional*	*Social*	Project management task/ AI Technique	*AI support*
3. Execution	Execution requires to PMs the coordination of people and resources. Cognitive intelligence helps in problem-solving and decision-making to solve issues that arise during project execution. Techniques like Earned Value Management (EVM) are used to track progress (Kerzner, 2017).	Managing team's social dynamics is crucial as maintaining morale. Emotional intelligence is required to address conflicts, motivate team members, and manage stress (Goleman, 1995).	Effective communication is mainly required to keep stakeholders and team members engaged. Social intelligence helps in fostering a collaborative environment and ensuring smooth interaction between diverse organizations and teams performing the project (Salovey & Mayer, 1990).	Task management/ robotic process automation (RPA)	Automate repetitive tasks such as updating status reports and managing routine communications (Aguirre & Rodriguez, 2017)
				Performance monitoring/ real-time analytics	Real time analytics can continuously analyze project performance data and report deviations from the plan, as well as suggest corrective actions (Mason & Hamblin, 2019)
4. Monitoring and controlling	This process involves assessing project performance and making necessary adjustments. PM's cognitive intelligence is crucial for analyzing performance data, identifying variances, and implementing corrective actions (Project Management Institute, 2021)	Resistance to changes or to technical/ organizational adjustments usually rise in team members or partner organizations; emotional intelligence is used to ensure continued team engagement (Goleman, 1995)	Social intelligence is applied with regard to communicating changes and updates to stakeholders effectively; in this way the PM can secure a continuous support and an effective management of their expectations (Salovey & Mayer, 1990).	Change management/ decision support systems (DSS).	DSS assist in evaluating the impact of changes on project scope, schedule, and budget by simulating various scenarios (Cioffi & Zheng, 2021)
				Quality control/ machine learning algorithms	MLA can analyze quality metrics and historical data to detect anomalies and predict potential quality issues (Khan et al., 2021)
5. Closing	Cognitive intelligence is used in this process by PM to review project outcomes, ensure all deliverables are completed, and capture lessons learned. These activities involve systematic evaluation and documentation of project performance (Kerzner, 2017).	Emotional intelligence is used to make final project review with sensitivity, acknowledging team contributions, and handling any final feedback constructively (Goleman, 1995).	Social intelligence is required and used to lead the transition of project outputs to operational use and for maintaining relationships with stakeholders for future projects (Salovey & Mayer, 1990).	Lessons learned documentation/ knowledge management systems (KMS) with AI.	Automatically gather and categorize lessons learned from project documentation and team feedback for future reference (Goes et al., 2020)

can support project managers in resource allocation and schedule planning, driving toward a more balanced and evidence-based approach in replacement of an approach based on anecdotal experiences or assumptions.

Execution Phase usually entails effective coordination and decision-making under pressure. Emotional intelligence is crucial in this phase, as project managers must orchestrate team dynamics and stakeholder relationships. Emotions and social relations easily and strongly overload and weigh on project managers' decisions. AI tools, namely robotic process automation, can process routinary tasks and status updates on behalf of the project manager, thus freeing him/her up to focus on critical interpersonal and value-added relations. Further, real-time analytics can produce continuous reporting and feedback on project performance, relieving project managers from operational tasks and freeing time and focus on relevant decisions, with lower stress and fewer bias.

During monitoring and controlling, biases arise from resistance to change and the tendency to consolidated and familiar solutions. DSSs can simulate various scenarios and evaluate the potential impacts of changes, enabling project managers to make more rational decisions based on data rather than intuition. Machine Learning Algorithms (MLAs) can provide quality metrics and analysis to detect anomalies, acting as proof or counterintuitive insights that counteract confirmation biases prevalent in performance assessments.

In the closing phase, cognitive and emotional biases can affect the evaluation of project outcomes and lessons learned. AI can, by the mean of Knowledge Management Systems (KMS), improve this project manager's phase. They automatically gather and categorize lessons learned from project documentation. This way the valuable insights are not overlooked due to cognitive biases or emotional attachments to particular outcomes, fostering and grounding a culture of continuous improvement.

Incorporating AI into project management brings opportunities to mitigate and control biases in project managers' decisions. Data-driven insights, predictive analytics, automated processes, support and improve project managers' cognitive, emotional, and social intelligence, resulting in more impartial and efficient decision-making. Human and artificial intelligence can join together in a virtuous and sustainable interaction by framing and mapping the project managers' tasks and the AI's ones. More investigation is needed to better understand how AI can be used by project managers and the ability and awareness on how to actively prevent bias.

9 Conclusions

This study elucidated the critical role of biases in modern project management, particularly in uncertain environments where project managers are called to decide quickly upon scares and changing information. The analysis of the project management process, reveals that cognitive, emotional, and social intelligence are integral to effective project managers decisions across all phases. Heuristics, while beneficial for simplifying decision-making, lead to significant biases that adversely affect project outcomes.

Unlike some similar studies focusing on AI potential gain for project management (Chong et al., 2017; Cioffi & Zheng, 2021), we utilized a qualitative framework, integrating analysis of AI applications in combination with the project management process, which provides a broader perspective on potential solutions, complementary to that of the mentioned studies. It is however to remark that both studies agree on the prevalence of cognitive biases in project management-.

Moreover, while traditional approaches to decision-making in project management persists like that of (Project Management Institute, 2021), this chapter suggested that AI can significantly enhance cognitive processes and should be considered in modern decision-making process models. NLP for stakeholder analysis, predictive analytics for risk management, can mitigate biases directly by offering data-driven insights and indirectly by automating repetitive tasks. Additionally, AI-driven decision support systems can contain the tendency and the risks associated with a fully heuristic-based decision. This chapter, besides providing to practitioners a prospective driver for the beneficial use of AI in decisions, contributes to the ongoing discourse on biases in project management by forwarding an AI-centric approach, which appears to offer a fruitful avenue toward more objective and effective decision-making practices in project management.

References

Aaltonen, K., & Kujala, J. (2010). A project lifecycle perspective on stakeholder influence strategies. *Scandinavian Journal of Management, 26*(4), 381–397.

Aguirre, S., & Rodriguez, A. (2017). Robotic process automation: The next generation of business process management. *International Journal of Information Management, 46*(1), 291–298.

Arkes, H. R., & Blumer, C. (1985). The psychology of sunk cost. *Organizational Behavior and Human Decision Processes, 35*(1), 124–140.

Asch, S. E. (1951). Effects of group pressure upon the modification and distortion of judgments. In H. Guetzkow (Ed.), Groups, leadership, and men (pp. 177–190). Carnegie Press.

Atkinson, R. (1999). Project management: Cost, time and quality, two best guesses and a phenomenon. *International Journal of Project Management, 17*(6), 337–342.

Banerjee, A. V. (1992). A simple model of herd behavior. *The Quarterly Journal of Economics, 107*(3), 797–817.

Busenitz, L. B. (1997). Differences between entrepreneurs and managers in large organizations: Biases and heuristics in strategic decision-making. *Journal of Business Venturing, 12*(1), 9–30.

Cambria, E., Poria, S., & Gelbukh, A. (2013). Sentiment analysis: A multi-faceted problem. *Computational Intelligence, 29*(3), 547–567.

Chand, S. (2024, October 1). *Decision types: 6 types of decisions every organization need to take*. Retrieved from Your article library: www.yourarticlelibrary.com/decision-making/decision-types-6-types-of-decisions-every-organization-need-to-take/25660

Chong, A. Y., Chan, F. T., & Zhou, L. (2017). Predictive analytics in Project Management: A case study of a large construction project. *Journal of Construction Engineering and Management, 143*(10), 128–149.

Cioffi, J., & Zheng, Q. (2021). Decision support systems in project management: Applications and opportunities. *Journal of Decision Systems, 30*(1), 41–60.

Drummond, H. (1996). Escalation in decision making: The tragedy of Taurus. Oxford University Press.

Elmansy, R. (2015). *The decision-making process designers should use daily*. Retrieved from Designorate: http://www.designorate.com/decision-making-process

Floricel, S., & Miller, R. (2001). Strategizing for anticipated risks and turbulence in large-scale engineering projects. *International Journal of Project Management, 19*(8), 445–455.

Flyvbjerg, B. (2006). From Nobel prize to Project Management: Getting risks right. *Project Management Journal, 37*(3), 5–15.

Flyvbjerg, B. (2009). Survival of the Unfittest: Why the worst infrastructure gets built and what we can do about it. *Oxford Review of Economic Policy, 25*(3), 344–367.

Flyvbjerg, B. (2021). Top ten behavioral biases in Project Management: An overview. *Project Management Journal, 52*(6), 531–546.

Gardner, H. (1983). Frames of mind: The theory of multiple intelligences. Basic Books.

Gardner, H. (1986). *Frames of mind: The theory of multiple intelligences*. Basic Books.

Goes, P. B., Huang, M. H., & Lai, K. K. (2020). AI in knowledge management systems: Enhancing lessons learned and decision-making. *Information & Management, 57*(8), 348–359.

Goleman, D. (1995). *Emotional intelligence: Why it can matter more than IQ*. Bantam Books.

Goleman, D. (1998). What makes a leader? *Harvard Business Review, 76*(6), 93–102.

Griffin, R. (2012). *Fundamentals of management*. South-Western Cengage Learning.

Hodgson, D., & Cicmil, S. (2006). *Making projects critical. Palgrave Macmillan*. Palgrave Macmillan.

Janis, I. (1972). *Victims of groupthink: A psychological study of foreign-policy decisions and fiascoes*. Houghton Mifflin.

Jouzdani, J., O'Connor, T., & Adams, R. (2016). Optimization algorithms for project scheduling and resource allocation. *European Journal of Operational Research, 249*(1), 34–49.

Judge, T. A., Colbert, A. E., & Ilies, R. (2004). Intelligence and leadership: A quantitative review and test of theoretical propositions. *Journal of Applied Psychology, 89*(3), 542–552.

Kahneman, D. (2011). *Thinking, fast and slow*. Farrar, Straus and Giroux.

Kahneman, D., & Tversky, A. (1973). On the psychology of prediction. *Psychological Review, 80*(4), 237–251.

Kahneman, D., & Tversky, A. (1979). Prospect theory: An analysis of decision under risk. *Econometrica, 47*(2), 263–291.

Kahneman, D., & Tversky, A. (1982). In I. D. Kahneman, P. Slovic, & A. Tversky (Eds.), *The simulation heuristic., judgment under uncertainty: Heuristics and biases*. Cambridge University Press.

Karau, S. J., & Williams, K. D. (1993). Social loafing: A meta-analytic review and theoretical integration. *Journal of Personality and Social Psychology, 65*(4), 681–706.

Kerzner, H. (2017). *Project management: A systems approach to planning, scheduling, and controlling* (12th ed.). Wiley.

Khan, M. A., Khan, M. A., & Khalid, N. (2021). Machine learning approaches for quality control in projects. *Quality Engineering, 33*(4), 507–522.

Loch, C. H., Solt, M. E., & Bailey, E. M. (2008). Diagnosing unforeseeable uncertainty in a new venture. *Journal of Product Innovation Management, 25*(1), 28–46.

Loewenstein, G., Weber, E. U., Hsee, C. K., & Welch, N. (2001). Risk as feelings. *Psychological Bulletin, 127*(2), 267–286.

Lock, D. (2020). Project management (10th ed.). Routledge.

Loomes, G., & Sugden, R. (1982). Regret theory: An alternative theory of rational choice under uncertainty. *The Economic Journal, 92*(368), 805–824.

Lovallo, D., & Kahneman, D. (2003). Delusions of success: How optimism undermines executives' decisions. *Harvard Business Review, 81*(7), 56–63.

Mahmood, K. (2021). AI for mitigating bias in decision making. *Journal of Project Management Technology, 3*(1), 180–191.

Mason, C., & Hamblin, D. (2019). Real-time data analytics in Project Management: A review. *International Journal of Project Management, 37*(6), 757–770.

McGraw, A., Mellers, B., & Ritov, I. (2002). Searching for the limits of overconfidence and uncertainty. *Journal of Behavioral Decision Making, 15*(3), 261–282.

Meredith, J. R., & Mantel, S. J. (2014). Project management: A managerial approach (8th ed.). Wiley.

Mumford, M. D., Zaccaro, S. J., Harding, F. D., Jacobs, T. O., & Fleishman, E. A. (2000). Leadership skills for a changing world: Solving complex social problems. *The Leadership Quarterly, 11*(1), 11–35.

Nelson, R. (2005). Project retrospectives: Evaluating project success, failure, and everything in between. *MIS Quarterly Executive, 4*(3), 361–372.

Nonaka, I., & Takeuchi, H. (1995). *The knowledge-creating company: How Japanese companies create the dynamics of innovation.* Oxford University Press.

Oxford University Press. (2024, August 20). *Oxford learner's dictionary.* Retrieved from https://www.oxfordlearnersdictionaries.com/definition/english/bias_1?q=bias

Pich, M. T., Loch, C. H., & De Meyer, A. (2002). On uncertainty, ambiguity, and complexity in project management. *Management Science. Management Science, 48*(8), 1008–1023.

Pinto, J. K. (2013). *Project Management: Achieving competitive advantage* (4th ed.). Pearson.

Pinto, J. K., & Slevin, D. P. (1987). Critical success factors in effective project implementation. *IEEE Transactions on Engineering Management, 34*(1), 22–27.

Polanyi, M. (1966). *The tacit dimension.* Routledge.

Project Management Institute. (2021). *A guide to the Project Management body of knowledge (PMBOK® guide)* (7th ed.). Project Management Institute.

Robinson, S. P. (2018). *Organizational behavior* (18th ed.). Pearson.

Salovey, P., & Mayer, J. D. (1990). Emotional intelligence. *Imagination. Cognition and Personality, 9*(3), 185–211.

Schwenk, C. R. (1986). Information, cognitive biases, and commitment to a course of action. *The Academy of Management Review, 11*(2), 298–310.

Sharma, N., & Verma, P. (n.d.). Data-driven decision making in Project Management through predictive analytics. *International Journal of Project Management, 39*(2), 90–101.

Shepperd, J. A., Klein, W. M., Waters, E. A., & Weinstein, N. D. (2018). Taking stock of unrealistic optimism. *Perspectives on Psychological Science, 8*(4), 395–411.

Spencer, L. M., & Spencer, S. M. (1993). *Competence at work: Models for superior performance.* John Wiley & Sons.

Taboada, I., Daneshpajouh, A., Toledo, N., & de Vass, T. (2023). Artificial intelligence enabled Project Management: A systematic literature review. *Applied Sciences, 13*(8), 5014–5027.

Taylor, J., & Tomaschek, A. (2020). Predictive analytics in Project Management: Leveraging data for better decision making. *Journal of Project Management, 35*(4), 22–28.

Thorndike, E. L. (1920). Intelligence and its uses. *Harper's Magazine, 140*, 227–235.

Turban, E., Sharda, R., & Delen, D. (2011). *Decision support and business intelligence systems* (9th ed.). Pearson.

Tversky, A., & Kahneman, D. (1974). Judgment under uncertainty: Heuristics and biases. *Science, 185*(4157), 1124–1131.

MIX
Papier aus verantwortungsvollen Quellen
Paper from responsible sources
FSC® C105338

If you have any concerns about our products,
you can contact us on
ProductSafety@springernature.com

In case Publisher is established outside the EU,
the EU authorized representative is:
Springer Nature Customer Service Center GmbH
Europaplatz 3, 69115 Heidelberg, Germany

Printed by Libri Plureos GmbH
in Hamburg, Germany